A Kipper With My Tea

also by Alan Davidson

Mediterranean Seafood
Fish and Fish Dishes of Laos
Seafood of South-East Asia
Dumas on Food (*with Jane Davidson*)
North Atlantic Seafood

A Kipper With My Tea

Selected Food Essays

Alan Davidson

MACMILLAN
LONDON

First published 1988 by
MACMILLAN LONDON LIMITED
4 Little Essex Street London WC2R 3LF
and Basingstoke

Associated companies in Auckland, Delhi, Dublin, Gaborone,Hamburg, Harare, Hong Kong, Johannesburg, Kuala Lumpur, Lagos, Manzini, Melbourne, Mexico City, Nairobi, New York, Singapore and Tokyo

British Library Cataloguing in Publication Data
Davidson, Alan
A Kipper With My Tea: selected food essays.
1. Food
I. Title
641.3
ISBN 0-333-47408-2

Typeset by Wyvern Typesetting Ltd, Bristol
Printed in Hong Kong

Contents

Part Five: Seafood

Part Six: Asia

Part Seven: Cheese

Part Eight: Tailpiece

For my sister Rosemary

Preface

During the last twelve years, besides labouring on an enormous book of my own and publishing other authors' books, I have written a number of shorter pieces, mostly on subjects which particularly interest me.

The discipline of being told that one has only 750 (or 2000, or whatever) words is often beneficial. It makes one think about what it is that one really wants to say, and how to say it briefly.

So I am grateful to my editors at the *New York Times, Connoisseur,* the *American Scholar,* the *Virginia Quarterly, Cuisine,* the *Journal of Gastronomy, Technology, Departures,* the *Guardian,* the *Sunday Times,* the *Times Literary Supplement,* the *Three-Course Newsletter* and others for thus helping me both to compress and express my thoughts. And from *Punch* comes the curious little item on page 3, included because it was my first paid piece of writing, in 1946, and had to do (sort of) with food and drink.

Some of the texts printed here have had 'cuts' restored. A few have been trimmed of material of purely ephemeral interest, or otherwise tightened up, while a few others have postscripts added.

Alan Davidson
World's End, Chelsea
1988

Introduction

Confronted by a patchwork quilt, one is curious to know its history. Similarly, eyeing the essays in this book, a reader may ask: who is this man, and why does he go on about these things?

I had some literary ambitions in my youth, of the sort which led me to compose feeble imitations of poems by Matthew Arnold.

As a small boy I caught a few small eels in a stream at Whitley Bay. And I took a mackerel, just one, off Whitby when I was about ten. A little later, I caught quite a lot of crayfish in the River Wharfe.

As straws in the wind, these were hardly perceptible. The result of my only 'fishery' activity during the war was highly, and horribly, perceptible, but without significance. As officer of the watch in an aircraft-carrier, I observed a whale heading across our bows. I altered course, but my judgement was wrong or the order came too late, for the aircraft-carrier bisected the innocent creature.

In 1946, back from the war, I fancied my prospects as a humorist. *Punch* took a piece from me in 1946 (see page 3), and a magazine called *Oxford Viewpoint* published several pieces while I finished my studies at Oxford. One of them was described as 'delightful' by Evelyn Waugh, in a letter which I saw but never got a copy of, alas.

During the next dozen years I wrote and wrote: but my output consisted of minutes written in the Foreign Office and reports from Embassies abroad. No doubt the experience has left its mark on my style.

In 1961 I and my family were sent to Tunis. The fish there were excellent, but their names (Arabic, French, Italian) were puzzling. From an initial promise to my wife Jane that I would give her an explanatory list for use in the market, a doomed idea for someone as ignorant of the subject as I was and unable to find any relevant books, I progressed to writing and publishing a booklet on the seafish of Tunisia. The metamorphosis from ignoramus to author was brought about by rascally Sicilian fishermen, whose dynamiting of fish in the Gulf of Tunis caused an Italian Delegation to come to Tunis, accompanied by a real expert, the greatest on Mediterranean fish, Professor Giorgio Bini. The problem discussed by the Delegation was, obviously, political.

They did not need an expert, so Bini had nothing to do, until I persuaded him to teach me the rudiments of ichthyology.

The interest, partly taxonomic and nomenclatural, partly culinary, which I then took in fish might have evaporated but for a coincidence. A colleague in the Embassy had known Elizabeth David in Cairo during the war. He sent her the booklet, she wrote about it in the *Spectator*, and years later when it had been long out of print she persuaded her editor at Penguin, Jill Norman, that it should be turned into a proper book covering the whole Mediterranean. So in 1972 I tasted the pleasures of being the author of a real book, and desired the same again.

The desire was suppressed for years, while I worked, now higher up, in the Foreign Office. Long days of anxious activity, interrupted nights, weekends in the office, all this caused the fish in my life to submerge; but they were still there, deep down.

In 1973 we were sent to Laos. A change. The pale faces, hurried steps and anxious looks of Whitehall faded from the screen, to be replaced by beautiful, composed, golden-skinned people. The 'Whitehall warriors' who waged so ferociously with pen and ink their interdepartmental battles gave way to Americans, Russians, Vietnamese, Chinese, fighting a real war. And I was exposed to temptation. I was now in a country whose fish had never been properly catalogued, and whose cookery had never been described in print.

Leaning heavily on the kindness of a Japanese expert who had been brought by the Americans to remedy the first deficiency, and helped in the second respect by the loan of the manuscript cookery book of the (now late) King's (then late) chef, I produced *Fish and Fish Dishes of Laos*. The destiny of this work seems clear: to be the only book on the subject. It was and remains unlike my other books on two scores. First, it was not a rearrangement of existing knowledge, but provided some new information. Secondly, it showed a profit, initially for the Laotian Red Cross and then, later, for me.

The machinery which rewards government servants with honours as they climb up the ladder came into play and provided me with some letters after my name just after *Fish and Fish Dishes of Laos* was published. Lao friends assumed cause and effect. Why else, they must have thought. Why else indeed? Or for what better reason? Of course I knew it could not be so, but I did not deprive my friends of such a charming illusion, so flattering to Her Majesty The Queen and Her Majesty's Government.

Laos has no coastline, so the fish I had been dealing with were all freshwater species. I was now inspired to turn back to the sea and start work on *Seafood of South-East Asia*; and to think of other, future books, and how I could get to write them. Vientiane, the capital of Laos, is small, so social rounds which would take a whole evening in Bangkok, New York or London could be accomplished in an hour. Many of my evenings and most weekends were quite free for writing. It would not be so in another capital, and certainly not in London. Should I quit diplomacy and become a writer?

My family, arguing that ten more years of official life would make me intolerably pompous, favoured quitting. The matter still hung in the balance when the Head of Personnel Department, in the course of an Asian tour, visited us. He spoke of the future, hinted at a posting back to London, and remarked apropos of this, and in encouraging tones, that he had always thought of me as a 'good Whitehall warrior': spine-chilling words, bringing into lurid relief my family's worst fears. I decided to quit.

This comprehensible sequence brought us back to London and set me to work writing *North Atlantic Seafood*. But I could see that the supply of seafood themes would not last indefinitely (though I still hope to do the Caribbean and West Africa); and also that in my new role I should think of writing about other things. So I undertook to write the *Oxford Companion to Food*, a work on which I still labour. This broadened my interest to include all aspects of food and cookery all over the world, in all periods of time.

The shuffling of the cards seemed so far to have been accomplished in an orderly way. But the joker had still to emerge. Accidentally I became a publisher. Time-Life Books, planning their mammoth 'Good Cook' series and perhaps realising that a counterweight was needed to offset the deadening effect of their own bureaucracy, hired an outstandingly creative artist and writer, Richard Olney, to be master-mind of the series. Sparks flew as he applied his creativity. One rule invented by the bureaucracy was that every recipe in the books had to come from a published source. There was one which Olney simply had to include, but for which no suitable published source was available. I asked him what would happen if someone started up a semi-academic journal on food history and the recipe appeared in the first (and probably the only) issue. 'That would be fine,' he said. 'I'd win.' So I did and he did. But ten years later the journal is in its 30th issue, and Prospect Books (the ten-year-old cuckoo in our basement) has also published over two dozen books. Among the many results of this has been a further widening of my interests, especially in the field of old cookery books.

'How much cooking do you do?' is a question I have sometimes – well, once or twice – been asked. The answer is not all that much: I tend to head for the library rather than the kitchen. But I make marmalade every year, lots and lots of it, and I have cooked multitudes of fish dishes, and I do dinner every Friday night. Otherwise I go to the kitchen for experimental purposes, like seeing what happens to bones if you pressure-cook them for a long time (answer on page 31). In short, I'm not much of a cook. And I keep company with bold Alice Waters (who must be almost unique among American cookery writers in this respect) in not answering to the term 'gourmet'.

So, there it is: all you need to know in order to make some sense of my patchwork quilt. All except for one thing. Why 'A Kipper With My Tea'? High tea, Scots style, has always been, at least since the age of four, my favourite meal. And I really like kippers.

Part One
A Personal Miscellany

Just Half a Cup for Me, Please

'Half a cup, please,' said Harold.

He gave me a meaning look as Joan manipulated the tea-pot. She handed back the cup, and he took it with the easy triumph of a conjurer producing a rabbit from his hat.

'You see, George?' he said, putting the cup down in the centre of the table and looking at it with disfavour. 'I asked for half a cup and I have got a whole cup. It always happens. There must be some strange kink in women which makes them do this. Is it that they never hear what we say, or is it that the sound of pouring tea bewitches their ears and paralyses their fingers? Whatever is its cause the situation fills me with foreboding. I can see little hope for a world split into two such irreconcilable factions – on the one hand men, thwarted, passionate beings, for ever on their knees, begging for half a cup of tea; on the other hand women, cold, dreamy creatures, perpetually handing them full cups with uncomprehending smiles.'

'Well, don't let it get cold,' said Joan.

Harold drank moodily.

He reverted to the subject later in the evening while we sat in the Red Lion, filling in time before the church social which Joan had bidden us attend at eight o'clock.

'Sometimes,' he said wistfully, 'I used to dream of meeting a girl who was completely mistress of herself when pouring out tea. But that was a long time ago; I didn't realise the difficulties then. The roots of this problem are as deep as time itself. Woman has always been behind the tea-pot, or its equivalent. It is there that she finds her fullest self-expression, and to meddle with her there is to invite disaster. I once knew a girl in Chichester who was driven by her brother's scorn to discipline herself in this matter. After a time she could manage three quarters of a cup; but the strain imposed on her was dreadful, and she developed a repression of unusual dimensions.'

We drank deeply and pondered the memory of this semi-paragon.

Shortly after eight we arrived at the social. Joan recognised our arrival with an approving nod from the far corner of the hall, where she was lavishing sandwiches on the butcher and baker (we have more candlesticks than we need).

We sat down in little green chairs and looked round us in what we considered to be a jolly manner. We longed for something with which we could toy, to conceal the awful fact that we never knew what we were supposed to do at functions of this kind.

It was then that the girl in blue came over to us. She was a remarkably pretty girl. 'Can I bring you two some tea?' she asked in a low musical voice.

'Yes, please. Only half a cup for me,' replied Harold, looking up solemnly into her brown eyes.

While she was away I glanced interrogatively at him. He shook his head, but this did not deceive me. Hope was gleaming in his eyes: and when she came back the hand which he stretched out for his cup was not quite steady. With the fascinated expression of a man who peers into a crystal and sees his destiny, he looked over the rim of the cup. It was precisely half full.

In a series of magnificent gestures he placed the cup aside, stood up, and took the girl's hand in his. He opened his mouth, and I grew pale, knowing the type of long emotional speech which a far less occasion than this could elicit from him.

But the girl anticipated him. 'I'm terribly sorry,' she said, 'but it's all there was in the pot.'

1946

'An Omelette and a Glass of Wine'

Publication this month of Elizabeth David's latest book*
provides an occasion for re-assessing the work, past and
current, of the doyenne of Britain's writers on food
and cookery

The blue front door in a quiet Chelsea street gives on to a hall in which cartons full of books, ever-changing but ever-present, define the narrow gangway to the kitchen. And it is in the kitchen – with its pine table, its orderly clutter, and its french windows opening on to a tiny patio – that one talks to Elizabeth David, if one has business with her, which I used to have as editor for a few of her essays.

In the midst of talk she will pause to check something in the oven or on the stove. A dish from her famous *Book of Mediterranean Food?†* More probably something simple for daily sustenance. The last time I came home from such a visit I could only report that she was cooking some potatoes in her beloved old 'diable'. Typically, my look of curiosity when she took it from the oven to see whether the potatoes were done evoked a commentary tinged with passion. The *only* way to cook English potatoes. The inside of the diable (a lidded, completely unglazed, clay pot) must *never* be washed. I am left dizzy with desire for my own diable, thinking ruefully of all the unsuitably cooked potatoes which I have eaten.

But the talk is not all of cookery; far from it. True, Elizabeth David's reputation rests on her cookery books, if they may be so classified. But if one thing is clear from reading them, and from talking with her, it is that she doesn't see cookery as a thing apart, a self-contained subject, a matter which can be dealt with just by writing out clear recipes. On the contrary, it is only one thread in a rich tapestry; a thread to be interwoven with many others – history, art of all kinds, literature. It is this sense of context, as well as her style of writing, which has lifted her books on to a level of their own.

*An Omelette and a Glass of Wine, London, 1984.   † London, 1950.

A conversation with her, for someone with a less developed sense of context, less wide knowledge, an inferior memory – all the defects which I, for example, exhibit – can be unnerving as well as stimulating. She shimmers, swerves and swoops from one matter to another with the grace and speed of a ballet dancer – and indeed moves around in like manner, offering a glass of chilled white wine or mineral water from her refrigerator, a set of impeccably corrected proofs from her kitchen table, a sight of a new book which she has liked, a smell of some strange spice which a friend has brought from afar, a painting which she acquired years ago – or a view of the potatoes in their diable.

The choreographer of this ballet is herself. Since time is precious to her, she always, automatically, plans how best to use it. One learns from experience that the pile of papers and books on the table represents the libretto according to which the conversation will be conducted; it looks like a haphazard pile, but in reality is as carefully planned as the subtle blend of colours in her clothes.

The comparison with ballet is not as far-fetched a simile as one might think. She has in her much of both actress and dancer; and I often think that she could have found her destiny on the stage. I mentioned just now new books which she likes. But there are also those which are not liked; and her negative reaction is no discreet English frown, but a Mediterranean display of shock and grief – her head will be buried in her hands, expressing anguish at missed opportunities, gaffes, inaccuracies, and other causes for lamentation.

In the introduction to her new book she recalls someone saying: 'It must be awful to be you. Always criticising everything, enjoying nothing.' On which she has two comments. First, 'if a food writer does not exercise his or her critical faculties to a high degree and with a backing of informed experience, he or she is not doing his or her job.' Second, the majority of the essays in the new book are expressions of enthusiasm, 'about benefits and pleasures, about good food, good wine, good cookery books'.

Reading the book bears this out: 5 heaped tablespoonfuls of appreciation for every 1 of condemnation. How, then, could the impression arise of an author always 'criticising everything'? I think because the criticisms are not only devastatingly witty, frank and well targeted, but also because they have – in her own words – 'a backing of informed experience'. The Iceberg Factor is at work. Only the tip is visible in what she writes, but it rests on a massive reserve of knowledge. It is a favourite theory of mine that readers can somehow tell when a writer has this invisible reserve, and that writing has greater impact when it is so fortified.

Readers are also quick to sense a situation in which an author seems to speak with knowledge which isn't really there; and, conversely, grateful to authors who don't hesitate to say that they do *not* know this or that. Here again, Elizabeth David has always been forthright. I was interested to read in her new book a passage from a 1961 review of Helen Brown's *West Coast Cookbook*.* This, she declared, 'throws light on scores of points about American ingredients and American cooking which, in my ignorance of the American continent, have always seemed to me most mysterious'. Another writer would have summoned up some second-hand scraps of knowledge about cooking in California, to give the impression of knowing all about it. Elizabeth David communicates with us in more genuine fashion, and we are in a way relieved to hear that there is something which is a mystery to her.

This particular mystery, by the way, has been partly dissipated. A seed was sown in 1961 which recently blossomed in a series of visits to California. These excursions represent a certain widening of her experience, geographically. But it remains true that Elizabeth David is, above all, a European and Mediterranean writer (although she had much of interest to say about Anglo-Indian cookery in *Spices, Salt and Aromatics in the English Kitchen*),† and that she has kept firmly to the principle of writing about what she knows, and only going into print when she is satisfied with the work she has done. This is one reason – bouts of ill health which subdue even her radiant vitality are another – why there are long intervals between her books. The new one is only the third since 1960, and the first since *English Bread and Yeast Cookery*.‡

There is another reason for the slow tempo of publication. As the bread book demonstrated, she has become much more deeply involved in history. At present she is working on a book which deals with the history of ice and ice cream; and the amount of research going into this is prodigious. When it is finished, it will be a contribution to scholarship as well as a fascinating read. Looking ahead, I can foresee how some reviewers, like doomed lemmings, scampering over the cliff edge, will take the occasion to refer to her as our leading 'scholar cook'. They will do so in ignorance of the fact that this phrase is one which immediately produces the head-in-hands grief syndrome. She does *not* like to be so categorised. Indeed she is eminently someone on whom it is inappropriate to stick any label, for her high renown is based firmly and precisely on the fact that she is different.

1984

* Boston, 1952.   †Penguin, 1970.   ‡London, 1977.

The Seven Wonders of Konya*

Even as a schoolboy, in the days before my buffer memory was full, I never could remember what the Seven Wonders of the World are, so when our Turkish hosts reminded us that three of them are in Turkey I could only suppose they were right. Perhaps we even saw one of them while we were there. But the seven things which filled me with wonderment were all to do with the Konya Congress.

I realised that this was going to be different from the symposia I had attended previously in Oxford, Adelaide, and Cambridge (Mass.), and it certainly was. One remarkable difference was the degree of *press interest*. On the first evening, at the inaugural cocktail party, one could hardly move for the trailing wires of photographers (television included), or see for the glare of arc lights, or draw breath except to answer questions, premature then, but soon to become highly familiar: what did we think of Turkish food? – what were our impressions of the Congress? Recalling the low-key apparition of occasional members of the press at Oxford, equipped with at most a discreet, pocket-sized, recording apparatus, I fell to wondering: whence this burning interest?

The Second Wonder was the *food*. Two banquets a day, and no repetition. It was all marvellously good, and most of it unfamiliar. A dinner in Konya comprised sixty local specialities. Perhaps someone managed to taste them all. Already bloated from an *alfresco* lunch at which three whole lambs, roasted in a sealed *tandur* oven, had been consumed, I warily dodged my way down to the fruit and dessert section. Quince stuffed with rice was a revelation. So was 'marrow jam', which wasn't the sort of jam we make, but produced by first soaking small round slices of marrow (courgette), then combining them with grape juice which had been boiled down to a viscous liquid, almost black.

* In 1986 an international congress on culinary history was held in Istanbul and Konya, Turkey.
   The illustrations are by Mary Lane Macatee, an American artist who lived and worked in Turkey for parts of her life.

The impression we thus received of almost infinite variety, fortified by the general euphoria, was soon eliciting comments to the effect that Turkish cuisine had been called by someone (no one could remember who) one of the three (or five, said some) great cuisines of the world, and that this was surely so. Treated as an expression of emotions of strong approval, this sort of statement is appropriate. Taken more seriously, it leads, I think, to the conclusion that, while one can identify the three highest mountains in the world, a similar approach to cuisines raises hopelessly complex questions of definition and criteria, and about the cultural background of the would-be judges. Too timorous to enter such a maze, I simply record my own astonishment (although I had been

to Turkey several times before) at the range of dishes offered to us
(while noting that many of these seemed to involve lamb, aubergines,
rice, or all three) and, with the benefit of reflection in tranquillity,
identify what I really enjoyed most of all: the bread; the honey
(someone gave me a whole comb from the environs of Mt Ararat); and
ayran (the yogurt drink).

But we had food for the spirit too. Konya is the home of the Mevlâna
sect and of the *whirling dervishes* who are their best known manifes-
tation. While in Istanbul we were taken to see them whirling, and I
suppose that I was not alone in expecting something quite different
from what we witnessed, which was a religious rite of an intensively
impressive kind. To the accompaniment of their special music, the
dervishes – eight of them, varying in age and under the direction of a
venerable arch-dervish – revolved dreamily in hypnotic patterns in a
very large octagonal room, round the perimeter of which, fenced off by
railings, we spectators sat in a condition verging on awe. We had been
prepared for the spectacle by a leaflet which pointed out that:

> whirling is the inevitable condition for existence. Any being that
> doesn't whirl cannot exist. The common similarity among exist-
> ing beings is that electrons, protons and neutrons of atoms
> forming their structures are whirling. The human being too whirls
> just like everything else does . . .

Thus the macroscopic whirling of the dervishes mirrors the invisible
sub-microscopic whirling which goes on within us all.

All this was thought-provoking; but what was the special message
here for food historians? Efforts were made afterwards to explain in
allegorical terms ('Why are you cooking me?' asked a chickpea) the
special role which food and cookery play in the beliefs of the Mevlâna
sect, but my comprehension stopped short at the bare fact that it has
such a role, and that one of the hero-figures for the sect is a thirteenth-
century chef, Ates Baz-i Veli, declared to be 'Mevlâna's and *world's first
chief cook*'. He died in 1285, and we were taken to see his tomb, an
octagonal structure just outside Konya. Arriving like tourists, in a
municipal bus, we left like true pilgrims, on foot, the bus having
reversed into a field to turn round and having been unable to get out
again.

Our organisers, who consistently showed a flair for dealing with
derailments of the programme and putting us back on schedule, dealt
with this and other problems effectively, but confessed at the end of the
Congress that they were dissatisfied with the arrangements they had

made to deal with the complication of bilingual proceedings, in Turkish and English, without the provision of simultaneous interpretation. There was a problem here, but it was greatly attenuated by the emergence of the debonair Dr Debeş, from the university in the Turkish Republic of Cyprus, as an unofficial interpreter of masterly skill. Many a bridge built he between the non-English speakers and the non-Turkish speakers.

This leads to consideration of the *great variety of papers* delivered at our formal sessions, a third in Istanbul and the rest in Konya. These were tightly organised. Fifteen minutes had been allowed for each paper, and this ration was not exceeded. Those who spoke about their papers came off better than those who read them and who were politely arrested in mid-paragraph when the 15th minute came. The most striking performance came from the Turk who delivered his paper in Turkish in 7 minutes, then repeated it in English – another 7 minutes, so one to spare. Time for discussion was promised for the end of each session, but was only available once, after the first session. On this occasion no one had any questions or comments. None of us had yet grappled with the forms which had been circulated on which we were to inscribe our questions in writing. We might have adapted to the system eventually, but after this initial response we found that discussion time was bounced forward from one session to the next, and finally and decisively bounced into limbo at the end.

However, many of the papers were excellent and, although the Congress had no official theme, they hung together surprisingly well. Several addressed directly or indirectly the subject of Turkish food abroad – what Raymond Sokolov referred to as 'the Turkish diaspora'. Here we had a survey by Jeremy Round of Turkish restaurants in London; an admirable paper by Maria Johnson on 'Turkish contributions to flour-based confectionery in the Balkans'; a piquant study by Berthe Meijer of the food habits of Turkish guest-workers in the Netherlands; and papers on how Turkish cookery was perceived in England in past centuries. Additional dimensions were added to this sub-theme by the ruminations of Paul Levy – ever alert to the fact that today's trends are tomorrow's history – on what is happening in the restaurant world generally; and by a brilliantly lucid extempore talk from Yan-Kit So, reflecting her paper on restaurants in Hong Kong. Some of the Turkish papers, being so far without a translation, remained opaque to most of us, but those which had been translated were full of interest and showed that culinary history is thriving in Turkey.

Of the papers referred to above on English perceptions of Turkish

cookery, that by Gillian Goodwin, who dealt with the seventeenth century, was broadly based, taking account of travel books and other sources besides cookery books. That by myself and Jane Davidson, covering the eighteenth and nineteenth centuries, was based entirely on the evidence of cookery books, and showed these to contain virtually nothing in the way of authentic Turkish recipes. The great exception to which we drew attention was the rare little *Turkish Cookery Book* by Turabi Effendi, published in 1864 (and in a second edition in 1884). We circulated the text of this to everyone, as an appendix to our paper, and expressed the hope that a Turkish participant could throw light on the origin of the book, and tell us who Turabi Effendi was.

The result of this enquiry was, for us, an *electrifying illumination*. A certain Turgut Kut, researcher at Gelişim Publishing House in Istanbul, stepped forward with shining eyes and offered us his bibliography of Turkish cookery books,* displaying an entry for Turabi Effendi's book and explaining that it was in fact a translation of the first proper Turkish cookery book, *Melceü't-Tabbâhîn* by Mehmed Kâmil (1844). Dr Kut assured us, before we were interrupted, that he also had

---

* Published in 1985.

information about Turabi Effendi, and we resolved to seek him out in the night train to Ankara, to which we were about to be shepherded, or some other suitable venue, but learned later that he had not been able to travel on from Istanbul. So the rest of the story will have to follow later. Perhaps it is well that such a momentous discovery ('This alone justifies the whole Congress!' exclaimed one colleague) should be delivered in instalments.

My Seventh Wonder must be *Nevin Halıcı*, the moving spirit of the whole Congress, an archimageiric presence with the dedication and face of a Byzantine saint, radiating an almost tangible calm and tirelessly catalysing contacts between the visitors and the home team. Among the gifts which we were given, none was more welcome than a set of the books she has written, enshrining traditional Turkish recipes of which many risked being lost from sight. We all hope that these may be translated into English and made more generally accessible. Indeed my own answers to the questions constantly asked by Turkish promoters of tourism etc. (Is Turkish cuisine sufficiently known abroad? What can be done to spread knowledge of it?) is that a sine qua non is the publication in English of basic works such as Nevin Halıcı's.

Let it not be thought, however, that Nevin Halıcı lacked a counterpart among the visitors. Claudia Roden, whose enthusiasm both helped to inspire the event and suffused it throughout, played this role with inexhaustible grace and wit, so that we had the benefit of two leading ladies.

1986

On the Trail of Giant Gooseberries

On 6 August last year the geese at the village pub in Egton Bridge, North Yorkshire, became over-excited and paraded up and down the grass in a manner even more ridiculous than usual. They must have been infected by the local excitement over the annual Egton Bridge Old Gooseberry Competition, held on that day. No doubt they will be infected again on 5 August of this year, for the competition is an annual event which has reputedly been going since 1800 and shows no signs of dying out. On the contrary, last year's event, which I attended, saw the establishment of a new Egton Bridge record: a berry weighing nearly two ounces (60g).

Gooseberry competitions are not recommended for thrill-seekers; but for those who relish quaint and out-of-the-way aspects of English rural life, uncluttered by busloads of tourists, they are perfect.

The growing and eating of gooseberries is very much a British activity. I say 'British' because the Scots as well as the English have the right climate and plenty of enthusiasm. But the craze which began in the eighteenth century for growing giant gooseberries was really an English one.

The gooseberry bush, unlike the apple tree, can be grown in a very small garden. So it provided an outlet for the horticultural enthusiasm of the workers living in small terraced houses, usually with a tiny garden attached, in the growing cities of the Industrial Revolution. Manchester in Lancashire was one such, and it was there, in 1786, that the first national register of gooseberry competitions was published. But the centre of gooseberry gravity shifted eventually to Cheshire and Yorkshire, and it is in those two counties that the ten surviving competitions are held.

Len Dowson, the secretary of the Egton Bridge competition, is a serious-looking geography teacher, whose brow is furrowed by mild anxiety when he discusses its history. As far back as the records go, the competition has been announced as 'founded in 1800', but he hasn't been able to find the evidence for this. Research in nineteenth-century newspapers continues, and everyone hopes that it will be concluded by 2000, so that the celebration of the 200th anniversary will rest on a firm foundation.

The competitors are not commercial growers, but amateurs. Some come from as far as thirty miles away, but since the competing fruits have to be picked on the morning of the competition and delivered by 2 pm, that is about the limit.

Recalling that there had been a small outcrop of gooseberry competitions in the USA in the nineteenth century, I asked Len what would happen if an American competitor appeared on the scene, having flown over on Concorde. He replied drily that the Rules Committee would take a look at the matter before there was any possibility of such a dramatic event being repeated. Gooseberries grown in a different climate were not likely to be welcome. But the committee, of practical Yorkshiremen, would not be likely to waste time on a hypothetical and improbable event.

Certainly, the competition is an intensely local occasion. On the eve of last year's event we were sitting with Len in the local inn (the Horseshoe Hotel, Egton Bridge, not to be confused with the Horseshoe in neighbouring Egton), standing each other pints and poring over his records. Looking only at the faces (and ignoring the clothes, and the cars outside), we could easily imagine ourselves in a group of medieval English yeomen. Nor, I wager, have the accents and the gooseberry talk changed appreciably in the last hundred years. Len's father was a grower. Some of those present had been 'growing' for over half a century.

The competition takes place in a spacious village schoolroom. The pace of activity in the morning is subdued. The three weighmen and two judges are closeted in the small room where the special scales are kept. Competitors arrive with their gooseberries, and each is weighed. About every ten minutes a weighman comes out into the main hall with a plate of weighed berries and an inscribed card upon it, and deposits this on the competition table. In another corner the volunteers who run the raffle write names on the tickets and tear them in half. That's all.

By 4 pm weighing is completed and visitors begin to make their slow way round the long table. There's a lot to look at. This is no simple competition for the one heaviest gooseberry. There are separate classes for red, green, white (very pale green) and yellow berries. Since all the berries are green until ripe, and it is hard to ensure that berries attain full ripeness on the exact day of the competition, most of the berries look green; but many of them are really reds, yellows or whites, and part of the judges' skill consists in correctly classifying them. 'Maidens', as new members are known, have their own prizes, and there are also prizes for the heaviest twelve and the heaviest six. A complex rule-book ensures that no one wins too many prizes, and that a high proportion of the contestants win something. The prizes, such as a home-cured ham and pieces of gardening equipment donated by local firms, are on the table too, together with the silver cup for the champion berry.

Last year's new record was established by a berry of the yellow variety Woodpecker (which has been the most frequent winner since 1943), entered by B. Harland. Its weight, at 30 drams 22 grains, was breathtakingly close to two ounces (a figure as talismanic to gooseberry growers as the four-minute mile once was for athletes), and a full 13 grains heavier than the best red, which was of the nineteenth-century variety Lord Derby. The champion was a big berry, certainly, but the first time I went round the table I missed it, bemused by the endless platefuls of giants and the complexity of the inscriptions on the little cards.

The afternoon visitors evinced only muted excitement: low murmurs of appreciation, technical comments, and occasionally a pawky Yorkshire joke. It was in the evening, during a boisterous raffle of potted plants (bleeding hearts and stars of Jordan) to raise a few hundred pounds to keep the competition going for another year, and with a silver band from the nearby village of Stape playing vigorously, that the atmosphere became jollier. In the late evening, at the Horseshoe Hotel, it was jollier still.

We had a hearty dinner at the inn, listening to the growing volume of noise, always dominated by the silver band. 'Oh yes, they keep going, drinks are on the house and they keep going,' observed the waitress. Recalling that I had not been able to persuade any of the growers to say anything about eating gooseberries (their eyes widened – eating gooseberries? – no, it seemed there was nothing to be done with them once they were weighed), I asked whether ever, at the inn . . . The answer was yes, there was a large gooseberry pie on the menu, served with cream. It was patently home-made, having that becomingly untidy look which good pies should have; and the berries, plump to bursting point after their cooking, had just enough acidity to balance the sweet cream. 'When the Saints Come Marching In' boomed through the windows. 'The gamekeeper's berries,' said the waitress, 'grown just over the river, quite big too, should have been in the competition.'

We went outside. The band played on, foaming glasses of ale beside most of the players. 'On Ilkley Moor Baht 'At' was followed by 'The Lord Is My Shepherd', in a secular and religious counterpoint which presumably reflected the make-up of the band. The geese continued to process, quacking but unheard above the din; 'Lead Thou Me On' was an apt accompaniment to their efforts. In the parlour a couple who were on their way from Scotland to the south of England, and who had booked their room in ignorance of what would be happening, resolutely carried out their 'read before bedtime' ritual, glancing up in temporary appreciation when 'Edelweiss' was played.

1986

A Dutch Treat

Way back in the 1950s, when we lived in The Hague, we would have Saturday lunch at a fish restaurant called Saur's, a 1930ish building perched unobtrusively at the end of the beautifully conserved Lange Voorhout. One could sit on stools round the kidney-shaped 'oyster bar', or at little tables flanking the bar, or out of doors. (There is an upstairs dining room, but that is for the wealthier people, prices about 18 per cent higher.) Wherever one sat, the economical dish to have was 'Saur's Fish Dish', essentially pieces of whatever fish were abundant that day, in a white sauce flecked with this and that, and surrounded by whorled mounds of mashed potato, lightly browned on top – served in an oval, shallow gratin dish. Delicious, always, and adopted into our family repertoire, where it has remained ever since.

In 1978 I went back to The Hague on fishy business and confidently asked at Saur's for my fondly remembered dish. The waiter, elderly and hard-pressed, told me firmly that they did not have it; and that they never had had it. He claimed to know what had been served since Saur's opened and that my crystal-clear memory was flawed, the mere imagining of a deranged foreigner. Having argued the point briefly and hopelessly, I retreated, resolving to prove myself right with another waiter and in another year.

The year was 1987, Mijnheer Van den Ende the waiter. A charming and perceptive man who, like most of the staff, has been at Saur's for ages and ages. He grasped the problem at once and applauded my detective work when, after examining the current menu, I put my finger on *Poisson crème au gratin*. Yes, that must be it. He regretted that the name had been changed. How confusing for old customers, of whom many returned after a very long lapse of time – my own 33 years was by no means a record. They did their best to keep everything the same, since that was what all their customers desired.

I had the rechristened Saur's Fish Dish, and it was exactly as I remembered. The fish which chanced to be in it on this occasion were salmon and turbot. The sauce was the same as ever, and the mounds of mashed potato might have had their whorls put on by the same hand which was at work in the 1950s.

Saur's have indeed adhered to the formula with which they began, and to the décor. The latter has all the charm of something which was (sort of) planned in the first place and has since been overlaid with harmonious but haphazard accretions, such as a mirror with a (?1950s) mermaid, anchor in one hand, guitar in the other; a severe 1980s white pot with a tropical fern; and a huge four-branched candelabra from the beginning of the century, surmounted by a towering pyramid of flowers. This sort of thing mitigates the rather sombre effect produced by the mural painting which was presumably the starting point of the original décor.

So, has anything changed? Yes, the prices of course. *Poisson crème au gratin* now costs 30 guilders (£9); and this is a real change, since in the 1950s it cost only the equivalent of about £4. A whole grilled sole now costs fl 58.50, while *Les filets de sole* are only fl 29.50 *à la meunière* and 36.50 *à la Dieppoise*. *Les suprêmes de turbot (à l'Ambassadeur, à la Catalane*, etc.) are all fl 56.50.

Everything is still as good as we remembered it, including the smoked eel, the memory of which we have long cherished as the 'best we have ever had', a memory now confirmed. Their suppliers, by the way, are Gebr. Kraan of Oude Wetering. And Saur's themselves have a small shop where this and other products, including excellent bisques which they make and can themselves, may be bought.

In case you wonder, no, there is no trace whatsoever of nouvelle cuisine influencing this establishment. It is as impervious to passing fashions as are the strictly protected eighteenth-century buildings which make up most of the Lange Voorhout. On both counts, the conservatism of the Hagenaars wins our heartfelt gratitude.

The same applies to our other favourite fish place in the city of The Hague-plus-Scheveningen (Scheveningen is the fishing port, formerly separated from the capital, now joined to it). This is the Havenrestaurant, by the side of the inner harbour at Scheveningen, a bustling place at which you must be prepared to queue. If dining, be there well before 7 pm, as they close early; if taking lunch, turn up in very good time. Try to look Dutch or, better, go with Dutch friends. The waiters are amiable enough, but they work at top speed and dealing with hesitant, inarticulate foreigners slows them down.

The food at the Havenrestaurant is very simple: the freshest of seafoods, straight from the boats, and good chips. If 'zeewolf' (*Anarhichas lupus*) is on the menu, ask for it; it is an uncommon fish and excellent.

1987

'Please Put the Table on the Bill'

'Two lunches, that's 130 francs [£13], and you'd like to take the table too? Right, that's another 5000 francs [£500].'

One of the best bargains in Paris for a light and delicious lunch can become expensive if you take up the offer of the proprietor, Jean-Pierre Rémy, to sell you the antique table off which you have eaten – or for that matter the table at which someone else is eating, or the plates, the silver . . . anything!

Of all the *salons de thé* which have been springing up like mushrooms in the centre of Paris, Délices et Orgues is the best for a 'total experience'. It is in a beautiful and quiet street in the Marais, a perfect area for browsing among antique shops while en route to the new Picasso Museum. The few other people in the salon (there are only four or five tables, depending on whether one has just been sold) are going to be beautiful/artistic/mysterious – and certainly possessed of exquisite manners. You may think that people choose where to eat, but a place like this can truly be said, by its special quality, to select its clients.

Rémy is a pianist – he was the last accompanist to play for Lucienne Boyer ('Parlez moi d'amour'), and only last year he closed down his salon for a month while he went to Japan to accompany Cora Vaucaire. So he holds recitals and small concerts in his salon, which resembles in shape a side chapel in a French cathedral, and indeed is part of the architecturally distinguished Rohan-Chabot mansion, which in turn backs on to the superb houses of the Place des Vosges. There are works of art displayed, too, and the atmosphere is of a tranquillity and refinement rarely found in a place where you pay to eat.

There is, by the way, a message in the name. There are three nouns in French which are masculine in the singular and feminine in the plural. Two of them are 'délice' and 'orgue'. So the name of the salon makes a statement of two themes: pleasure and music. But it also subtly implies, for those who know their grammar, the third noun in the offbeat trio. And what is that? Amour.

Jean-Pierre prepares the food, and it's very good indeed. The 65 franc lunch offers all this:

- a choice of five salads, for example an avocado salad on a bed of oakleaf lettuce, with tuna, small fresh vegetables, and tomato sauce, every ingredient perfect;
- either the *plateau des fromages* (cheese tray) or hot cheese on toast – the cheese is heated almost to melting point but retains its shape until you probe with a knife, when it 'relaxes' over the toast;
- a choice of *pâtisseries* brought daily by a young *pâtissier* of the *quartier*, who is quite brilliant;
- extra-good bread and butter;
- a *pichet* of wine, or beer or tea.

Tea (choose from 33 varieties) and coffee are both of the highest quality. Indeed everything is. Last time I went, it was the day after a pretentious and deeply disappointing meal at a two-star restaurant, which cost well over 400 francs (£40) a head. The recollection of this had been chafing me all morning, and I was in the mood for something simple and good, and for a really friendly ambiance. Which is exactly what I got.

You emerge from Délices et Orgues feeling refreshed in every way, and not least by talking with Jean-Pierre. If you have bought your table, you will also feel wildly exhilarated.

1986

An Ambiguous Ambigu

An ambitious exhibition, called *Les Hommes et leurs Aliments*, was held early in 1987 in the Cité des Sciences et de l'Industrie, a vast exhibition hall on the outskirts of Paris. The show had its moment of glory when a seventeenth-century '*ambigu*' (supper buffet) was laid on at midday for French television.

The exhibition committee included bevies of top food historians, so the repast was authentic, and delicious. It also included designers and publicity hounds, so it was eye-catching and photogenic – not just the huge table of sevententh-century dishes but also the bewigged flunkeys and the musicians who played seventeenth-century music.

The paradox is that for all the lavishness of the *ambigu* and the grandiloquence of the brochures distributed to the press, the exhibition itself was trivial: a few panels of information, and a couple of computer games. One of the games was scholarly ('If you were giving a banquet in the seventeenth century which of the following items might you serve?'). The few who essayed this scored very low marks. The other was about diet, contributed by the Alimentarium Museum which Nestlé have established in Switzerland: it takes a long time to answer all the questions about yourself and what you eat, especially as they presuppose that you are Swiss (what happened to the rest of the world?). I tried both. On the diet game I accidentally translated my height in inches into a grotesquely small number of centimetres, so had just been told to manage on a dwarf-like quantity of calories when an attendant switched the computer off – 'It must not run while the television cameras are working!' This was typical of the occasion. Here was someone attempting to take the exhibition seriously and finding himself unplugged as a potential nuisance to cameramen.

The explanation for this ambiguous event is that the exhibition was a mere trailer for a much larger and more costly show which was awaiting finance before it could be constructed and sent to tour the big provincial cities. The *ambigu* was laid on to impress possible sources of finance. If any such were present, they were heavily disguised, but perhaps the right people saw it on TV. Anyway the food historians and the TV technicians had a right feast, described in the souvenir menu as: *Ovalle à sept bassins, huit assiettes et seize pourcelaines*. The 31 items included: *Un grand pasté de gaudiveau à la françoise entouré de trois pâtés de lapins froids*; four salads – *anchois, persepierre, olives, citrons*; *Des baignets d'abricots* (liked by all) and *Des compotes de chair d'orange*, the bowls of which shone like suns on the white table, echoing with additional luminosity the whole oranges in the *Pyramides de fruits* which, obelisk-like, provided the vertical elements in the composition.

Two things are clear. '*L'homme*' in the title of the show is a Frenchman, not a citizen of the world; and the historical focus is more on aristocratic fare than on that of ordinary people. No doubt this is to be expected, given the way in which the most famous French writers on gastronomy have concentrated on such matters, and the reverence still paid to these writers. But I had hoped wistfully that the exhibition might signal an extension of culinary horizons, both geographically and socially. True, there was the gloomy-looking man from Alimentarium and his switched-off quiz; but he hadn't had to drive far to get into France, had he?

What is not clear is the real purpose of the whole thing. However, let us not overlook the incidental but interesting benefit of a subsidised tuck-in. If the show does attract finance, and swells to the proportions desired by the organisers, it will make a lot of sense to turn up on a day when there is an *ambigu* and pay the additional fee for that. The food is real, and eating it is a genuinely illuminating experience, especially if unilluminated by the lights of TV crews.

1987

Attacking a Lamb with our Fingers

Returning from an international food congress held at Istanbul and Konya, I wrote a piece called 'The Seven Wonders of Konya' (see page 8). In fact there was one more thing to wonder at, a different sort of thing, which sticks like a burr in my mind.

My wife and I had taken a paper to the congress, about English perceptions of Turkish cookery in the eighteenth and nineteenth centuries (see page 129). In this we had occasion to quote from a remarkable book, entitled *Domestic Economy and Cookery for Rich and Poor; containing an account of the best English, Scotch, French, Oriental and Other Foreign Dishes* . . . , published in 1827 and 'composed . . . by A Lady'. In her chapter on Oriental Cookery the Lady has the following passage about eating with the fingers:

> The Levantines far surpass us in the healthiness and excellence in dressing meats, though their unceremonious manner in presenting it, the way they squeeze it in their hand, &c. is at first not very agreeable to strangers, who do not take into consideration their frequent ablutions: besides, the true amateur of good living knows how much higher flavoured meats are from the hand than in any other mode. We, from prejudice, go into other countries in the proud superiority of our own customs and manners; and as the vulgar first attract our notice, we generally mistake their manners for those of the country. Were one of our fashionables to go down into one of our remote counties, and see a boor stuff a large wooden or horn spoon, full of some coarse food, into his wide open mouth, with his eyes shut, it were odds if he ever again ate with a spoon; declaring, perhaps, that pretty tapering fingers were expressly made to feed man more delicately.

I was pleased with this passage. I recalled how much had been eaten with the fingers in Laos, by the Lao and by us too, although often with the interposition of leaves between fingers and meat. The whole idea seemed fine.

Then, in the garden of a villa near Konya, we came up against reality. Our host had had three lambs slain and roasted whole in a sealed pit oven, out of doors. We shared the general sense of pleasurable anticipation as he bade his gardener break the seal on top of the oven. Gather round, he told us, the smell will be marvellous. It was indeed appetising. But as the gardener lifted out the scorched corpses, doubts attacked us.

The lambs had been small, and they looked smaller still after being sheared, cleaned, trussed and hung for hours in the fierce heat. A pathetic sight, in severe contrast to the large, live, hungry human beings who crowded round with exclamations of joy, those of them who were yoked to photographic apparatus jostling and clicking.

We sat at round picnic tables, eight to a table, eight to a lamb. At our table, someone (predictably, the familiar anecdote was bound to come to life) plucked out the eyes, announcing that they were the choicest morsel. Our unease was increased. But we set to work with our fingers, as directed, plucking morsels of meat. This was not the neat, easy operation which might have been expected. The flesh was still so hot that it was difficult to handle the gobbets. On the surface, it had been cooled by contact with the air; but, a finger poked in to prise a piece off would be slightly burned. I wondered how the Lady of 1827 would have coped, and recalled that Alexandre Dumas had been in a similar predicament near an oasis in Tunisia a long time ago (and that he had also described his difficulties frankly). Still, we managed, and of course the meat was delicious, no question about that.

What was left of the lamb's head had been decorated by placing sprigs of flat-leaved parsley between its jaws. What happened after the eyeball incident was that another lady of the party reached forward, parted the jaws and plucked out the tongue. She did this with finesse, her own uncooked tongue peeping out between her uncharred teeth as she concentrated on the task. Another great, although diminutive, delicacy, it seemed. I regularly have a slice of ox-tongue for lunch at home, but I declined my share of this morsel.

Not far away was a fountain, with towels laid out beside it. Naturally, we all wanted to wash our hands when we had finished feasting on the lamb. Naturally? Or was there something more to the want?

In a sense, this experience was banal. How often have we reflected that it is one thing to buy a piece of meat in a shop, another to take part in or even witness the events which lead up to the presentation of the sanitised fragment on the shelf!

On this occasion we had not been there for the slaughter. Judging by our reactions to the aftermath, this would have been too much for us. Even the rosewater dispensed by our host would have failed to leave us feeling clean.

Banal, yes, for you readers, and for me too if I were reading what someone else had written. But the occasion made a sharply etched and lasting impression on me, which I have felt impelled to record. I shan't again quote so lightly pieces about the charm of eating with the fingers, because the phrase will henceforth bring the image of the feast in the villa garden into my mind's eye.

1987

Funeral Cookbooks

There is a custom which I have met only in Thailand, whereby a person composes a small cookbook before her or his death, so that it can be distributed as a keepsake to the mourners attending the funeral.

The recipes, typically no more than a score, are likely to be those which the deceased especially enjoyed. They need not have been composed or used by the deceased, but often are. Sometimes they incorporate little anecdotes and attributions.

The design of the booklets, and the specifications to the printer, may reflect very careful consideration. I have one with a beautiful white card cover on which appears a luminous red sun. The typography and layout are such that a professional designer had clearly been at work.

I know of only one person, a Thai lady, who made a point of collecting these hard-to-find ephemera. She was murdered by her gardeners in Bangkok and I never learned what happened to the collection. The items are hard to find because they are printed in small editions, just enough for the expected number of mourners; and those who receive them usually keep them.

The idea is attractive. With what better keepsake could one depart from a funeral? What other would equally well keep one's memory green among friends? If one is to issue some sort of posthumous message, avoiding anything egotistical or hortatory, is not a simple message about enjoyable food the best that could be devised? It is true that one could equally well compose a list of 'books I have enjoyed', but that might seem didactic, even patronising; whereas a little bouquet of recipes arrives on a more relaxed note: 'take them or leave them, it's up to you, I just wanted you to have them.'

So I have thought about this, off and on, for years. If I was in the Thai cultural framework, I would long ago have put together my favourite family recipes and worked out an exquisite design and cover for them. Every two or three years I would be updating it, modifying the design, thinking of even greater refinements, perhaps adding an appendix giving biographical particulars of my forebears whose recipes would be used, maybe even a tiny index; and would there be scope for some drawings, and who should do them?

However, I am not in the Thai culture, and I hesitate to import this item from it, with the attendant risk of causing surprise and perhaps even criticism in the damp and muddy driveway of the crematorium. Although, naturally, hoping that the hypothetical booklet would not be printed until long hence, I am prey to gloomy imaginings about its reception.

'A bit odd, don't you think?'

'Yes, but of course he *was* a bit odd.'

'I think I'll give mine to Oxfam tomorrow.'

'Hmm, wouldn't it be more correct to keep it for a while?'

'Yes, but what for? We're knee-deep in cookbooks already. Still, you may be right. By the way, did you say anything to the family about it?'

'No, I wondered whether to, but I thought not. Between ourselves, I heard that the whole business of getting it printed in three days had been a nightmare for them.'

'Yes, I'm sure it was. It's all rather embarrassing, isn't it?'

Yet sometimes I hear other voices, surprised in a pleasant way, enthusiastic, warm in the autumn sunshine which plays on the group at the crematorium door.

'My dear, I think it was a wonderful idea! And so original! I'm going to treasure my copy . . .'

What, then, will happen? Something or nothing? Time will have to tell. But will anyone be listening when time tells? Probably not, save perhaps a lone ethnologist collecting data on the transferral or non-transferral of funeral customs from one culture to another.

1988

Part Two
Food Science

The Joy of Cooking Under Pressure

When did science and technology first encounter the cook's domain? I suggest that they made their entry, hand in hand, on 22 May 1679, when Denys Papin demonstrated to the Royal Society in London what we would now call a pressure cooker. He called it a 'digester' and designed it to soften bones, a process useful for 'cookery, voyages at sea, confectionary', and other diverse purposes.

Born and educated in France, Papin had come to England in 1675, and worked under the celebrated early physicist Robert Boyle for several years. Unlike Boyle, who tended to display mandarin symptoms, Papin had a sense of scientific *noblesse oblige* and a fondness for disseminating his lore. Thus he wrote *A New Digester* (1681) 'in the vulgar tongue', for 'housekeepers' and others who might benefit from the new technology he described. Although properly scientific, a large part of this 54-page book consists of descriptions of experiments designed for the kitchen. There were 17 for cooks, 10 for those preparing 'victuals for voyages at sea', four for confectioners, five for people making drinks, and only nine for 'chymists' and dyers.

Certainly it was the use of the digester for cooking that attracted attention. John Evelyn records in his *Diary* that on 12 April 1682, he attended a Royal Society supper, at which the results of cooking meat and fowl in the digester were exhibited and eaten. The 'hardest bones of biefe itself, & mutton, were . . . made as soft as cheese.' Evelyn paints a happy picture of the assembled sages turning the now friable bones into crumbs that 'one may strew on breade & eate without harm.'

You can probably figure out how Papin's machine worked by looking at *A New Digester*'s diagrams. *A* is a hollow brass cylinder, closed at the bottom and open at the top. *B* is a shorter brass cylinder, open at the bottom and fitting exactly on to *A*. The projections *CC*, the two iron bars *DD*, the removable iron bar *EE*, and the screws *FF* serve to keep *B* firmly on top of *A* when the contraption is in use and pressure builds up.

Inside *A* and *B* is *G*, 'another hollow cylinder made of glass, pewter, or some other material, fit to receive those things that are to be boiled:

this being filled and stopt with a cover exactly ground to it, and pressed upon it with a screw.' *G* is surrounded completely by water inside *A* and *B*. Note also that the rod *LM* has a weight suspended from it at *M*, holding down the valve *P* with a force equivalent to six times the normal air pressure. The entire contraption was heated by lowering *A* into a furnace, and Papin's design included clever indicators showing the amount of pressure and the temperature inside *G*. The latter was measured by a weighted thread swinging to and fro every second, with provision made for placing a drop of water in a cavity in the top of the weight and observing how many seconds elapsed before it evaporated.

Papin's first two experiments were devoted to seeing what would happen to a breast of mutton in the interior container *G* under varying degrees of heat. Neither experiment produced satisfactory results. Success finally came with experiment three, when he discovered the right temperature to render mutton 'very well done, the bones soft, and the juyce a strong gelly.'

Let me briefly review the principle of pressure-cooking and the circumstances in which it is most useful. At ordinary atmospheric pressure (15 pounds to the square inch) water boils at 100°C. As the pressure increases, the boiling temperature increases too. Thus, at 30 psi the temperature of boiling water and its steam is not 100°C but 120°C. The pressure cooker contains steam under abnormally high pressure, and anything in it is therefore cooked at a higher temperature. For many cooks the advantage in this lies in increased speed of cooking. But speed is not what Papin was after, nor is it what interests me. The more important question is whether this method of cooking affects what we may loosely term quality. Papin found that the flavour and texture of some things he cooked in his engine seemed better than normal. But the trend of his comments is to the effect that things were 'as good', and this is in line with what culinary experts would say today, as far as soups, vegetables and braised meats are concerned: quicker, but not better.

Bearing in mind the title of Papin's work, however, what about bones? Can they be softened in a pressure cooker to a mere pulp? This would be a real feat: one could produce a thick concentrate of bone that could be used to add calcium in large doses to certain foods and could also be used as an alternative to flour (currently so heavily frowned upon by the adherents of the nouvelle cuisine) for thickening sauces. With this in mind I have been conducting experiments with our own pressure cooker, a model that provides up to 15 pounds additional pressure and whose instructions do actually say that marrowbones can be reduced to a pulp in it. Not quite so, I found. Having taken chopped marrowbones and given them four successive two-hour treatments instead of the two treatments prescribed in the instructions, I found myself left with rock-hard bones projecting from what was left of the liquid.

This, I reflected, did not conflict with Papin's findings. His engine multiplied the pressure by six or even ten times, whereas our pressure cooker merely doubles it. But my faith in our instruction booklet was shaken. Luckily I tried once again. The result seemed to be the same. The projecting bones were by no stretch of the imagination softened, not even the least bit. So I started to disinter the mess from the cooker, ready to discard it. At this stage enlightenment came. When I got down to the bottom of the cooker, I found that the bones there were stuck to the metal. Using a heavy knife to pry them off I found to my delight that they *crumbled*. It quickly became clear that those pieces of bone that had been in superheated liquid throughout the experiment had indeed been softened to the point of edibility, while those sticking up and subjected only to superheated steam had not.*

The latter safely disposed of in the garbage can, I set to work on the former and found that I could produce a thick paste with the aid of a pestle and mortar. I moistened this paste with a little cream, divided it into three batches of about three tablespoonfuls each, and added to these, respectively, one pounded clove of garlic, one teaspoon of desiccated coconut, and one half teaspoonful of a hot Tabasco-type sauce that I had brought from Thailand. Each of the three potions was cooked very gently and stirred for a few minutes and then tasted with some plain boiled rice. All were excellent in flavour, although rather too thick for normal use. Diluted with a little of the marrowbone stock, freed of all traces of fat, each turned into a sauce of conventional consistency.

That was the end of the scientific road: success. But I had also achieved some positive culinary results along the way, which I now impart in the form of detailed instructions.

* This calls for an explanation. The emeritus professor of physics at Oxford University whom I consulted thought that there were two hypotheses to consider: first, that the immersion in liquid, as opposed to steam, was especially conducive to the crumbling of the bone; and second, that the temperature of my pressure cooker was in fact perceptibly higher at the bottom, where the flame was playing on it, than higher up, and it was for this reason that the bottom layer of bone succumbed while the pieces sticking up did not. While unwilling to commit himself without conducting experiments using my pressure cooker, he inclined strongly to the latter explanation. It seems plausible to me, too, and explains why Papin's digester, which was so constructed as to have a uniformly high temperature in and around the inner cylinder, achieved better results than our simpler domestic machine can.

Obtain from your butcher a marrowbone (it will usually be a shinbone) and cajole him into chopping it up into fairly small (say, six or eight) pieces. Put these in your pressure cooker, add the amount of water indicated in the instructions (3 pints, 1½ litres, for ours), bring to pressure, always following the instructions that accompany your own pressure cooker, then cook at 15 pounds additional pressure for two hours. (The instructions will say at 15 pounds, but what they mean is 15 pounds additional, since the normal atmospheric pressure, as noted above, is already 15 pounds to the square inch.) Reduce pressure, open up, lift out the bones, strain the remaining contents of the cooker through a moderately fine strainer, rubbing as much as you can through, and leave this liquid to cool. When it has cooled, there will be a thick layer of marrowfat on the top. Remove this and you're in business.

The ideal use for the marrowfat is frying croutons. No other fat is as good; it is rich and flavourful and has a relatively high burning point. Keep some frozen for use whenever you need croûtons.

In making biscuits, substitute this marrowfat for the butter or other fat you would normally use. But remember that marrowfat has a strong flavour, so do not use it for biscuits that do not have some other ingredient, such as cinnamon, that will subdue this flavour without banishing it altogether.

What you have left after removing the marrowfat is, as you would expect, excellent stock.

In my experience this extraction of marrowfat and stock from bones is best done in a pressure cooker. So, as you eat your marrowfat biscuits, you can reflect with pleasure that it was a seventeenth-century scientist who made possible their confection, and with regret that he did not go on to explore other means of improving cookery.

This careful experimenter, with his interest in foods, flavours and textures, might well have advanced by a century the nascent science of cookery if he had chosen to continue his work in the culinary field. As it was, Denys Papin spent much energy in trying to convince the world that the steam engine offered a profitable substitute for the institution of slavery; his memory is honoured for engineering rather than gastronomic reasons, and certainly much less than his bone-melting achievements warrant.

1981

Tastes, Aromas and Flavours

When scientists deal with these matters, they draw a clear distinction between tastes and aromas. Tastes are what we detect with the taste buds in our mouths, mostly on the tongue. Aromas are what we smell. As for flavours, these are the complex products of combinations of tastes and aromas such as even a simple dish is likely to present.

Taste Buds and Tastes

Our taste buds are elongated cells which terminate in what are called gustatory hairs. They are extremely small. The greatest concentration of them forms a kind of V shape on the upper surface of the tongue, just visible as tiny nipple-like protuberances and officially known as the vallate papillae. However, such papillae occur elsewhere on the tongue; and on the soft palate, the pharynx and the epiglottis. All of them are inside the mouth. None are to be found in the hairs of a man's moustache, for example (although this might be a convenient arrangement, for which a precedent is provided by the taste buds to be found in the barbels of a catfish, which enable this creature to 'pre-taste' foods before admitting them 'through the barrier of its teeth', as Homer might have said if he had paid attention to the matter).

At one time it was thought that the taste buds were arranged in groups, for example those responding to sweetness on the tip of the tongue. However, although there is some truth in this notion, the actual arrangement is much less tidy, and may even be subject to change with the passage of time.

The taste buds are specialised. Some respond to sweetness, others to an acid taste, and so on. I shall attempt to describe the mechanics of this response.

The taste buds, or receptors, work by detecting the characteristic shape of the molecules of tasty substances, as the latter drift or eddy over them in the mouth, dissolved in water. If the shape of a molecule matches the shape of a receptor site (as a key matches a lock), the two lock together, usually just for a moment, and the receptor is thereby stimulated. The degree of stimulation is variable, and so is the time taken for the stimulation to register. This latter factor accounts for the phenomenon of 'aftertaste', which may of course also be caused by remnants of food remaining in the mouth.

The strength of a taste depends partly on the number of molecules of the tasty substance which are present. The more there are, the greater the chances of collisions (which happen in a fortuitous manner) and momentary locking between molecules and receptors. But numbers are not all. Quality matters too. For example, molecules of saccharin exert a stimulation on 'sweet' receptors which is 500 times more powerful than those of sugar can achieve. The saccharin molecule resembles the sugar molecule in shape. Quite what gives it this greatly enhanced power of stimulation is not known. But some other facts, of a fascinating character, have come to light in this general area of study.

Some tropical plants have been found to contain chemicals which, although they do not themselves taste sweet, have the power of making anything else taste sweet. Research has been done on one such substance, miraculin, which is present in the 'miracle berry', *Synsepalum dulcificum*. Its molecule apparently locks itself into place on the side of a sweetness receptor site, distorts the receptor slightly and jams a 'sugary' part of itself into it. The effect produced by this aggressive behaviour is to override the tastes of other substances. Another chemical, in the leaves of the plant *Gymnema sylvestre*, has exactly the opposite effect. It 'shuts off' the sweetness receptors for hours, so that sugar tastes like sand.

Despite their minute size, delicacy and specialisation, our taste buds are rather 'blunt instruments'. The accepted view is that they can only distinguish for us four tastes: SWEET, BITTER, ACID and SALT. These terms are not invariable; thus the term SOUR may be used instead of ACID. It has, incidentally, been suggested by some authorities that there may also be an ALKALINE taste, while others have proposed adding

ASTRINGENT to the list. But I think that I am right in saying that the only serious candidate nowadays for the honour of being a Fifth Taste is METALLIC. On this assumption, the tastes may be laid out thus for inspection:

SWEET	BITTER	ACID (sour)	SALT	(?) METALLIC

And it is generally agreed that our taste buds have a rather limited capacity for distinguishing even these.

To illustrate this last point, I draw on the experience of Richard Olney. When conducting a class in the art of wine-tasting, he made some experiments. The members of the class were given samples of water to sip, the samples having been invested with different tastes, as follows:

1 sugar added
2 quinine added
3 lemon juice added
4 salt added

The additions were made in quantities known to be clearly above the threshold of perception of the average person with properly functioning taste buds. The students were then asked to identify the tastes. Only half of them scored full marks. Although this result surprised the participants, it would not have surprised anyone versed in the workings of the taste buds. It is well established that the sensitivity of the taste buds varies greatly from individual to individual, and that a substantial number of people are 'taste-blind' for one or more of the tastes which most of us can distinguish. In addition, there are linguistic problems. The terms 'bitter', 'acid' and 'sour' are often confusing for people who have not been trained in their use.

Incidentally, the taste buds can only detect tastes if the matter containing them is in solution. That is to say, the gustatory hairs react to liquids, not to solids. The liquids may be taken as such (for example, a glass of lemon juice) or may be formed by the dissolution in our saliva of the substance in question (for example, if we put some dry salt into our mouths).

In fact, when we talk of something tasting 'salty' we mean that saltiness is the predominant taste. We do not often eat pure salt, or something which contains nothing but ingredients of a salty taste. And much of what we eat, so it seems to me, has no taste in the strict sense of the word; i.e. it is neither sweet, bitter, acid nor salt, but 'neutral' in its effects on our taste buds. This may be because it does not stimulate any of them, at least not noticeably. Or it may be because all four kinds of taste buds are affected in a balanced way, the results cancelling each other out. A food containing sugar, salt, mild acids and some bitter elements may taste bland and 'neutral'.

It is interesting to look back at earlier classifications of tastes. One of the first authors to show a scientific interest in both tastes and aromas was Père Polycarpe Poncelet, whose *Chimie du Goût et de l'odorat* was first published in 1755 and later, in a new edition, in 1774 (the version which I have used). The very title of his book demonstrates an awareness of the distinction which I have made above, between tastes and aromas; and it is noteworthy that he does not himself find it necessary to explain the distinction, but assumes that it will be familiar to his readers.

The number of tastes discerned by Père Poncelet was seven, and he avers that it is no coincidence that the number is the same as the number of musical notes. In his opinion, an analogy can be made between musical harmonies and harmonies of taste. Three of his tastes (*acide, doux, amer*) correspond to three in the standard list. *Piquant* (hot, fiery, peppery) is an addition which would seem justifiable to many, although I shall suggest further on that this belongs to a different category of sensations and should not be counted as a taste. *Fade* (weak, stale) seems to be less of a taste in its own right, but rather a qualification which could be applied to a taste such as sweet or sour; or a negative term meaning 'tasteless' or insufficiently seasoned. *Austère* is used, presumably, in the same sort of sense as our 'sour', the English term 'astringent' being perhaps the best one to use as a translation, since it has been used by some authors as an alternative to 'sour' and also has a wider meaning which corresponds to the broader sense of *'austère'*. Finally, *aigre-doux*, like our 'sweet-and-sour', patently applies to a combination of tastes rather than to a single taste. So Poncelet's list may be regarded after all as constituting five tastes, with a sixth term for absence of taste (or a weak, unsatisfactory taste) and a seventh for what was then a familiar combination of two contrasting tastes.

Let us now consider whether Poncelet was right in including 'piquant' as a taste. In doing so, we should also consider the possibility that 'coolness' or 'coolth' should be added to the list, since there is at least one substance, menthol, which creates a feeling of coolness in the mouth – or at least in the open mouth, since a flow of air seems to be necessary to create the effect.

In looking at these questions we have to recall a point which has already been noticed, namely that the taste buds are specialised in function, one kind responding to sweetness, another to saltiness, and so on.

Thus a new question emerges. Are there taste buds which respond to piquancy or pungency (the quality responsible for the burning sensation produced by hot chilli peppers, for example) or to the coolth induced by menthol? The answer is that there are not. Hotness, in the sense of piquancy or pungency, and coolth, although they belong to the category of sensations which occur in the mouth and do not depend on our sense of smell, are different from the standard tastes in that they do not represent the reaction of taste buds which are, so to speak, designed to be receptors for them, but constitute an effect which is felt by the whole mouth. The scientific explanation of this is that the piquant effect impinges on pain receptors, not on taste buds. The effect is in fact pleasurable if these receptors are not overloaded; but the reverse if they are assaulted by something overpoweringly piquant and 'hot'. Note, however, that they can become habituated to such assaults, as the ability of Mexicans and others to consume very hot chilli peppers demonstrates.

Finally, the question of the possible 'metallic' taste. Here again, it seems clear that there is no special set of taste buds involved. On the other hand, the evidence that it is the taste buds which react to the taste is strong. The 'metallic' taste is usually generated by salts of iron, copper and tin; and is frequently observed as an aftertaste. The presence of tannin makes the taste of copper more noticeable; whereas the presence of salt, sugar, citric acid and alcohol has the contrary effect. Not surprisingly, the metallic taste is often associated with foods stored in metallic containers, since the uptake of metal into the food may be on a sufficient scale to generate it by this means.

What lessons are there for the cook in all this?

The first point is that when a recipe bids you 'taste and correct the seasoning' it usually means that you should check what you have made for saltiness or sweetness, so as to ensure that the finished dish is neither too salty nor too sweet. It may, of course, mean more than this; for example, in a dish flavoured with tarragon it may mean that you should check that the tarragon flavour is neither too strong nor too weak. But generally speaking it refers to saltiness and sweetness. In this connection it is interesting to note that the culinary vocabulary of the Lao language (which is a relatively unsophisticated language, lacking tenses and other such devices) includes a single word which means just this: 'taste and check that the dish is neither too salty nor deficient in salt'.

What recipes do not usually say is what you should do if a dish turns out to be too salty. (The remedy for the converse situation is obvious enough – add more salt.) The answer is usually that you should add a little sugar or other sweetening agent, such as honey, in order to compensate for the excess salt.

A further point for the cook to note is that the strength of a taste is partly dependent on the temperature of the dish, and also on its consistency. A liquid will have a stronger taste than a gel or a solid, simply because, as already noted, a taste can only be registered by the taste buds if it is furnished by a substance which is in solution; and if the substance is already in solution when it enters the mouth the taste will be more immediate and stronger.

The relationship between taste and temperature is worth exploring in greater detail, since it has quite complicated implications for cookery. The tastes of sweetness and bitterness cannot be detected at all in food or drink which is either very hot or very cold. The limits of perception appear to be between 86°C at the hot end of the scale and freezing point at the low end. Experiments have been conducted over a narrower band of temperatures, to take into account the circumstance that feelings of pain might obliterate perceptions of taste at the extremes. This experimental band ran from 17°C to 78°C. The result was to show that a sweet solution of given strength tasted more than five times as sweet when its temperature was raised from 18°C to 35°C. Thereafter, as the temperature went higher, it tasted less sweet. (When the experiment was pushed beyond the limit of 86°C, no taste of sweetness at all was perceived.)

It is for this reason that puddings taste sweeter when hot; and that hot stewed fruit may seem too sweet while the same dish, after being allowed to cool, seems just right.

The above concerns sweetness. If we divert our attention to other tastes we find a quite different pattern. The taste of bitterness seems to thrive on cool temperatures. Over the range 17°C to 78°C it becomes less strong as the temperature goes up. Moreover, the decrease is not constant. It starts slowly and becomes much more rapid towards the top of the scale.

These considerations provide a scientific basis for being particular ('fussy', some would say) about the temperature at which foods are served. They also throw up some puzzles. For example, what are we to make of the fact that a high proportion of the world's population seem to care very little at what temperature their food is served? Is it that a lukewarm temperature is, generally speaking, least likely to produce unfavourable effects over the whole range of tastes?

The strength of a taste may also, paradoxically, be increased by the addition of a contrasting taste. Experiments by the German scientist

Kiesow, published in 1899, show that a taste stimulus which was so weak as to be below the threshold of perception would nevertheless become perceptible when the contrasting taste was added. For example, a salt taste is not normally perceived in a solution of less than 0.04 per cent salt. But if a sweet taste is added the average person is then capable of perceiving a salty taste when the concentration of salt is only a tenth of the threshold level, i.e. as low as 0.004. As for sweetness, the level of perception may drop to one-fifteenth of what it usually is if a salt or bitter taste is added. It is this phenomenon which explains why puddings and sweet cakes may be made to seem sweeter by adding a pinch of salt to the ingredients. This is useful to know, since many people like a sweet taste but wish to minimise the amount of sugar in their diet.

Aroma

So far we have been dealing with tastes in the correct and narrow sense of the word, i.e. sensation perceived by the taste buds. Now we come to the sensations perceived by the sense of smell. The first thing to be said is that the number of aromas (or smells or odours – the terminology is optional, although I shall use aroma consistently) is infinite. The second is that we normally detect the aroma of a foodstuff before we detect its taste. This applies particularly to compound dishes, which almost always have a perceptible aroma, e.g. when the lid is taken off the soup-pot, but also applies to the great majority of single, unprocessed ingredients. The aroma continues to impinge on our olfactory sense when the food is placed in the mouth; indeed it may become stronger, as it has an easy passageway up from the mouth to the olfactory nerves behind the nose. But it is the aroma that we first sense.

One interesting feature of food aromas, about which – as about many other matters – I first learned from *The Origin of Food Habits* by H. D. Renner,* is that they can be quite different in the kitchen and in the dining room. The reason is that the kitchen is usually full of food smells, and that anyone working there will before long become physiologically fatigued in registering their presence, with the result that, in so far as they persist unchanged, they become imperceptible or barely percep-tible. In the dining room, on the other hand, the aroma arrives with the dish and exerts its full effect on our senses for some time.

This point illustrates the principle of saturation, which is connected

* London, 1944.

with but not identical to the principle of satiety. Saturation is also illustrated by the experience of spending some time in a cheese shop. The aroma of cheese is at first very strong. But after a while our organs of smell are saturated by it. It then becomes difficult for us to detect a cheese aroma properly even when sampling a piece of cheese.

Satiety comes as a result of consuming a large quantity of the same dish or foodstuff. The initial impact of its aroma diminishes gradually and eventually reaches vanishing point. This is a good reason for serving moderate portions of a number of different dishes or foods. It may also, as Bender suggests, account for our tending to eat rather quickly a dish which we particularly like. We are anxious to finish it before the principle of satiety begins to diminish our pleasure. (He also suggests that the converse consideration impels us to eat slowly something whose aroma is displeasing. Before we are finished, we shall be much less aware of the aroma.)

Although we have been discussing aromas here, the same principles apply to tastes. At the beginning of the chapter, I proposed the equation: TASTES + AROMAS = FLAVOUR. I shall come back to this shortly, since the cook's essential concern is with flavours rather than with tastes or aromas considered separately. First, however, let us consider the contrast between tastes, whose number is finite and small (whether you count them as four, five or six), and aromas, which can plausibly be said to be infinite in number and which seem to defy classification. Some people have tried. Here is the classification proposed by H. Zwaardemaker, quoted by E. C. Crocker in his book *Flavor*:*

ETHEREAL	AMBROSIAL	HIRCINE
AROMATIC	ALLIACEOUS	REPULSIVE
FRAGRANT	EMPYREUMATIC	NAUSEATING

What is one to make of this? It may be of some help to know that hircine, for example, means 'goaty'. Even so, most of us would find it difficult to fit the majority of aromas into this framework.

Not all classifications of aromas are as complex. Linnaeus had a list of seven. Hans Henning, a German psychologist, produced a list of only six fundamental kinds of aroma, expressed in understandable terms:

SPICY	RESINOUS
FLOWERY	FOUL
FRUITY	BURNED

* New York, 1945.

This is an interesting list, because the terms are descriptive rather than analytical. They echo our natural tendency to say that something smells 'like' or 'of' something else; or at least the first four do so. But it seems to me that anyone should be able to think, in two minutes, of half a dozen aromas at least which do not fit any of Henning's categories. And I have yet to find a set of categories which seems to be of any practical help in dealing with aromas. One is constantly brought back to drawing a specific comparison. Smelt (the fish) smell of violets. That is a helpful statement. To observe that they have a flowery aroma is hopelessly vague.

Much work is being done at present on refining the classification of aromas, and also on synthesising them. But the problem of devising a system of nomenclature which can be used by the lay person, one which does not involve long and impossible-to-memorise names of chemicals, is unsolved. In the field of natural history we are fortunate to have the Linnaean system of nomenclature which permits everyone, whatever language they speak, to know what animal or plant is being discussed. It is unfortunate that no such convenient tool has yet been devised for identifying aromas; and perhaps none can be devised.

Flavour

At this point it will be apparent that if tastes are married to aromas, as they are to produce flavours, the whole problem of description becomes even more difficult. And here I stop.

1980

Cookery: an Art, a Skill or a Science?

Early English cookery books, for the most part, echoed classical writings in ascribing to the various foods properties affecting health and also dispositions. Foods were described as excitatory, carminative and so forth; and these general qualities were often accompanied by specific attributes, such as the power to cure or mitigate this or that disorder of the body or mind, or alternatively to make it worse. (There was, for example, a long-standing idea that salmon encouraged leprosy!) Indeed many of the early cookery books were a combination of what would nowadays be separate books on, first, the properties of foods and their medicinal powers; second, their production – for example, dairy work and animal husbandry; third, their preservation – salting and smoking, etc.; and, fourth, the ways of cooking them.

These matters did not go hand-in-hand in all the books of the period, but they did so often enough to show that the subjects were thought of as a natural combination. At this stage, however, there was little reflection on the different methods of cooking. The writers showed no sign of realising that the effects of food, whether nutritive (a term not then understood in its present sense) or curative, might be changed by varying the manner of cooking them.

With this preamble I come to the question of my title.

Let us start with the view that cookery is a *skill*. The idea here is that cookery is essentially something which you learn from your elders, like, say, sewing, and that you may or may not have a natural gift for doing it well. Cookery books are thus in the nature of *aides-mémoire*, serving to remind you of how something is done rather than to teach it in the first place. Anyone trying to translate into contemporary terms the recipes of the fifteenth and sixteenth centuries will quickly realise that a lot of knowledge is taken for granted. (It is interesting to note in this connection that a high proportion of French books on cookery have gone on making similar assumptions right into this century, and that it is only recently that the majority of French cookery writers have changed to the practice of giving full and explicit instructions.)

Next, the *art* view. This, necessarily, has to be combined with the skill view. If cookery is an art, then according to the normal usage of the terms 'art' and 'artist' it is only done well and properly by a limited number of people – corresponding in practice to the great chefs of the time. They not only possess skill, they are the artists, who stand out like mountaintops among the foothills. Lower down come the vast majority of practitioners, who go through similar but less complicated and subtle motions in their kitchens and who are no more than artisans. One might draw a parallel with metalwork. There is a gulf between one of the great silversmiths and the people in his workshop, despite the fact that they did similar work and turned out products which fell into the same category. The art view has also survived in France with greater tenacity than elsewhere, although we find echoes of it in China – and also Japan.

Finally, the *science* view. This is not represented in the early cookery books, except tacitly by the assumption that the choice of foods and combination of foods is a branch of the science of medicine or at least a close ally thereof. It is only later that we shall come to the small excitement provided in this essay, namely the first mention of cookery as a science, or at least as a part of a science.

Let us now take a look at the titles of cookery books in the English language of the sixteenth, seventeenth and early eighteenth centuries. Almost all of them have short titles and long titles. It was the custom to fill the title page with a lengthy description of the contents of the book, amounting to a kind of prospectus, and the terminology used in such 'extended titles' is often of as much interest as that employed in the main title.

The earliest English cookery books, up to the latter part of the seventeenth century, tended to use titles incorporating words like 'Delights', 'Jewel', 'Treasury' and 'Cabinet'. The thought here seems to have been that the best recipes were like hidden jewels, to be discovered when the author opened his or hers or somebody else's cabinet or closet. One of the most famous of such books is *The Closet of the Eminently Learned Sir Kenelme Digbie, Kt., Opened* (1669); but there were many others, such as *The Queen-like Closet or Rich Cabinet* by Hannah Wolley, published the following year.

This general idea of recipes as hidden treasures is primarily a reflection of the 'skill' conception. It was echoed in the use of another word which appears in several titles or sub-titles: 'Mystery'. Charles Carter's book of 1730 was entitled *The Complete Practical Cook*, but sub-titled *A New System of the Whole Art and Mystery of Cookery*.

It will be noted that Carter used the word 'Art'. He was by no means the first to do so. The work of Jos. Cooper (1654) bore the title *The Art*

of Cookery; and the phrase 'the whole Art of Cookery' appeared two
years later in the sub-title of Monsieur Marnette's *The Perfect Cook*.
But it was in the eighteenth century that the titles chosen for cookery
books laid most emphasis on its being an art. The most famous of the
eighteenth-century cookery books, that of Hannah Glasse, is called *The
Whole Art of Cookery Made Plain and Easy* (1747); but she also wrote
(or, rather, lifted from a less well known, earlier, author – a confectioner called Lambert) *The Complete Confectioner or The Whole Art
of Confectionary Made Plain and Easy*. In this latter book she unveiled
yet another connected art, that of making artificial fruits.

These early writers strove, within a rather limited framework of
terminology, to keep their works distinct from each other by avoiding
the use of the same title. But most of their works had elaborate sub-
titles; and if the word 'art' is not in the main title it is likely to appear in
the sub-title. Thus in the same year in which Mrs Glasse's book on
confectionery was published (1760), Ann Cook produced a work called
Professed Cookery, a novel title, but the author described herself as
'Teacher of the True Art of Cookery'.

A similar view prevailed on the other side of the English Channel.
There were fewer French cookery books in the first half of the
eighteenth century in France than in England. Indeed there were
remarkably few. But something of a renaissance occurred in the 1740s,
when what was called 'la nouvelle cuisine' (the very phrase now current
in the 1970s and 1980s) made its appearance in the last work of Vincent
La Chapelle (1742) and in Menon's works (from 1739 on). La Chapelle
was a transitional author. The first version of his work, *The Modern
Cook*, plagiarised Massialot, who was at that time (1735) the grand old
man among French cookery writers and whose own work stemmed
back to the previous century. But La Chapelle, who seems to have been
capable of innovation as well as plagiarism, can be seen in the successive
editions of his work to be moving in a new direction. Menon, whose
most famous work, *Les Soupers de la Cour*, first appeared in 1755,
completed the move and proclaimed himself, albeit anonymously for no
author's name appeared on the title page, the herald of the nouvelle
cuisine. It is interesting to note that the full title of his book continues
'. . . ou l'Art de travailler toutes sortes d'alimens', and that he ruminates
in his 'Avertissement' (preface) on the nature of the art of cookery. An
intriguing sidelight is cast on what was then the French attitude towards
cookery books when he argues that chefs should not blush to be seen
reading them, since practitioners of other arts such as architecture
openly read manuals on their subjects. He insists that, despite the
importance of practical work in the kitchen, a knowledge of the theory

of the art of cookery is required. In discussing this need he almost sidesteps into the realm of science by referring to the properties of foodstuffs, the nature of and difference between flavours and so forth. But he always comes back to the terms 'art' and 'artists'. (The fact that two of his earlier works have titles which begin with the French word *'Science'* is, incidentally, not an anticipation of later developments, since the word is used simply in the sense of 'knowledge'.)

After Menon's contributions, there was another long lull in the production of French cookery books, while the steady stream of English works on the subject continued to appear. It would be pleasant to find that one of the more deserving English writers was the first to take up the theme of cookery as a science. However, so far as I can discover – and I would positively like to be corrected on this point – the distinction was reserved for the co-authors Francis Collingwood and John Woollams, whose book *The Universal Cook, and City and Country Housekeeper* was first published in 1792. Their preface begins by disavowing any intent 'to discover what was the food of our first parents in the garden of Eden, or in what manner they performed their culinary operations: it is sufficient for us to know at present that Cookery is become a science . . .'. It is true that they also refer to it as an art, in traditional style, but they then immediately repeat the term 'science' with emphasis. Not that their book is scientific in its approach. On the contrary, it is just a collection of recipes of which most come from earlier sources, prefaced by some unimpressive 'General Observations'. Still, there we are: our first recorded statement in an English language cookery book that cookery is become a science. This is the statement which rings in the period when cookery really was so treated, the era of Count Rumford, Liebig, Mathieu Williams, Mrs Kellogg and the other luminaries of the nineteenth century.

If the nineteenth century was the period when the scientific view held sway, why is it that the twentieth century is different? After all, most people nowadays subscribe to the skill (for most people) and art (for some few) approach, even if they are prepared to acknowledge, uneasily, that science has something to do with the matter.

The explanation, I think, is that nineteenth-century expositions of the scientific principles of cookery were, while usually mistaken, comprehensible. Few people read Liebig, but many grasped his message, and it was, imperfectly perhaps but recognisably, echoed in some cookery books.

What has happened since then is that in this, as in so many other areas, science has taken itself out of the reach of ordinary people. Questions such as 'Why use a copper bowl to beat egg-whites?' turn out

to require, in effect, a book by way of answer, and a complicated book
at that. Those few intrepid writers, such as Harold McGee, who seek to
explain such matters in a comprehensible manner have an earnest
audience, for there is still a feeling that there must be a scientific
explanation for every culinary phenomenon, and that if we could grasp
it we would be better cooks. But the difficulties are such that the
counter-feeling – 'oh well, if we know what to do, that's enough, we
can't expect to know why' – prevails. And so it is in other matters of
everyday life. After all, we operate electric devices successfully without
understanding electricity. We use here a skill which can be taught; we
may apply ourselves to develop it into an art; but we do not profess to be
scientists.

1981

Part Three
The Good Things of Life

Green Salad without Lettuce?

Shortly before I set off on a journey round the world, on fishy matters bent, someone faced me with two questions. What is happening to green salads? Could we be moving into a sinelactucate (i.e. without lettuce) mode?

For Britons the concept of a green salad without lettuce is about as easy to play with as that of, say, a world without time, or space. But I said I would try.

Twenty thousand leagues and fourteen cities later, I had concluded that the treatment of green salads is indeed changing; that sinelactucism is practised, warily, by a few adventurous spirits (although the retreat from the Iceberg is more often in the direction of other, rarer, lettuces than away from lettuce altogether); and that the changes taking place, although bearing on their surface the usual froth of fads and crazes, are important. I had not been offered Iceberg once on the ground, and had declined it eleven times in the air. I had also picked up a number of ideas for new ingredients; a dozen from Japan alone. I impart just a few of them in this essay, prefaced by a peep into salad literature.

There isn't much of this in any language. So far as English is concerned, one could say that no one has ever bettered the first work on the subject: *Acetaria, A Discourse on Sallets*, by John Evelyn, 1699.* This polymath, who was a friend of Pepys, defines our subject with a nice turn of phrase, saying that, as to 'the business in hand, we are by *Sallet* to understand a particular Composition of certain *Crude* and fresh Herbs, such as usually are, or may safely be eaten with some *Acetous* Juice, *Oyl, Salt,* &c. to give them a grateful Gust and *Vehicle.*'

Passing on to give an extensive catalogue of salad ingredients, Evelyn first prepares his readers for some surprises by observing that people in other countries have a more eclectic attitude than Anglo-Saxons; thus 'the more frugal *Italians* and *French* . . . gather *Ogni Verdura*, any thing almost that's *Green* and Tender, to the very Tops of *Nettles*,' so that 'every Hedge' can yield a salad. He proceeds to list 73 salad ingredients (with a postscript on exotic items such as tulip bulbs), of which 55 are greens, and the remainder 'white' or 'pickled'.

* A facsimile reprint was published by Prospect Books, London, 1982.

He also showed himself thoroughly familiar with some of our recent 'discoveries'. Oak leaf lettuce, purslane, rocket, and many others figure in his recommendations; and he firmly states that neither rocket nor tarragon should be omitted from any salad containing lettuce.

It is remarkable that Evelyn so clearly anticipated two general trends which are noticeable now, nearly three centuries later: 'See what the Italians and French do', and 'Look in the hedgerows'.

Such thoughts found few echoes in the eighteenth or nineteenth centuries, or in the first half of the present century. The *Edgewater Beach Hotel Salad Book** is probably the greatest salad book of this period. It quotes some of Evelyn's ideas in an appendix, but by way of saluting a predecessor rather than adopting his ideas. The index of the book lists about 750 salad recipes, but none for Green Salad! Everything seems to involve fruits, or at least tomatoes.

Other, more recent books have redressed the balance. The outstanding one of the eighties is *The Salad Garden* by Joy Larkcom.† This has a wealth of possibilities described and illustrated in colour. Joy Larkcom, who grows the greens at her farm near Cambridge, offers a unique combination of horticultural and gastronomic expertise, all spiced with history (she too is a fan of Evelyn) but carefully adjusted to the practicalities with which most of us have to contend. A favourite mixture of hers, which I ate before setting off round the world and which served as a standard for comparison, is the first in my collection.

Joy Larkcom's *Purslane and Flower Salad*. Succulent purslane leaves, the basis of this composition, are a perfect foil for

* Chicago, 1926.   † New York and London, 1984.

nasturtium, pot marigold and borage flowers. Variegated nasturtium leaves and sprigs of redcurrant are added.

From the same source: *Simple Green Salad*. Two kinds of lettuce are used: Little Gem and bronze Trotzkopf, garnished with variegated lemon balm leaves and borage flowers.

In Seattle I found that Donna Jean Zentner of the Café Optimum was also making liberal use of flowers, including pinks, violas, evening primrose and candytuft, to set off the 28 different greens which she regularly uses according to the season and her whim. She likes to include wild greens in her compositions. A fine place to go for the unexpected. Typical of the mixtures you might meet is the following:

sweet cicely (lacy, delicate)
anis hyssop (small, purple)
sorrel (to provide a larger leaf and heavier texture)
arugula (rocket, with spicy, deeply indented leaves)
curly seakale (sliced very thin, like a julienne).

All these have different shapes, colours and textures. Donna said that she might add spinach, or bibb lettuce (to provide a sort of basis, but in discreet quantity so as not to compete with the unusual items). Better still, she added, would be miner's lettuce (as she calls purslane). Then she would need a flower, perhaps candytuft, which is sweet and delicious and easy to obtain. And there might be a sprinkling of finely chopped herbs, in small quantities, for added flavours: variegated mint, lemon balm, etc.

Further south, in Berkeley, California, I asked Alice Waters of Chez Panisse about the delicate greens with touches of pink and red which she likes to use. Her grower, Andrea Crawford, operates just a few blocks away, on a small plot which must be one of the most intensively cultivated pieces of land anywhere. There I beheld the salad ingredients growing thickly together, mostly to be gathered in the seedling stage although a few are allowed to flower. The standard mixture which Andrea grows for Chez Panisse is:

Frisée (curly endive) de Louviers;
Red Salad Bowl, a fine red oak leaf lettuce, which she plants very densely;
rocket;
curled chervil.

The restaurant is constantly devising new formulae, however. Small-seeded mâche (corn salad) is intersown with bronze-leaved mignonette for them. And there is always a bed of *mesclun*, a traditional Provençal mixture which the people of Nice claim as their own (stipulating rocket, dandelion and baby lettuce), but which exists in scores of different forms. Andrea's mesclun has rocket and red oak leaf lettuce and at least four other greens (an element of chance innovation being introduced by her practice of sprinkling the last seeds from other nearly empty packets over the bed).

Mesclun has its Italian counterparts, such as the Roman *misticanza*, made from at least seven (but possibly many more) wild greens. Those who wish to explore Italian ideas will do well to start with Joy Larkcom's book, since her interest in the subject was kindled by a journey through Italy when she investigated the various *saladini* or small salad herbs which are used regionally (and she identifies everything in a manner which enables one to order the right seeds).

But it is time to move to the other hemisphere.

Meals in the Orient have a place for salad greens, but not for anything called a green salad. Visiting Japan, Korea, Taiwan and South-East Asia I kept my eyes open for any greens which could be lifted out of their oriental context and placed to advantage in my green salad bowl.

In Japan, scouting through the placid lanes of ancillary shops lying beside Tokyo's great fish market, I found various herbs, all intended for use with fish. The prettiest, and just about the most expensive, had reddish stalks and small, glossy green leaves. They came in very small bunches, and were patently edible. 'What does one do with these?' I asked. A long speech was made. The interpreter said she was telling me to take home a bunch of the *hama-bofu* and first to sit down and admire its beauty for at least twenty minutes. Then I could use it to garnish *sashimi* (raw fish). I smiled assent but in my heart I knew that I was going to try it in a salad. It was a great success. Just a couple of the aromatic stalks per person suffice. The taste is pleasantly acid and refreshing. But what is it? *Phellopterus littoralis*, a plant which grows wild on sand dunes near the sea and which may be met on the Pacific coast of North America as 'corkwing'. I later gathered it in the Pescadores Islands (it is *sang hu ts'ai* in Chinese) and saw it in the Philippines. Full grown, it is not much good; but the youngest shoots are delicious.

The Japanese have another winner, which they call *shiso*. This is *Perilla frutescens*, which comes in two main varieties, green-leaved and red-leaved. The latter is used for colouring *umeboshi*, the pickled 'Japanese plums' (really a kind of apricot) which one is supposed to eat before breakfast to clear the system. The former is milder in flavour and just right for a salad. Its leaves are of a very pretty shape.

Moving to Korea, and elbowing my way through the *kimchi* (pickled vegetables, especially cabbage) which fills Korean markets, I found some fresh greens, but they mostly seemed to be asking to be put in a soup. However, the salad accompaniments to the best dinner of my stay included a sensationally good white item, *toraji*. This is the root of the Korean bellflower, *Platycodon glaucum*. Pickled, cut *en julienne*, then added to a salad in discreet quantity, it contributes not only a different colour but also a distinctive texture and an interesting flavour.

Reflecting on all this, and on what I found in the Philippines and Malaysia too, I finally realised an obvious truth. *Of all the important areas of gastronomy, that of green salads is the one which offers most scope for being creative and inventive.* Toss old formulae out of the window, taking care that they do not land in your window-box (which will now be full of your own special mesclun), and you're on your way.

1985

On the Esculent Fungi

Many phantasticall people doe greatly delight to eat of
the earthly excrescences calles Mushrums . . . They are
convenient for no season, age or temperament – Venner, *Via Recta ad Vitam Longam,* 1620

English is the wrong language for this article, for the English, as the quotation from Venner and a hundred others which could be cited demonstrate, are notoriously shy of edible fungi. They are not alone in this. The Scots, Welsh and Irish keep them company, and so do the Dutch. A tight little knot of North Sea non-fungus eaters, which has spawned correspondingly negative nodules in other continents: Canada and the USA, South Africa, Australia, New Zealand, the Indies West and East.

Arabs are also wary. When I was in Tunisia recently, seeking evidence of the consumption of the desert truffle which the Romans so enjoyed, I was assured that Tunisians abstained not only from this elusive delicacy but also from the chanterelles and other choice species which grow in the woods near Ain Draham – to the sole benefit of Europeans. The Arab 'no-mushrooms-please-they-might-be-dangerous' zone extends from Morocco to the Persian Gulf.

Elsewhere in the world, mushrooms are valued and people usually know how to distinguish the edible from the toxic varieties. The degree of enthusiasm varies from region to region. Perhaps no other people can match the Russians in this, although the Scandinavians and central Europeans, and the Chinese too, might think themselves no less mycophilic.

I introduce this strange adjective, which simply means 'mushroom-loving', not to parade the fading remnants of my classical education (an edifice which four decades have reduced to a state of ruin more advanced than that which afflicts the Parthenon after two millennia), but to prepare the way for a further injection of classical terms, this time in the form of the Latinised scientific names of the species. In the whole vast area of food studies, there are two patches where the student will remain perpetually immobile on his launching pad if unwilling to use scientific names. One is that of fish and seafood (see page 170), the other that of edible fungi. In each instance the explanation is the same. There is a very large number of species to be considered, often differentiated by characteristics imperceptible to the lay person and almost always confused by a plethora of common names which even within the confines of a single language looks like a telex message from the tower of Babel.

There are, incidentally, other parallels. Both fish and fungi are now beginning to be cultured or cultivated on a large scale. And both are being 'intercontinentalised'; a process aided by modern transport but still hampered by failures to grasp the relationships between species here and species there.

However, fungi are even more muddling than fish. A fish is a fish, but a fungus may be anything from a blob of slime to a growth of mould to a toadstool or mushroom. Which brings me to the matter of definitions.

What then is a mushroom, and what is a toadstool? Mushrooms are good although not always so (for one can speak without self-contradiction of poisonous mushrooms). Toadstools are harmful. This rule holds good in many languages. It is of considerable antiquity in English. The *Grete Herbal* of 1526 says of 'mussherons' that: 'There be two maners of them, one maner is deedly and sleath them that eateth of them and be called tode stoles . . .'

The derivation of mushroom, which is first recorded as an English word in the ninth century, is uncertain; but it seems likely to have come from '*mousseron*', a French term which nowadays applies to various small mushrooms. Toadstool, spelled thus, appears in the seventeenth century. It had been known from the fourteenth century in the form 'tadstole' and in the fifteenth as 'tode stole' and – an interesting variation – 'toodys hatte'. Rival theories have been put forward, but the simple notion that the name is derived from toad and stool seems most plausible. John Ramsbottom, in his excellent *Mushrooms and Toadstools*,* reproduces a quartet of photographs from the London *Times* showing a toad approaching a toadstool, mounting it, and finally perched snugly on the 'stool'.

Scientists, in modern usage, give mushroom and toadstool the same definition: the fruiting body of a fungus of either the Order *Agaricales* (the one which includes the common field mushroom and the closely related cultivated mushroom) or the Order *Boletales* (in which the cep or king bolete is famous). There is such a gulf between everyday usage and this definition, which rests on fine points of structure and excludes many fungi which are commonly known as mushrooms, that it seems unlikely to win support outside scientific circles.

I prefer to retain a more general meaning for mushroom, applying the term to the fruiting bodies of any fungus in a category which includes edible species; but especially to those species which are unequivocally edible† and of conventional cap-on-stem appearance. I believe that

---

* London, 1953.
† The dividing lines between edible and toxic species are sometimes uncertain. There are many species of which the experts can only say: 'upsets some but eaten by others with impunity.' It is therefore best to eat only the unequivocally edible species, and always to identify positively any mushrooms gathered from the wild. In many countries there are special facilities for having mushrooms identified. The most charming is the Norwegian 'Sopkontrol', a mushroom control point which is established at the railway station in Oslo during the season, so that mushroom-hunters returning from their excursions can have their harvest checked.

there is a general trend, except in purely scientific works, to give the word this wider meaning.

The meaning of toadstool, in contrast, remains static, and understandably so; toads can't, after all, be expected to sit on fungus of any shape or form. So a toadstool is still a fungus of conventional appearance, looking as though it might be edible, but perceived as harmful.

Most of the fungi which are widely eaten have the conventional mushroom appearance. But some do not. Truffles are an outstanding exception – and such an outstanding one that I must exclude them from this essay lest there be room for nothing else. So are puffballs and such odd items as *Sparassis crispa*, the prized 'cauliflower mushroom', and species of the genus *Auricularia*, the Chinese 'wood ear' and 'cloud ear' mushrooms.

In the realm of fungi which are eaten on a small scale or only in certain places the list would be much longer, including for example *Sarcoscypha coccinea*, the eye-catching scarlet elf cup which is eaten in the Jura (added, with a dash of kirsch, to a fresh fruit salad, according to one French authority).

Incidentally, the potential of the cup fungi as delicate and decorative containers for other foods – they would make a welcome change from those mingy little artichoke hearts in which petits pois are often nested – seems to have been overlooked even by those (such as the chefs who are still clambering aboard the nouvelle cuisine chuckwagon, having failed to notice that it is now stationary) who could be expected to pounce on any novel idea of this sort. Indeed, it would be fair to say that the wealth of different forms and textures which edible fungi exhibit has been exploited, even by the Chinese and Japanese, in an oddly selective way. Could the ancient fear of unfamiliar fungi still be at work; or is the problem, in part, one of deficient documentation?

One extraordinary feature of fungi is that the literature about them is of very recent origin. To be sure, they were mentioned by classical authors; but their nature was not understood. The fact that the fruiting bodies (the part of the plant which we observe, gather and eat) spring up so quickly led early authors such as Dioscorides to produce fanciful theories about spontaneous generation. (These ideas lingered on well into medieval times and beyond. Lyly, writing in the sixteenth century, could still declare that snails crept out of their shells, turned into toads, and then, feeling the need of something to sit upon, fashioned toadstools for themselves.) It was only in 1729, when Micheli published his *Nova Plantarum Genera*, that the subject began to have a scientifically acceptable basis. Linnaeus, the great Swedish natural historian of the mid-eighteenth century, failed to absorb fungi into his scheme of things; indeed, he created a genus with the defeatist name *Chaos* to accommodate fungal phenomena for which he could not provide a better home. But the honour of his country was saved by another Swede, Fries (1794–1878), who built on the work of the Frenchman Persoon (1761–1836) and perhaps did most to establish a basis for the classification which is still used.

The peculiarity of fungi is manifest in many ways, one of which is that scientists are not agreed on whether they belong to the Plant Kingdom or should be assigned a Kingdom of their own. Nor can they agree on how many Classes and Orders there are.

However, they do all divide them up according to the manner in which their spores are borne. Thus we learn that fungi of the Order *Ascomycetes* (including morels and cup fungi) have spores enclosed within bags; while the spores of *Basidiometes* are borne externally on gills (as in the common field mushroom) or a spongy network of tubes (for example, the whole group of boletus mushrooms). This and similar distinctions are important for the mushroom-hunter but afford only intellectual satisfaction for the cook; they do not bear on work in the kitchen.

But the cook does have an interest in knowing that the main groups of edible fungi, and many of the species within them, are of global distribution. This is not surprising, since their spores are so light that they can easily be blown from continent to continent in the upper atmosphere. What is surprising is that so little has been done to link up the fungi of one continent with those of another. Until recently, I supposed that the dried mushrooms which I encountered in every oriental food store were something peculiarly oriental. Eventually someone drew my attention to a clump of 'wood ear' (*Auricularia* sp) growing on a tree trunk a few blocks from my home in Chelsea, London, and I began to see the light. (Worse still, I had thought that the *funghi porcini* in Italian delicatessens were uniquely Italian, whereas they are really ceps, of the species *Boletus edulis*, usually called cèpes de Bordeaux – which I of course, if I may continue to expose my former state of ignorance, had regarded as the private property of the French, although they occur in many European countries and are widely distributed in North America.)

'Only connect,' the Forsterian exhortation which sticks like a burr to my mind, has recently guided my efforts to produce, as part of a larger project, a world manual of edible fungi. It has led me into out-of-the-way places, including a Chinese bookshop in Shanghai, where I flourished a crude drawing of a mushroom and emerged half an hour later with a paperback manual on Chinese mushrooms of that province, mercifully equipped with the Latin names of the species. Many an old friend from Europe found I there. So the Chinese have morels, do they? Why are they not more noticeable in Chinese cookbooks (I mean the ones published in China, as well as western works)? And what do the Chinese do with the *Russula* mushrooms? Questions such as these multiply to such an extent that one could write a small book consisting of 'Unanswered Questions about Fungi in Asia (and Africa)'.

Unanswered questions are hardly a recipe for a best-seller. But if Mr Valiant-for-Truth makes a sufficiently persistent Pilgrim's Progress, some of the missing information emerges. At the Herbarium of the Royal Botanic Gardens at Kew I recently interviewed an enthusiastic mycologist, Dr Pegler, who has often lifted his eyes above western horizons and the narrow confines of taxonomy. Besides writing more general works, he is co-author of 'The Edible Mushrooms of Zambia'* which tells us that chanterelles, including *Cantharellus cibarius* (the principal chanterelle of Europe), occur in Zambia and are eaten by Zambians. The monograph also contains the first scientific description of the largest edible fungus in the world, *Termitomycetes titanicus*, whose cap occasionally reaches a measurement of almost 1 metre (say, 3 feet) across.

I remarked that it seemed odd that such a prominent fungus – it rears its great bulk from termite mounds – should only now have received official notice, and that the oversight was even odder if the huge things were edible.

'Yes,' said Pegler, 'it is incredible, especially as it is the best mushroom in the world to eat.'

'What? Better than the cep, the morel, the oronge . . .?' I recited the familiar list.

'Yes. I think so, anyway.'

Probing further into the matter, I learned that Pegler's co-author, Piearce, is a scientist working in Zambia who happens to take a particular interest in the edibility of fungi as well as in their taxonomy. A happy coincidence. But it leaves one wondering what further surprises, apt to upset our established view of the subject, may be in store when experts similarly interested in edibility fetch up in other African and Asian countries.

My interest in finding out more about little-known edible fungi may seem like an academic pursuit, but the subject is one which could turn out to have practical importance if new cultivable species are identified.

---

* D. N. Pegler and G. D. Piearce, in *Kew Bulletin*, 35(3), 1980.

In the seventeenth century the French began to explore possibilities of cultivating the common mushroom: Olivier de Serres, in *Le Théâtre d'Agriculture des Champs* (1600), suggested a way of doing this, and in 1678 the botanist Marchant demonstrated to the Académie des Sciences how mushrooms could be 'sown' in a controlled way by transplanting their mycelia – the filaments which spread through the soil like fine roots and eventually produce the fruiting bodies which we eat. John Evelyn, in his *Acetaria* of 1699,* described French practice at that time in terms of a 'hot Bed of Asses-Dung' which was impregnated with mushroom parings etc. and watered, and lasted for two or three years. During the eighteenth century, cultivation of *Agaricus bisporus* began to take place on a large scale in the vicinity of Paris; which is why the small button mushrooms of commerce are called *champignons de Paris*. Their cultivation has now spread to many other parts of the world, and is regularly reviewed at international congresses on mushroom cultivation.

Study of the proceedings of these congresses shows clearly that a major change has taken place in the last few decades. Instead of only one, a dozen species of mushroom are being commercially grown. Some had been cultivated before, on a cottage industry scale; others had not. All the newcomers, including quite exotic items such as *Pleurotus ostreatus* (the oyster mushroom) and *Tremella fuciformis* (the white jelly mushroom which the Chinese like so well), are already or may soon become the basis of major operations; and mushroom-growers are realising more and more that most of these species can be cultivated anywhere in the world if enough trouble is taken to create the right conditions. The common European mushroom has for some time been grown in Taiwan. What is more interesting is that the Japanese *shiitake* is now being cultivated in the USA.

Mushrooms will never be a staple food. But they are more important in nutrition than is generally realised. Despite their high water content they supply appreciable quantities of protein, with virtually no fat, and they also play a useful role as flavouring agents for staple foods which need to be made more tasty if they are to be attractive. As often happens, gastronomic interests and concern for world food supplies here coincide. And it is notable that mushroom cultivation, although sometimes requiring energy, does not compete for scarce resources with other kinds of food. The growing media are often waste products, and agricultural land is not needed.

As a footnote to the merits of mushrooms, I should mention that the

---

* Reprinted by Prospect Books, London, 1982.

Chinese, predictably, consider some to be aphrodisiacs. But neither they nor anyone else seems to have speculated on the possibility that by eating mushrooms we could somehow absorb their remarkable physical force. Tales of paving stones caused to rise up from their bed by a few small mushrooms are familiar. An experience which befell Sir Joseph Banks in the eighteenth century was even more dramatic. He left a cask of wine in his cellar for some years. Returning, he found that a fungal growth proceeding from the wine had completely filled the cellar and had become so hard that it had to be hacked away with an axe; and that the cask, now empty of wine, was firmly pinned against the ceiling by it.

One topic on which, to put it mildly, much work remains to be done is that of mushroom cookery. The idea of a 'single theme cookbook' has so far been largely confined to the West, and most occidental books on mushroom cookery have a routine air to them. Those few which reflect a real interest on the part of the author, and therefore have real interest for the reader and cook, include one each from England, France and the USA. Jane Grigson's *Mushroom Feast** is – as always with this author – learned, poetic and practical. Paul Ramain's *Mycogastronomie†* is the distillation of a lifetime of study, and deserves to be better known. *Wild Mushroom Recipes* from the Puget Sound Mycological Society‡ is an inspiring handbook and includes recipes for edible fungi in some of the less well known genera (*Armillaria, Sparassis, Hydnum*, etc.). It also displays some knowledge of oriental practice.

Cookbooks apart, one may sometimes learn from manuals, scientific or popular, on mushrooms. Caution is needed here, since many authors of such books have lacked direct experience of cooking or even eating their subject matter and yet – conscious of the curiosity which their readers might have on this aspect – have felt bound to include at least some comments on 'edibility'. Such comments tend to be copied from one book to the next. But there are honourable exceptions, such as the vast work by Charles McIlvaine§ and the slighter volume from the Reverend Charles Badham.

McIlvaine was a supreme optimist. Whereas many authors of mushroom books, haunted by visions of readers collapsing in agony after eating toxic species, pile warnings and cautionary tales upon each other to such an extent that their works seem to be funerary rather than

* London, 1975.
† Paris, 1954; Marseilles, 1979.
‡ Seattle, 1973.
§ *One Thousand American Fungi*, revised ed., Indianapolis, 1902; reprinted West Glover, Vt., and London, 1973.

culinary, he tends in the opposite direction and positively spurs on the hesitant. 'Reputed to be harmful,' he will observe, 'but never did me any harm!' And even species of moderate merit excite him to lavish praise; I have lost count of the number of mushrooms which he declares to be 'second to none'. His enthusiasm is infectious, and he makes clear that he has himself experimented with a high proportion of the thousand fungi he describes.

Charles Badham, the clergyman whose *Esculent Funguses of Britain* went into its second edition in 1862, was a man in whom caution and enthusiasm were agreeably mingled. The purpose of his book was to introduce the ultra-suspicious English to mushrooms which they were neglecting (and continue to neglect). Mushrooms, he declared, were to be eaten 'with discretion not à discrétion'. But his eloquent prose, fortified by the assurance that in a single summer he and his friends had eaten thirty-one species,* must surely have won over some of the hesitant. Hark to his song:

> I have indeed grieved, when I reflected on the straitened condition of the lower orders this year [1847], to see pounds innumerable of extempore beef-steaks growing on our oaks in the shape of *Fistulina hepatica* . . . Puffballs, which some of our friends have not inaptly compared to sweet-bread for the rich delicacy of their unassisted flavour; *Hydna* as good as oysters, which they somewhat resemble in taste; *Agaricus deliciosus*, reminding us of tender lamb-kidneys; the beautiful yellow Chantarelle, that *kalon kagathon* of diet, growing by the bushel, and no basket but our own to pick up a few specimens in our way; the sweet nutty-flavoured *Boletus*, in vain calling himself *edulis* where there was none to believe him . . .

Badham gives summary instructions for cooking the various species, rather than full recipes such as are found in the more recent books mentioned above. Those of Ramain are the most detailed; but they belong to the French classical tradition and will not appeal to all. His recipe for 'Oronges [*Amanita caesarea*] à la Lucullus' is furnished with a typical italicised preamble (*La meilleure façon de savourer ces magnifiques cryptogames! C'est une recette de haute gastronomie . . .*)

---

* A creditable number, but soon to be outdone. William DeLisle Hay, the author of an *Elementary Text-book of the British Fungi* (1887 – the unexciting title conceals a rich store of culinary information), reveals by his personal comments on various species that he had tried about 200 of them. But all such figures are overshadowed by a recent Italian author who claims to have sampled over 1250.

and goes on to demand a rich veal and chicken stock, canapés cut from a special kind of pain brioche, a roux-based sauce with Sauternes and tarragon, and (come back to the kitchen, we haven't finished yet) a whole array of secondary canapés coated with a purée of fresh foie gras. Hmm. What was that phrase of Badham's about 'the rich delicacy of their unassisted flavour'? I think I prefer that approach. However, not all mushrooms have a richly delicate unassisted flavour; indeed most of those eaten in Europe and North America, being ordinary cultivated mushrooms, do not. Ramain, in a passage with which I sympathise, unleashed his italics and exclamation marks against these, describing them in their 'button' form (and in my free translation) as watery globs of rubber-substitute. Yes, they do need assistance. But let the golden mean be followed in this, as in other aspects of cookery: do not mask good natural flavours, but be ready to supply desirable additional flavours where they are needed.

I conclude with an anecdote which points up the difficulty, in the present state of the literature, of tracing the more obscure edible fungi.

One evening in December 1983 my wife and I flew into Seattle. Ours was the only flight of the day which could land there; the big-time publishers were all safely grounded by weather conditions. We had come to secure a major prize: the first good book on Tibetan cookery, by a Tibetan bartender whose name, rendered into English, is Flat-headed Thunderbolt. We signed him up, and then went through the illustrations which he had done for the book. One showed a Tibetan on hands and knees, scrabbling amongst sparse vegetation. What was he doing? Ah, said the Thunderbolt, he is searching for something uniquely Tibetan, a strange item which is a worm in the winter and changes to a mushroom in the summer: a very precious foodstuff. I knew better than to deny the possibility, although the tale struck me as odd and my mind wandered back to Linnaeus's category of *Chaos* in search of a place to file the information.

Months later, in Singapore, a publisher showed me a book on Chinese herbs. This referred in imprecise but convincing terms to a similar phenomenon – something called 'winter-worm/summer-grass . . . believed to be a lowly worm which creeps about in winter, undergoes a metamorphosis through spring to become a leaf in summer, dries up in autumn to drop like a shrivelled twig and begins its crawly cycle all over again. This strange animal/vegetable is found mainly in China [in the south-west, near Tibet]. . . .' The author gave the name Cordycepts, which was clearly part of the scientific name.

I only had to go 4000 miles, to New Zealand, for the next clue. Thumbing through the pages of a book on New Zealand fungi, to see what European species grow there, I came on *Cordyceps robertsii* and a picture showing 'the mummified body of a soil-dwelling moth caterpillar killed by the fungus. When the fungus has used up all the nutriment provided by the insect tissues, it sends up a brown stalk which is the only part that appears above ground . . . thickened at the apex like a tiny bulrush. . . .' So! The winter worm is really a caterpillar, and it doesn't survive its metamorphosis into an odd, grasslike mushroom. Nor is it unique to Tibet, or even to China, or even to the northern hemisphere. But Mr Flathead's information was, broadly, correct.

Back in London, I appealed to a Chinese friend who can read the Chinese encyclopaedia. Armed with my clues, she quickly found the right entry, confirming and amplifying my 'discoveries' in a humiliating way (the information was there all the time – but how could one have known?). From her own experience she was able to add that the dried fungi are indeed a valued foodstuff, and that the Chinese use them in a rich chicken broth, to be eaten late in the evening since *Cordyceps* is both a restorative and an aphrodisiac.

This was almost the end of the trail. The real end came when my friend made me a bowl of the soup – an event which had no perceptible effect on me but which should help to fix my image as one of Venner's 'phantasticall people'.

1985

Nuts

Nuts are festive, mysterious, symbolic; and supremely versatile. In prehistoric times they were a staple food, and they still are in some places, but the changed value of human labour has turned them into a luxury food in the western world.

For the connoisseur Edward Bunyard, they played only one role: to go with the wine as part of dessert. Writing of English cobs, handsome in their 'russet livery', he advised that the husk should not be removed before bringing them to table, 'as it is a decoration and nothing which facilitates the leisurely consumption of nuts is to be discouraged. The quiet selection, removal of the husk and leisurely handling in the crackers are nineteenth-century virtues deserving all encouragement'.

Not all nineteenth-century connoisseurs displayed these virtues. We have it on the authority of Charles Pierce, *maître d'hôtel* to the Russian Ambassador in London, whose gossipy book *The Household Manager* enjoyed a vogue in the 1860s, that in the grandest houses nuts were shelled and peeled, and then served up in bowls of salted water, so that diners had no work to do, not even adding salt.

Bunyard's essay* was written long before the desire for fast foods started to dominate the scene. It breathes the spirit of the previous century, when desserts and port were a lengthy ritual and classical allusions were bandied to and fro with an ease which would be disconcerting at a 1980s dinner table. After quoting the obscure author Eupolis as calling for Naxian almonds and Naxian wine, he refers blandly to 'lines too well known to need quotation' from Phrynichus, Heracleus of Ephesus, and Plutarch.

Hmm. I have but to tap my own forehead to identify one former classical scholar who would have to search his reference books to discover who Phrynichus was. But Bunyard's words are a useful reminder that our western attitudes to nuts stem largely from the Greeks and Romans of antiquity. It is from them that we inherit and conserve the idea that nuts and wine go together, and that nuts are to be

---

* In *The Anatomy of Dessert*, London, 1929.

savoured with discrimination and relish; in short that they are a matter for the connoisseur.

Mixed up with this conception are two less hedonistic strands of thought. One is that nuts loomed large in the diet of the anthropoids who preceded the human race, and that they are therefore a particularly 'natural' food. The other is that they are exceptionally nutritious, as indeed most of them are. Both these strands have conspired to give nuts a unique mystique for vegetarians, and for others too. That I concentrate here on the pleasures which nuts afford implies no disrespect for these other aspects, but a feeling that they are better handled in journals of anthropology and nutrition.

There are, however, two aesthetic aspects which contribute to the mystique of nuts. One is that they are all packaged by nature, and often in an exquisite manner. It can be argued that the eggshell is nature's finest container, and it certainly scores top marks for delicacy; but it is not impermeable, and the debris of a broken eggshell is unattractive. Nut shells are stronger and provide interesting debris, as a multitude of still-life paintings attests. Cracking a nut open is a unique experience. No one has seen the nut before, nothing from the outside world has touched it, it has an unrivalled virginity.

Also, it represents power. A nut is a tree in embryo. A Brazil nut, for example, is capable of becoming a giant of the jungle, towering 200 feet up and dwarfing the *castanheiros* who quickly but cautiously gather its huge seedcases when they plummet to the ground. This kind of thought, which comes to mind when a Brazil nut is popped into the mouth, is a source of additional pleasure for those of a romantic and imaginative cast of mind.

Such persons will also take pleasure in the resemblance between a walnut kernel and the human brain, and in other aspects of nut symbolism. Max Ernst's disturbing painting 'Oedipus Rex' – so disturbing that I will not even describe it – opens a window on one such aspect . . .

An examination of all the various uses of 'nut' in the *Oxford English Dictionary* brings others, of a less sinister character, to light. The old use of 'nuts' to mean 'sources of delight', as in 'To see me here would be simply nuts to her', or to mean 'crazy about' ('Johnny and Gregory were nuts on their pet') is pleasantly straightforward. It seems more appropriate than the modern 'nuts to you', which invites the question: What are these nuts which are unwelcome? Perhaps there is some connection with the odd colonial usage, whereby 'nut', at least in Australia, signified 'a long, lank, lantern-jawed, whiskerless, colonial youth'; or with 'nut' meaning 'crackpot'.

But nutty flights of the imagination take second place for most of us to the more palpable pleasures of eating nuts. And these have become more readily available thanks to modern techniques for preserving nuts. It is true that most nuts keep and travel well, especially in the shell, but they do become stale and even rancid in time. And there is nowhere in the world where all, even a majority, of the choicest nuts grow. (The two Georgias, one for each superpower, do quite well, and California and Turkey are good places, but the box which lists my top ten nuts shows that even these favoured regions can only score about half marks.) So, in the past, the nut connoisseur faced serious problems. Now, however, it is possible to shell and process nuts where they are grown and to vacuum-pack them so that they stay fresh quite long enough to travel half way round the world.

These problems, by the way, have never bothered the French. Their traditional perception of the nut world is that three excellent nuts grow in France (the walnut, the almond and the hazelnut); and that's all there is to the matter. (Well, maybe four, since they do prize their best chestnuts, the famous *marrons*.) French connoisseurship is shown mainly in the consumption, in their seasons, of the three nuts in fresh, 'green', form; and by French ability, unrivalled anywhere else, to distinguish between varieties; a score of walnut varieties, for example, ranging from the very large Bijou of the Grenoble area to the small Noix noisette which is just the size of a hazelnut.

The list of the top ten nuts would contain one surprise for Phrynichus, and indeed for Bunyard. It includes a recent 'discovery', the macadamia nut, the only food indigenous to Australasia which has rocketed to the status of an international delicacy. It received its botanical name, honouring Dr John Macadam, in Melbourne in 1857, but it is only in the last few decades, when plantations of improved varieties in Hawaii have multiplied, that it has acquired star status. The rapidity of its climb to fame suggests that other obscure nuts may have a bright future in the next century.

The list also includes one nut which is not really a nut, but the seed of a legume: the peanut. The definition of 'nut' fascinates botanists and philologists, but is a real bore for the average person, who knows what a nut is and doesn't want to be told that, whatever his definition may be (does it include sunflower seeds?), it won't stand up to informed scrutiny. So far as I am concerned, what people call nuts are nuts: even the Chinese water chestnut which is a bulb, and the chufa nut which is a tuber. Even so, there is something to be said for distinguishing between true nuts, which grow on trees and are expensive, and other 'nuts' such as the peanut.

My Top Ten			
Nut	Grows in	Top nut for	At its best
Almond	California Spain	flavouring power	'green'; roasted and salted; in marzipan
Brazil nut	Brazil, in the wild	size (?)	for dessert
Cashew nut	India, Africa SE Asia, Brazil	eccentricity (grows out of end of fruit)	roasted and salted; in confectionery
Chestnut	Europe, W Asia	starch content	roasted; in chestnut purée as marrons glacés
Macadamia nut	Australia; Hawaii	all-round richness	roasted and salted
Peanut (=groundnut)	USA (especially Georgia); Africa, Asia, Latin America	nutritional quality	in home-made crunchy peanut butter
Pecan	USA (south and centre)	oil content	for dessert; in pecan pie
Pistachio	Iran; Turkey; California	colour	garnish & decoration; in ice cream
Pine nut [or pignon]	Near East [south-west USA]	price and protein	in pilau dishes; in tea (Arab style)
Walnut	California; Turkey & Greece; China; Soviet Union	sculptural quality	for dessert; in cakes; pickled (English style)

The trees which bear nuts represent a considerable investment for the producer. A pecan tree will only start bearing after six to ten years, an almond tree after about four years. And they won't grow anywhere. Ninety-nine per cent of almond production in the USA, the world's largest producer, is in north-central California. The pecan has a much more extensive range – from the South-East (it is the official state tree of Texas) and the South-West (Georgia produces more pecans than any other state) up to Illinois. But it is difficult to propagate, and the machinery needed – tree shakers, harvesters, shelling equipment, electronic sorters, etc. – represents a lot of dollars.

The peanut is not expensive, because the plant is an annual, and relatively easy to process. So peanut butter is the commonest nut butter. Is it also the best? Such questions are hard to consider with complete objectivity, when prices vary so much; even the keenest-witted people sometimes fall prey to the fallacy that if something costs more it must be better. And nut-butter tastings are rare events. I can only say that hazelnut butter is a strong competitor, but that peanut butter, of the crunchy kind, seems to me to have the edge.

Peanut butter must, by law in the USA, contain at least 90 per cent peanuts. This is feasible because peanuts are cheap. The costly nuts could hardly be treated this way; indeed the tendency is to incorporate them in tiny amounts in other things like ice cream. If there's a law about the minimum contents of pistachio ice cream, it probably says a fraction of one per cent.

However, this sort of economical practice is acceptable, because a little nutmeat goes a long way in providing flavour and texture, and everyone can enjoy them in this way. *One* macadamia nut, after surgery with a razor blade, can make *four* people happy.

There is an interesting parallel here between West and East. Asians also make a little nut go a long way. But in most of Asia, and in much of Africa too, and the Near East, nuts are as prominent in regular cookery as they are in confectionery and bakery and as tidbits.

This is not true of the West, and the contrast puzzles me. After all, early Arabic cookery is a main trunk from which many branches of western cookery stem, and the Arabs used nuts a lot in their cookery and still do. In medieval Europe this influence was strongly apparent. Almonds, especially, were an important ingredient in court dishes; and at a humbler level the chestnut and even the acorn and beechnut were the basis of, or an important ingredient in, many substantial dishes.

What has happened to all this? Well, England provides one dismal example. Everyone there knows 'blancmange', a tasteless, opaque, white 'jelly' which is mainly cornflour and artificial flavouring. Yet five hundred years ago 'blanc manger' ('white eats') was a precious dish made by court cooks with milk of almonds.

I hope that someone, some day, will write a ruminative work on nuts which will illuminate some of these mysteries and pull together both the contrasts and the parallels in the uses of nuts in the two hemispheres.

By then, of course, some of the contrasts may have been ironed out. When I lived in Laos in the mid-1970s, I felt that I was making a discovery in learning all about the coconut. In some ways, of course, this is the top nut of all, but it doesn't figure in my list because it is so large and 'different' (imagine the reaction of B if asked by A whether he would like a few nuts at the end of lunch, and if, when he said 'yes please', A then staggered into the dining room with a load of coconuts). Anyway, the use of coconut cream in cooking was news to me, and good news, but back in London in the 1980s I find that coconuts are everywhere and a surprisingly large number of people know just what to do with them. There is even a shop where you can buy a South-East Asian 'rabbit' which combines a comfortable seat with an apparatus for grating the meat.

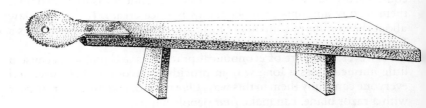

All the same, there are some oriental situations which seem unlikely to be reproduced in the West. One which I met in Laos is the mystery of the 'ma bok'. This is a really good nut, from a large tree of the jungle. It tastes like an almond. But what is really amazing is that it comes pre-husked by animal (or insect) labour. When the nuts fall in an area accessible to cows, the cows eat off the husk, leaving the nut, still in its shell, to bleach and dry in the tropical sun. The Lao come by after a while and gather them. I pointed out to a Lao friend that there aren't that many cows in Laos. 'No problem,' he replied, 'if a cow doesn't eat the husk, termites come out of the jungle and do the job for us.'

Lao recollections prompt a final, unanswered, question. Street vendors of nuts exist, but why are there no special nut shops? Not in Paris, not in London, not in New York. But, surprise, you could say that there was one in Laos. In the morning market in the capital, Vientiane, there was a lady whose 'shop' sold nothing but ma bok.

Rare and Up-and-coming Nuts

Some good nuts are only eaten locally, or are only being exported experimentally. Here are a few for which globe-trotting connoisseurs should be on the alert.

In Brazil? SAPUCAYA NUTS, from trees of the genus *Lecythis*, closely related to and almost as tall as those of the Brazil nut tree. Like Brazil nuts they are encased in a big, round, woody container, but there is a difference; that of the sapucaya has a detachable base or 'lid'. Whereas the whole container of the Brazil nut falls bodily off the tree, only the lid of the sapucaya comes away, allowing the nuts within to fall out singly or to be picked out by monkeys and parrots. Since monkeys can run faster than people, and parrots can fly, human collectors get only a few nuts. These are eaten locally, as dessert nuts or in chocolate and confectionery. Brazilians with gardens often grow trees for their own use. Befriend such a person.

In the Philippines? Meet the PILI NUT, a thin, cream-coloured nut, pointed at both ends and triangular in section. The sweet taste has something in common with the almond. The shell, alas, is inconveniently thick and hard, but the development of thin-shelled cultivars should qualify the pili for promotion in the international nut league.

In Japan? Try the JAPANESE WALNUT, a small walnut of very fine flavour, often called heartnut in the USA (where it is now grown on a small scale).

In China? That is the place for eating a GINKGO NUT. The pale green kernel is toxic when raw, but the Chinese can cope; they let the surrounding flesh rot away, then roast the nuts and eat them, enjoying the sweet taste. They also paint them red, the colour of happiness, and string them up in festoons as a wedding decoration.

In India? Enjoy CALUMPANG NUTS, the correct name of what are called 'almondettes' in western countries. This is a nut of the cashew family, with a flavour which recalls both almond and pistachio. Very popular in India for sweetmeats.

In East Africa? That is the region of the OYSTER NUT, a delicacy little known elsewhere, although Frederic Rosengarten* prophesies that its fine eating quality – it resembles the Brazil nut in flavour and is even more nutritious – may eventually bring it into general popularity. The plants which bear it certainly try hard enough; they are vines which scramble up over trees, covering an area the size of a small parking lot and sometimes crushing their hosts with the weight of their huge seed-containers, each containing a hundred or more of the oyster-shaped nuts.

In Indonesia? You'll be eating CANDLENUTS, there called kemiri nuts; but you may not know that you are since consumption of the raw nuts is

* *The Book of Edible Nuts*, New York, 1984.

barred by a toxin which is dispelled in cooking, and the kernels are usually crushed with other ingredients such as shallots, garlic and chilli peppers before they are cooked. This sort of combination produces the highly characteristic flavour typical of many Indonesian savoury dishes.

1986

Marmalade: an Unpublished Letter to *The Times*

I think it was in 1984 that Shona Crawford Poole, then *The Times* Cook, alluded to men making marmalade. I sat down right away and wrote the Letter to the Editor which appears below. It was never published, because it was never posted. I usually remember to put things in the post, and suspect that what was at work on this occasion was a subconscious fear of being typed as the sort of person who writes letters to *The Times*. If so, the subconscious fear won out, and I have escaped that danger.

Mind you, it may be equally bad to be branded as the sort of person who just never writes letters to *The Times*. But the revelation of this little episode is enough to clear me of that charge. I did write one.

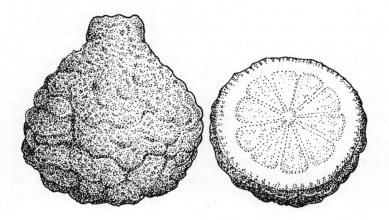

14 February

Sir,
  Shona Crawford Poole's advice on making marmalade (*Times* yesterday) included the comment that in many families a man

does it. So in this family; and I have now nearly forty years' experience in the art. I began with my Scottish grandmother's recipe, which the S.C.P. version closely resembles, although my grandmother had one more Ritual. Warming the Sugar, Warming the Jars, Putting the Pips in a Muslin Bag, Skimming the Froth, Fiddling with the Waxed Discs: all these and also Steeping the Cut Fruit Overnight beforehand. Gradually, as the decades have gone by and time has become more and more precious, I have introduced simplifications, cannily checking from year to year that the loss in quality of appearance has not been accompanied by a deterioration of flavour and that it is outweighed by the great saving of time and labour.

Here is my advice, for marmalade-makers of either sex. Forget about warming the sugar and the jars. Don't fret because your muslin bag has been lost; you won't need it. Stop searching for waxed discs of the right size; they too are otiose.

Buy 2 lb (1 kg) Seville oranges, a grapefruit and a lemon. Rinse them, nip off the tough little 'buttons' if they are still there, then quarter the fruit and put it in a large pan with more than enough water to cover. Simmer, covered, for about an hour. When the peel is soft, use a pair of kitchen scissors to chop it (in or out of the pan, whichever you find quicker). Add rather more than 2 lb 1 kg) sugar and stir until the sugar is dissolved. Then turn up the heat to produce a fast rolling boil. Rapid evaporation will reduce the proportion of water to sugar and fruit and permit the temperature to climb to setting point. It may arrive there quite soon (4 minutes is my record so far). So test for setting regularly, as S.C.P. advises. As soon as you have a positive result, remove the pan from the heat, let cool for 5 minutes, stir and then ladle the contents into clean jars, the kind which have screw-on air-tight caps. Fill them very full (no air, no mould), put the caps on loosely, read the newspaper for a few minutes, then tighten the caps and that's that. When you come to use the marmalade you will find that about every second jar does have some mould on the surface of the marmalade. Lift it off with a teaspoon before bringing to table.

The pips? I eat them; with pleasure.

It is fair to add that whatever law it is which says that for every hour saved in carrying out household tasks at least half an hour is restored by the introduction of new complications has been at work. My compensatory complication is to buy for each batch, from a shop selling South-East Asian fruits, one Kaffir lime

(*Citrus hystrix*, normally used for flavouring only, thick-skinned and knobbly). I add this to the oranges etc., finely minced. This refinement brings into play the Sub-law of Counter-compensation. You finish up with more marmalade for yourself. Forty per cent of British people find the flavour too sharp and say 'No, thank you.' The remainder find the flavour so sensationally good that they will be doubly grateful if given half the quantity.

1984

On the Scent of the Truffle

I wonder whether President Truman ever received, and tasted, the largest truffle of which a record exists: a giant which registered over 4 pounds on the scales. The Italian who dug it up in 1951 near Alba, in the heart of the Italian truffle country, sold it for 130,000 lire (equivalent, perhaps, to £10,000 now), and the food historian Leo Goldschmiet records that the businessman from Rome who bought it intended to offer it in homage to Truman. If he did, there would have been a pleasing contrast between gift and recipient; the simple eater from Missouri faced by a supreme example of the most expensive, subtle and mysterious of the foods known to man.

The Roman donor could also have reflected that he was giving to the leading personality of the New World the one Old World food which he could not possibly grow on his own territory. It is true that truffles are a world-wide phenomenon; and some species exist in North America, including *Tuber texense*, an edible white truffle which is used by Alice Waters at Chez Panisse in Berkeley, California. But no one has claimed that this, or any other truffle outside Europe, is a serious rival to the black truffle of Périgord, *Tuber melanosporum*, or the white truffle of Alba, *Tuber magnatum*.

The black truffle is probably at its best in Périgord, where conditions conspire to bring it to perfection, but it does grow in other parts of France, and also in Spain and Italy. The white truffle is found only in Italy, mainly in the vicinity of Alba. Of the dozens of species scattered over the globe these two stand alone, in excellence as in fame.

It was not always so. If our Roman had lived 1800 years ago and had wished to honour his own Emperor, he might well have offered him a specimen of *Terfezia*, the desert truffle which was brought to Rome from Arab lands, especially North Africa. 'Terfez', as the Arabs know it, is still found and may still, roasted whole, add lustre to a Sheikh's table in the Persian Gulf; but its reputation and consumption seem to have dwindled remarkably since classical times.

In those old times, and indeed until about a hundred years ago, no natural historian understood what truffles are and how they grow. Theophrastus thought that they were produced by the rain of thunderstorms; Dioscorides that they were a kind of root; Pliny that they were 'callosities of earth'; and Plutarch that lightning was a necessary condition of their formation. Even in the eighteenth and nineteenth centuries, when some learned men were beginning to sniff the truth, others continued to uphold quite false theories.

A truffle is in fact the fruiting body of a fungus which belongs to the category of mushrooms and grows wholly underground. Truffles are not the only underground 'mushrooms', but they are the only valuable ones of this habit. The plant itself consists of an extensive web of filaments so fine as to be invisible. And these filaments, known as the 'mycelium', link up with the roots of certain trees and shrubs in what is called a 'mycorrhizal' relationship. This relationship benefits both parties. From the point of view of the tree, the filaments of the truffle become extensions of its own roots and enable it to draw up more sustenance, notably minerals, from the soil. For the truffle, the tree gives nourishment in the form of products synthesised by its leaves. This remarkable exchange is not achieved by mere contact between the mycelium of the truffle and the roots of the tree. They are organically bonded together by a special growth called a 'mycorrhiza'.

At this point one begins to understand why the cultivation of truffles, which for obvious reasons has long been attempted, is on the one hand difficult (how to reproduce a natural phenomenon of such complexity?) but on the other hand possible (since young trees in a mycorrhizal condition can be transplanted). The would-be cultivator has to remember that the system only works with some kinds of tree (notably, but not exclusively, certain kinds of oak), in a limited range of climates and on certain types of soil (a limestone base being preferred). Maps are available showing where truffles grow in France – the sort of thing over which people who dream of creating truffle plantations overseas regularly pore. If they are eventually successful, fortunes will be made, since the demand for truffles far outstrips the supply and prices are sky-high.

Given the wealth which the 'black diamonds' of Périgord represent, it is odd that production should have fallen so dramatically from the level recorded a hundred or seventy-five years ago. In 1912 the Périgord-Quercy region alone put 280 tons of truffles on to the market. After the First World War harvests declined steadily until in the 1960s the whole of France was producing a mere 70 tons. Faced by this surprising trend, some people say that it has been exaggerated by the tendency of truffle-gatherers to dispose of their finds surreptitiously, in order to evade taxes. A similar tale is told in Italy. No doubt there is some truth in this; but it is incontestable that the supply of truffles has dwindled, and authors such as Jean Rebière have been able to explain why, and by what measures the trend can be reversed.

Rebière is the doyen of truffle experts in the Périgord, and lives not far from the little truffle museum which was recently opened in the village of Sorges, and which now serves as a base from which to take 'truffle walks' and study the appearance of places where truffles grow. One striking feature of these is the 'scorched earth' area round a tree which has a mycorrhizal relationship with truffles, especially the black truffle. Virtually no other plants, except for those which need no water, can grow in such soil, and the underground progress of the truffle mycelium can be charted by the spread of this barren ground. Rebière has come up with some intriguing pieces of information about circumstances which will help restore a former *'truffière'* to productivity again. Roadworks help a lot, especially if heavy bulldozers are used. And having a local basketball team use a piece of ground for their games is another favourable factor. Shock treatment, in short, works wonders.

Rebière's work* is so illuminating and the trufflers of his region so communicative (the café in the little village of Cubjac is a fine place for gathering information) that I will stay with the black truffle in the rest of this article, while assuring Italians that I have been to Alba too and have the highest respect for their white species.

The mycelium of the black truffle starts active growth in May and continues until July. The fruiting bodies are white when they first begin to form, then successively greyish and reddish, by which time they have reached full size. Finally, when they reach maturity, they are nearly black and veined white inside. There is often a long pause, perhaps of several months, between the time when a truffle reaches its full size and the time when it matures. This accounts for the length of the season, extending over five winter months.

Although some truffles break the surface of the ground at an early stage in their growth, most remain well underground. Skilled hunters may be able to detect from signs on the surface that a truffle is below; but the aid of animals or insects has to be invoked to ensure a full harvest. The aroma of a mature truffle can be detected by a pig or a dog, and it is these animals which have traditionally been trained to do the work. The pig has some disadvantages, especially for the truffle-poacher. A villain of this kind has to be able to make a quick getaway if spotted, and this is difficult if he is encumbered by a pig which has just found a truffle and is unwilling to part with it. Separating pig from truffle is anyway awkward. Dogs are nimbler and less possessive.

* *La Truffe du Périgord*, 2nd ed., Périgueux, 1981.

The helpful insects belong to the species *Helomyza tuberiperda*, and may be seen hovering over the spot where a truffle lies concealed. They hover with the ill intent of depositing their larvae on the truffles, little realising what an expensive baby-food they thus provide for their tiny offspring.

Even with these various aids, truffle-hunting is a skilled business, and one which is closely regulated. Truffling rights in a piece of land may be separated from ownership of the land itself. In truffle country one may see, from August onwards, stern notices announcing: 'Truffière Protégée par La Loi, Articles 388 and 401 du Code Pénal, Articles 173 et 177 du Code Forestier.' I looked up Article 388 and found that if I dug up a truffle in defiance of it I would be liable to a term of imprisonment (fifteen days to two years) as well as a fine. And if I worked by night, with human accomplices or a motor vehicle, I might spend five years in prison.

The severity of these penalties, and of those in Article 401 (even stronger), reflect the great value of the harvest. An expert hunter working in good terrain may gather the equivalent of six months' livelihood in a few weeks, if the summer weather has been right and the season is therefore a good one.

The season, as noted above, is long: from November through February, and even March, in the Périgord. The market is most active around Christmas and the New Year, but it is a popular misconception that most truffles reach maturity at this time. The explanation is simply that demand is then at its peak, since this is the season for making pâté de foie gras and the truffled turkey which is a traditional Christmas and New Year delicacy. Half a pound of truffles for one turkey!

When choosing truffles remember the following points:

- A good truffle is black, firm to the touch and dense; and of course has a fine strong aroma. Very large and very small ones may be perfectly good, but the preferred range of size is from 10 to 200 grams.
- Reject truffles which seem unduly dry and light in weight. They have probably been exposed to the air for too long, and have become dehydrated. (If such truffles have been soaked to restore them, they will have a bitter aroma and are to be rejected likewise.)
- Truffles which are soft and sweat when pressed are likely to have suffered frostbite and will be of a light coffee colour inside. Have nothing to do with them.
- A truffle which has no aroma is probably immature. It can be

allowed to reach maturity by being put back in the earth or stored in a sealed container.

Truffles will keep well for up to a week in a plastic bag from which most of the air has been expelled. If you need to keep the truffles for a month or two, cover them with oil. Either way, they should be in the vegetable compartment of the refrigerator.

Truffles can also be preserved in Cognac or Armagnac; or frozen (for periods up to several months). But for long-term preservation they should be carefully cleaned, placed in cans, sealed and sterilised. This works better than some people think. The first truffle I bought was a very small one in a tiny can. Awestruck by our extravagance, we kept it for ten years before judging that an occasion warranting its consumption had arisen. It was fine, although not quite as good as a fresh one.

The supreme method of enjoying truffles (and this is for wealthy connoisseurs only) requires whole truffles, unpeeled. Wrap them in several layers of cooking paper greased with goose fat, and roast them gently under hot cinders.

But this is for the *very* wealthy. The common run of millionaires will probably be satisfied with the slivers of truffle to be found in pâté de foie gras *truffé*. Buy this delicacy from a reputable source. A study of French court proceedings shows that, very occasionally, slivers of something else, such as terfez or even carrot, are dyed black and substituted.

There is a way of enjoying truffles for a few pence. The technique permitting this is only possible because of the quite extraordinarily pervasive power of the aroma of truffles. All you need yourself is some eggs; but you do need to know a friend who has some fresh truffles. You persuade this friend to let your eggs sit for a while in whatever receptacle is being used to keep the truffles. Then you remove the eggs and make an omelette with them. The truffle flavour will be highly satisfactory.

1984

Honey

In the first recorded love poem, written in India thousands of years ago, the author addresses his beloved as 'honeysweet': a note echoed ever since by poets, lovers, and all who have access to the product of the honey-bee.

That is now just about everyone. The honey-bees, *Apis mellifera* and relations, belong to the Old World, but early colonists took them to the New World, where they quickly settled down. Indeed in North America they took off across the continent by themselves, and were treated by the Indians, who called them 'white man's flies', as a warning that white men were not far behind. They penetrated down to Brazil and Chile, and also arrived in Australia and New Zealand, both now important honey countries, in the nineteenth century, thus completing their spread through all five continents.

The fact that there are no indigenous honey-bees in some parts of the world does not mean that there was no honey. Allied species such as the tropical stingless bees in Latin America make it. So do some ants, which act as living honey-stores, lolling inactive in their hives while holding the precious substance in their distended bellies. Australian aborigines apparently enjoy 'popping' such ants in their mouths. But this taste treat has not caught on. The honey of the honey-bees is best.

To be more exact, at its best it is best. There are infinite numbers of different honeys, including a few which are downright harmful and some which have a disagreeable taste or texture. The variations have multiple causes, notably the nature of the flowers from which the bees take the nectar that they make into honey.

What is this nectar? It is a watery solution of sugars, with traces of other substances; and the nectaries containing it are devices in the plant which act like 'sugar valves'. They are found in various parts of the plant, not just the flower areas, and even in non-flowering plants. But the flower nectaries have a special significance. By attracting bees, who collect pollen as well as nectar and who often fly away with a cargo of pollen stuck to their legs, they ensure the pollination of the plants. If a plant could speak to a bee, it would no doubt say: 'Help yourself to my nectar, but please take some pollen too.'

Nectar is not identical with sap, but nearly so. It is not a great over-simplification to regard it as a reservoir of sap. Sap flows in the plant at the times of greatest activity, typically in the spring when leaves are formed, and in the autumn when they change colour. So it is at these times that the stores of nectar are most needed and most available, and at these times that the bees do most of their foraging. Spring honey is in most regions held to be the best, and may be identified as such by small producers who sell direct, but the labels on commercial honeys don't say when it was gathered. Indeed they don't say much except for the country or countries of origin, sometimes a locality, and often the name of a flower (of which more below). They stay silent on the nature and extent of processing, which are matters of concern to the honey connoisseur.

Many such connoisseurs would cast their vote for unprocessed honey – still sealed in the wax comb in which the bees have encased it. This is straight from the bees, which is good. But the question arises: do you eat the wax comb? Some do. Apparently it has no nutritive value, passing through the body unutilised; and even if it is mashed up with the honey it doesn't slip down so readily. One forthright honey expert, pointing out that even the bees don't eat beeswax, declared that munching it down was about as sensible as eating the wrapper from a packet of sugar. His advice: cut it to the width of the knife blade, lay it upon the plate with the cells vertical, and press the blade flat upon it, when the honey will flow out to the right and left.

However, honey in the comb has become a rarity in the shops, and honey in jars has been processed, if only a little. At the least, the liquid honey has to be extracted, usually by centrifuge, from the wax combs in which the bees have deposited it. This exposes it to air, which results in a slight loss of flavour – some of the aromatic substances which contribute to the flavour are highly volatile. But worse may follow. On the way from the centrifuge to the pots in which it will be retailed, honey has to flow along pipes. It doesn't flow easily at room temperature, but will do so if heated. Mild heat does not cause problems, but higher heat does; and honey which has been 'overheated' will be of less good quality.

Heat is also used to make honey stay liquid, if it is to be sold as liquid. Flash heating dissolves any crystals, and is followed by rigorous filtering which removes virtually all solid particles. Since these include some natural constituents of the honey, this practice displeases scientists who might wish to establish the plant origin of the honey by examining the pollen grains in it. There won't be any in honey which has been treated this way.

Establishing the plant origin of a honey can be important, since the nature of the nectar remains the most influential determinant of the qualities of a honey, and that is why most honeys are identified on the label by the name of a flower. (Eva Crane, whose 608-page book *Honey: A Comprehensive Survey** is the standard reference, provides a 'short list' of 150 nectar-producing plants and describes the character-istics of the honey from each.)

If one is not equipped to study traces of pollen under a microscope, how can one tell what flowers the bees have visited? Sometimes one can't. The Governor of the Bank of England has a hive in the middle of London, and his bees have to be highly eclectic, making their choice from the hundreds of different garden flowers in city gardens. A friend who has a hive on his London rooftop believes that this 'polyfloral' honey is as good as any of the single-flower kind; and a recent experience in Turkey has convinced me too.

I was buying some honey from a merchant in Istanbul who had in the window huge pans into which suspended combs were dripping the precious liquid. A tall Turk intervened to tell me that I could do better than this, and that I must have the best – the best in the world! Two days later he swooped in his car to intercept me as I stepped from the night train to Ankara, thrust a long comb into my hands, announced it as 'from Bars, near Mount Ararat', and was gone before I could get out my notebook and ask what flowers had yielded their nectar for it. I later worked out that it must be polyfloral. (By the way, it *was* the best. I carried the dripping comb, secure in several layers of plastic, back to London and tasted it with Hymettus honey, Scottish heather honey and litchi flower honey; its flavour seemed to me the most subtle and delightful of all.)

Most apiaries, however, are situated in places where at any given time one flower is likely to be dominant in the collection area of the bees (usually not much more than a mile in radius, although sometimes greater); and if bees can consistently collect nectar from one kind of flower they will do so.

Clover, rape, heather – the 'big names' are numerous. In Australia, most honey is eucalyptus-based. However, there are many situations, and not only urban ones, in which the bees are gathering from a variety of flowers. In the south of France one meets honeys described as 'of the maquis'; they are based on nectar from a range of plants which bloom in the maquis. These mixed-origin honeys are often extremely good.

There are also 'blended honeys'; blended by man, not bees. By

* London, 1975.

analogy with tea, they need be none the worse for that, but I've never been convinced. The labels rarely, if ever, match tea language by saying, for example, 'a rich blend of rape honeys from Canada with a touch of coffee honey from Mexico' – they just say 'a blend', or 'produce of several countries'. The impression is that availability and price are the determining factors.

Honeys vary in appearance. The colour may be anything from whitish to nearly black, with surprising hues such as red (well, reddish – this from kiwi flowers) and green in between; but, as the term 'honey-coloured' suggests, the usual colour is amber or light brown. Darker honeys tend to have a stronger flavour.

Differences in consistency are just as striking. A liquid honey looks very different from one which has crystallised, whether to the consistency of butter or – as can happen – hard enough to bend a teaspoon. Yet the same honey may appear in both forms; indeed any liquid honey will eventually crystallise, or 'granulate', if left to itself. The speed at which this happens depends on the ratio between glucose and fructose, the two main sugars in honey. If the glucose is high, the honey granulates easily; and if it is very high, granulation may even occur while the honey is still in the comb. Clover and buckwheat honeys granulate quickly. Acacia honey, on the other hand, stays liquid for a long time, even for many years.

There is one category of honeys which is neither liquid nor granular, but a gel. The best known example is ling heather honey, from the flowers of *Calluna vulgaris*, but honeys from the flowers of carvi in India and manuka in New Zealand also have this characteristic. The reason for their different structure is their relatively high content of certain proteins. I recently compared heather honeys from the south of England, from Scotland and from Corsica. The strength of flavour varied but the gel consistency was the same.

The pleasure of eating honey is not diminished by the thought that it is better for you than other sweeteners. But is it? Analysis of any honey will show that it is largely composed of sugars; that there is some water; and that other elements, such as minerals and amino-acids, are present in quantities so small as not to matter much in nutrition. If one offered to a health food enthusiast a meal consisting of two large piles of sugar, three thimblefuls of water, and a pill containing miniscule amounts of minerals and amino-acids, he would start back in dismay. Yet the same person, were he to be presented with a helping of honey, would engulf it eagerly. One attractive explanation of this paradox is that honey contains something which analysts have not yet identified, a sort of super-vitamin.

I half believe this myself, having read a Russian book* which reveals the extraordinary longevity of beekeepers (not just in Russia – the same phenomenon has been noticed in many countries). Scholars who have studied the matter, and who can produce lists of scores of beekeepers who have lived to over a hundred years, believe that a combination of factors is at work – eating honey, consuming with it a certain amount of pollen, and the generally beneficial effects of a calm and productive way of life in a health-promoting environment. Noting that many of the famous centenarians of the Caucasus worked in apiaries, Naum Ioyrish observed that 138-year-old Safar Husein attributed his long life to eating honey and to working in an apiary; while 150-year-old Mahmud Eivazov considered that working in the open air, in his own bee-garden, was the best elixir for longevity. (None of these centenarians, by the way, advocated eating the so-called 'royal jelly' or propolis – 'bee glue' – other bee products for which some people lavish large sums of money; nor did they believe that apitoxin therapy, treatment by controlled bee stings, was suitable for very aged persons, although it can be useful in treating some ailments earlier in life.)

But, reverting to the question whether there can be something special in honey itself, what could the mystery substance be, and how can it have escaped analysis?

Perhaps the explanation, or a large part of it, is simpler. The sugars in honey, unlike the sugar we usually eat, can be absorbed by the human system instantly and easily. A lady I know in a remarkably small English village (population 26) where traditions date back unimaginably far, told me that she was fed spoonfuls of honey while giving birth to her daughter – nothing else would have filled her need for extra energy at a moment's notice.

There was a time when honey was cheaper than sugar. Indeed in Europe this was so up to about 1800. Sugar, which was originally regarded more as a medicinal item than as a culinary one, was then believed to have special and mysterious properties. Since sugar has become much cheaper than honey, and seems bound to remain so, this belief has evaporated. Could the same happen with honey? It seems not, since although honey is made for free by the bees, the maintenance of commercially productive apiaries is a costly business and by its nature not susceptible to the economies of what we mean by mass-production (although 'mass' production is surely the right phrase for work involving billions and billions of workers).

Still, one wonders. It is only just over a hundred years ago, in the

* *Bees and People* by Naum Ioyrish, trans. G. A. Kozlova, ed. H. C. Creighton, Moscow, 1974.

1860s, that the introduction of the 'Langstroth' movable frame hive revolutionised honey production. And there is still one factor which can be greatly improved: the bee itself.

The leading light in bee genetics, and one of the great beekeepers of all time, is the octogenarian Brother Adam of Buckfast Abbey in Devon. The abbey is famous for its honey, and he has been in charge of the bees, and an elaborate research programme, for sixty years. As he explains in his chronicle of long journeys to inspect bees, in various parts of the world* – places as remote as a Saharan oasis – there are many races of honey-bee, each with its advantages and disadvantages. Thus the Anatolian is very productive but tends to 'swarm'. The Syrian is bad-tempered. The Carniolan, on the other hand, is calm and hard-working, yet slow at making comb. The Italian has many good qualities, but lacks stamina.

The obvious solution is to produce crosses which will combine the good qualities and shed the bad ones. This is what is going on, and if it leads to a race of near-perfect bees the effects will be as far-reaching as the introduction of the modern hive.

But Brother Adam, when I went to see him, explained that these effects will be on the economics of honey production, not on the taste of the honey. That will still depend mainly on the source chosen by the bees, or presented to them; so our honey jars are likely to bear the name of a flower on the label for as far ahead as anyone can see.

However, Brother Adam, who seems well set to join the ranks of beekeeping centenarians, was willing to talk also of the quality of honey and to reminisce about the kinds which had pleased him most in his travels. The honey which he describes as possibly 'the loveliest in the world' is that from the Alpenrosen, a species of dwarf rhododendron which only thrives at high altitudes in non-calcareous regions of the Alps. The other honey which he says is of 'supreme' quality is that produced from rosemary on islands off the Dalmatian coast.

I suggested that the Buckfast heather honey has no equal. He acknowledged the compliment, while observing that the flavour of heather honey is too strong for some people. For those who are capable of appreciating it, he added, Buckfast is indeed best: it is made 95 per cent from ling heather, whereas in other areas the bees gather a significant proportion of nectar from bell heather.

Leading me out through the 'honey hall' below his offices, Brother Adam displayed the Buckfast heather honeypress, a beautiful and unique piece of machinery made to his design. It was spotless, so much

* Brother Adam, *In Search of the Best Strains of Bees*, Hebden Bridge, Yorkshire, 1983.

so that I wondered whether it was still in use. Yes, it was, but 1986 had been such a disastrous year for the bees that there had been no honeycomb to press between its stainless steel jaws. Even if there had been, I learned, it would all have been sold locally. Devon beekeepers, and not just the monks at the abbey, seem to take a pride in selling their honey locally, and at what they consider a fair price. The thought that the same produce might sell for much more to connoisseurs in distant places holds no appeal. This is an endearing trait, although exasperating for the distant connoisseurs. The moral seems to be that if you want the very best honey you have to go and get it, and that often means going a long way.

There is a final twist to the search for the 'best honey'. One of the Devon beekeepers explained to me that he and his wife always reserve for their own use what they count the very best. Their bees forage from bluebell, sycamore, clover and bramble – sometimes in a good season, hawthorn too. But, whatever the source of the nectar, the choicest honey is the small amount which adheres to the capping of the comb cells. This capping is sliced off before the comb is centrifuged to release its honey. If the cut-off cappings are drained, they will yield a little honey which contains – this is the secret – some pollen. It seems that when the bees cap the cells with wax they deposit this pollen there in case it is needed – like putting a little of something on the shelf just inside the pantry door. You'll never find this special honey marketed, but if you have beekeepers among your friends and they don't want it all themselves . . .

1987

Part Four
History

The Natural History of British Cookery Books

In many countries, when motorcars throng the roads during the holiday season, the authorities put up signs to indicate alternative routes, bypassing the best known and most frequented places along the way. Similarly, I shall steer clear, or almost clear, of some of the cookery writers on whom much – and in some instances excessive – attention has already been lavished and will instead conduct a tour along secondary roads, introducing not-so-famous authors whose import-ance has been underestimated.

The point of departure is clear. *The Forme of Cury*, a vellum roll on which are written the recipes of the chef of King Richard II, belongs to the very end of the fourteenth century and is the first work on cookery in the English language. It is not, naturally, a purely English work. What C. Anne Wilson, the historian of English food, has called, in a recent article, 'the French connection' is fully apparent. But the terms of Norman origin that are to be found in it are intermingled with others of Saxon derivation, and its claim to be the first English cookery book is indisputable and undisputed, despite the lapse of time (about three centuries) before it appeared in printed form.

The first printed cookery book in the English language was composed between 1470 and 1480 and printed in 1500, a conveniently memor-able date. There is one known copy of this book, in the library of one of the great country houses in England. When I last visited this house, the librarian, perceiving that I was unoccupied while my friend went about her business, casually passed it to me as something with which to while away the time. The sensations that pervaded me as I turned over its crisp, almost mint, pages were of my native Celtic intensity, although I preserved a properly English appearance of calm. The book is called simply the *Noble Boke off Cookry*. Robina Napier, who edited a printed edition of the manuscript version of the same book (which is among the treasures of another of England's stately homes), commen-ted on the similarity between many of its recipes and those that had been recorded in *The Forme of Cury* nearly a hundred years previously. She referred also to some recipes in French that had been among some law papers in the possession of a certain Mr Horwood. These were in the same hand as the manuscript of the *Noble Boke off Cookry*. Some were very close to the English version given in the latter document; others were more elaborate. Mrs Napier concluded that much of the *Noble Boke off Cookry* had its origins in French manuscript material even older than *The Forme of Cury*. She may well have been right. It is relevant at this point to make the rather obvious comment that when we look at the contents of old printed cookery books, we must assume that the recipes in them had been current for some time, perhaps quite a long time, before they found their way into print. Elizabeth David, in recording her search for the earliest English ice cream recipe, has emphasised the need to keep this time lag in mind; indeed, she has found that the earliest recorded English ice cream recipe is probably that of Grace, Countess Granville, written in her personal receipt book while she was still a girl, well before the end of the seventeenth century, by another hand. The earliest printed English recipe for ice cream seems, however, to be that in *Mrs. Eales' Receipts*, published in 1718.

In general, the sixteenth century was a productive one for English cookery books. Printed books on any subject were still relatively few in number. The output of cookery books in the whole of the sixteenth century corresponds no doubt to something like three weeks' output at the present time. Perhaps for this reason, the character and quality of the sixteenth-century books are easier to analyse and appraise than those of today's books, and the innovations that some of them represented are more apparent.

One feature of these early books is that many of them dealt with health and diet as well as with cookery. This combination was a persistent one (and is still to be found today) and reflected the medieval view, inherited mainly from Galen, that there are four elements; four qualities of which all substances including foodstuffs partake; and four humours that characterise human beings. Whoever was in charge of the kitchen, in a household that adhered to this view, was as much concerned to match the qualities of the food with the humours of the consumers as to pay attention to flavours, degrees of doneness, and the other things that preoccupy twentieth-century cooks. However, there was little original English writing along these lines. English authors tended to copy foreign ones, as when *The Secretes of the Reverende Maister Alexis of Piemont* was published in 1558. This and other kindred books had a relatively small cookery content. But some straightforward collections of recipes were published, such as *A Book of Cookrye*, compiled by 'A. W.' in 1591. I would count this among the very first, if not the first, English cookery book that can be read and used today without an extensive glossary. It can also be read without having to repair to one of the libraries possessing a copy or incurring vast expense in buying a copy, for it is among the volumes reproduced in the series 'The English Experience', a large collection of facsimile reproductions of early English printed books.*

I like the directness of the title of A. W.'s book. In contrast, many of the sixteenth-century books, such as that of Maister Alexis referred to above, made great play with the idea that they were revealing secrets or unveiling hidden treasures. To take a pair of examples, we have in 1573 *The Treasurie of Commodious Conceites, and Hidden Secrets* and in 1588 *The Good Hous-wives Treasurie*. This style of title was further developed in the seventeenth century, when the fashion was to refer to unlocking cabinets or closets (to reveal their secrets and treasures). Thus in 1639 appeared *The Ladies Cabinet Opened*, to be followed almost at once by an improved edition called *The Ladies Cabinet Enlarged and Opened*. The metaphor is beginning to escape control. It also invited competition. What would be the best cabinet to open? The author of *The Queen's Closet Opened* (1655) no doubt thought that she had climbed to the topmost rung of the ladder. Hannah Wolley's title, *The Queen-like Closet*, for the book that she published in 1670, seems rather anticlimactic after that.

In this discussion of titles, we have already strayed past 1600. It was in that year or thereabouts that the first edition of Hugh (later Sir Hugh) Plat's *Delightes for Ladies* was published. This book (of which a charming reprint with an extensive and illuminating introduction by its editors, G. E. and K. R. Fussell, appeared in 1948) will serve well to illustrate three points. The first is that Hugh Plat was not a cook, but a man of learning, an inventor, a farmer and a gardener. It was from this wide background that he turned his attention to cookery and the associated arts of distilling, perfumery and so forth. As the Fussells put it: 'He made two divagations. One was to write a book about gardening, the other was to produce *Delightes for Ladies*.' In fact, the second divagation took him through the garden and into the house, where the domain covered by *Delightes for Ladies* included both the kitchen and the stillroom. At that time, and for some time to come, houses had both, and it was not uncommon for cookery books to be organised in accordance with the internal layout of the house, one section being devoted to activity in the stillroom, where all manner of conserving and distilling were practised. (Houses commonly had a dairy, too, and the

* Published by Walter J. Johnson Inc., Norwood, N.J. and Theatrum Orbis Terrarum, Amsterdam.

THE
CLOSET

Of the Eminently Learned
Sir *Kenelme Digbie* K.ᵗ

OPENED:

Whereby is DISCOVERED
Several ways for making of
Metheglin, Sider, Cherry-Wine, &c.

TOGETHER WITH

Excellent Directions
FOR
COOKERY:

As also for
Preserving, Conserving, Candying, &c.

Published by his Son's Consent.

London, Printed by *E. C.* for *H. Brome,* at
the Star in *Little Britain.* 1669.

production and handling of dairy goods could also form a separate section or chapter in cookery books.)

So the first point is that some English cookery writers 'came in from the fields', so to speak; the second is that it was common not merely to give recipes for use in the kitchen, but also to cover all the activities concerned with food that went on in a large house and to supplement these with advice on other stillroom work. The third point to be exemplified by Plat is that English authors, who were not, of course, alone in this, took great pains over the introductions to their books. In the twentieth century, authors often see no need to explain why they have written their cookery books (although in many instances the question must pose itself to their readers). But in earlier times a preambular justification for the book was of importance and usually exhibited two characteristics: modesty, real or feigned and qualified or not qualified by self-praise; and a high literary style, whether success- fully achieved or not. Plat addressed his fair readers in verse, in an introduction that he called 'The Epistle', which carefully lists the subjects to be covered in enticing terms:

> *Of sweetes the sweetest I will now commend*
> *To sweetest creatures that the earth doth beare;*

He concludes – after explaining with some emphasis that 'painefull practice' and experience have qualified him to expose each 'secret' that he strives to teach – by commending the said secrets to his audience with a somewhat surprising metaphor and a final passage of diminuendo modesty:

> *Accept them well, and let my wearied Muse*
> *Repose her selfe in Ladies laps awhile.*
> *So when she wakes, she happely may record*
> *Her sweetest dreames in some more pleasing stile.*

Arnold Whitaker Oxford, in his classic work *English Cookery Books to the Year 1850,** lists fifty-five other books, either devoted to cookery or containing a significant proportion of material thereon, that were first published in the seventeenth century. It is interesting to observe that during this period certain specialised forms of the cookery book emerged. Thus 1653 saw the publication of *A Book of Fruits and Flowers* with recipes for them and for meat, biscuits and suchlike

---

* Reprinted by the Holland Press, London, 1913.

confections too. I think that the fruit and flower section of this book may be the first example of a technique that was rarely used since then but has been adopted by several authors in the twentieth century. This is to start by presenting the fruit or flower, with an illustration and description, and then to give recipes that are specific to it before going on to the next item. Another specialised work, published in 1699, was John Evelyn's *Acetaria: A Discourse of Sallets* (that is, salads). Some years previously Denys Papin published *A New Digester, or Engine for Softening Bones* (1681), which was certainly among the first, if not the first, book to be devoted in a suitably scientific manner to a piece of cookery equipment, namely what we now know as the pressure cooker (see page 31).

One of the best known books of that century, *The Closet of the Eminently Learned Sir Kenelme Digbie, Kt., Opened* (1669), also has a specialised bent: the number of recipes for making drinks such as meath, metheglin, hydromel, stepony and strawberry wine is very large. Like Sir Hugh Plat before him and a number of later authors, Sir Kenelme was a man of wide learning, with a questing mind and much natural curiosity. These characteristics are not exclusively British – far from it – but their application to matters of food and cookery is more noticeable in the history of British cookery books than elsewhere. I find much to admire and enjoy in the contemplation of these learned men and their works on the kitchen.

I have recently embarked on a study of 'science in the kitchen'. If the phrase be taken literally, then, as I hope to show, the period from about 1790 to 1900 was that in which it had most application, or found most expression. If, however, one takes it in a wider sense, then many of the earlier English cookery writers can be said to have brought science, or 'experimental philosophy', to bear on their subject matter; and this adds interest to their work by setting it in a wider context.

There were, of course, more simple and professional compilations of recipes made in the seventeenth century. It is common to point to *The Accomplisht Cook* by Robert May, which was first published in 1660 and ran to at least five editions. May was a professional cook of fifty years' experience. And a new genre was inaugurated with the publication of *The Family Dictionary* by 'J. H.' in 1695. But my own favourite among these businesslike books is that of William Rabisha, *The Whole Body of Cookery Dissected* (1661). This is a well-organised and practical book of recipes by someone who described himself as 'Master Cook to many honourable Families before and since the wars began, both in this my Native Countrey, and with Embassadors and other Nobles in certain forraign Parts'. Rabisha made a point, in the lengthy subtitling of his work, of saying that he was drawing on the culinary traditions of other countries, for example, of France, Italy and Holland.

This leads me to the questions: how far did English cookery writers go in using recipes from overseas, and when did a tendency to do so in more than a casual way become apparent? I am not referring here to the natural use of recipes that had in fact been imported long ago (such as those of French origin in *The Forme of Cury*), but to the deliberate introduction into English cookery books of recipes identified as belonging to another country. The answer is that, apart from a few translations of foreign works, there was little sign of this in the sixteenth century, not much more in the seventeenth (Rabisha being one exception), but a growing trend in that direction in the eighteenth (when cookery books were often sprinkled with recipes for something 'in the Dutch manner' or 'in the French style'). Only in the nineteenth century do we find any kind of systematic and eclectic approach to the gathering and presentation of foreign recipes.

A smaller question is linked with the larger ones, namely: when did English cookery writers first begin to indicate regional sources within England for their recipes? This question in turn leads to others. To what extent did early cookery writers give *any* indication of the sources of their recipes? And how much plagiarism took place? These questions find their answers in the eighteenth century, to which we now come. I shall give priority here to three writers whose work I greatly admire, although they are far less famous than, for example, Hannah Glasse.

Cambridge University appointed its first Professor of Botany in 1724. He was Richard Bradley, then in his mid-thirties and already distinguished for his botanical work and his inquiries into agriculture. On his death in 1732, Bradley was succeeded by a certain John Martyn, who appears to have been a man of many faults, both of commission and of omission. These faults he proceeded to attribute to his dead predecessor, with such effect that Bradley's reputation has been clouded since then until recent times, when scholars have probed into the matter and vindicated him. It is this unfortunate history, or perhaps the fact that Bradley's two cookery books were among the last of the forty-two books that he wrote, the second being the very last of all, that has caused a general and, in any other circumstances, highly surprising neglect of his work on cookery. As a symbol of what happened, I may take my own volume of Bradley. It is three volumes bound as one. The first is *The Country Gentleman and Farmer's Monthly Director* (sixth edition, with additions: 'Particularly some rules for breeding Pheasants, by a Gentleman', 1736). The second is the sixth edition (also 1736) of *The Country Housewife and Lady's Director*. The third is a work with the

same title, but described as Part II, first published in 1732 but here also
bearing the date 1736. Because the Farmer came first in the trilogy, the
book found its way on to the shelves of a specialist in antiquarian books
on agriculture. Fortunately, a colleague of his, one of the lynx-eyed
specialists in old cookery books of whom we have but three or four in
the United Kingdom, spotted it and realised that its real value lay in the
second and third volumes. The trilogy passed into my hands; I am
happy to have all three volumes, and in their present order, for Bradley
was another cookery writer who 'came in from the fields'. It was
his interest in botany, in the introduction of novel plants from the
New World and their acclimatisation in England, and above all in the
use to which the products of agriculture and market gardening were
put – for he was a most practical man – that led Bradley to round
off his numerous and learned works by directing his words to 'The
Ladies of Great Britain, etc.' (what does 'etc.' mean? – presumably,
all non-British female inhabitants of the globe) in an opening address,
which I insist on quoting for the sheer pleasure that the prose always
affords me:

> The Reason which induces me to address the following Piece to
> the Fair Sex, is, because the principal Matters contained in it are
> within the Liberty of their Province. The Art of Oeconomy is
> divided, as *Xenophon* tells us, between the Men and the Women;
> the Men have the most dangerous and laborious Share of it in the
> Fields, and without doors, and the Women have the Care and
> Management of every Business within doors, and to see after the
> good ordering of whatever is belonging to the House. And this, I
> conceive, is no less the Practice of these Days, than it was in the
> time of that great Philosopher; therefore it may seem necessary
> that I make some Apology for the Work I now publish, which, for
> the most part, falls within the Ladies Jurisdiction: but I hope I am
> the more excusable, as my design is rather to assist, than to direct.
> I may call myself rather their Amanuensis, than their Instructor;
> for the Receipts which I imagine will give the greatest Lustre or
> Ornament to the following Treatise, are such as are practised by
> some of the most ingenious Ladies, who had Good-nature enough
> to admit of a Transcription of them for publick Benefit; and to do
> them justice, I must acknowledge that every one who has try'd
> them, allow them to excel in their way. The other Receipts are
> such as I have collected in my Travels, as well through *England*, as
> in foreign countries, and are such as I was prompted to enter into

my List, as well for their Curiosity as for their extraordinary Goodness.

And so to the recipes. Bradley's introduction will already have shown that many of these come from individuals, whom he names. Many are also ascribed to places or regions in England. Earlier writers may have occasionally made such references, but Bradley seems to have been the first to grasp the idea of regional cookery and to see something of interest in it. He was an assiduous traveller and seasons his collection of recipes with many pleasing anecdotes, a habit dear to my own heart. As I wrote elsewhere: 'The wholly practical and methodical cookery book has its place on every cook's shelf. Yet a place is reserved too for the cookery book which can be dipped into outside the kitchen as well as used in it.' Bradley is the earliest author who fulfils this requirement of mine; and he fulfils it in a manner both instructive and entertaining. In discussing Stilton cheese, for example, he not only gives one of the earliest detailed accounts of it but also recalls his own visit to the Blue-Bell Inn in Stilton; and in explaining how to make 'Marygold Cheese' he describes vividly his own reactions to it. One has the feeling, in perusing his pages, that here is a real human being communicating his own experiences and thoughts to us across the centuries, in a manner so idiosyncratic that it must have been his natural style, and with so many attributions and expressions of thanks (especially to the ladies who wrote to him, imparting their favourite recipes, after his first volume had appeared, and whose missives constitute a large part of the second volume) that even the faintest suspicion of plagiarism is banished.

Mention of plagiarism leads me to Mary Cole, a redoubtable opponent thereof. Her book *The Lady's Complete Guide; or Cookery and Confectionary in all their Branches* was first published in 1789. It provides ample evidence, if any were needed, that plagiarism was rife among the seventeenth-century cookery writers. It was not uncommon for the more heinous offence of pirating a complete book to be committed; and this was done on a transatlantic basis in the latter half of the century when whole books on cookery, published in England, were republished in North America without so much as a by-your-leave. But what aroused Mrs Mary Cole's wrath was the manner in which certain writers simply lifted recipes from other books and stuck them into their own, without a word of acknowledgement.

Mrs Cole herself made great use of cookery books that had appeared earlier in the century, such as the admirable *The Experienced English Housekeeper* (1769, and a score of later editions) by the enterprising Elizabeth Raffald (who is said to have borne sixteen daughters and who engaged in business activities such as innkeeping, founding newspapers, and publishing the first directory of Manchester); *The Lady's Assistant* (1775) by Mrs Charlotte Mason; *The Professed Cook* (1769), which was a translation by Clermont of the French book *Les Soupers de la Cour* by Menon; the well-known book by Hannah Glasse, *The Art of Cookery Made Plain and Easy* (1747, and numerous further editions extending into the nineteenth century); and many others. The feature that distinguished Mrs Cole's book was that she said plainly whence her recipes came. This does not apply to quite all of them, for some are unattributed and must be assumed to represent her family or personal receipts, and for others there was no written source. But the majority of her recipes have attributions – many have multiple attributions – showing that she had studied two or three versions of the same recipe and amalgamated them into what she thought the best prescription. This was indeed conscientious. More recent writers, who have been good enough to acknowledge the source of a recipe when lifting it bodily from some other work, have not thought it necessary to explain the origin of amalgamated recipes; on the contrary, they have felt that by using more than one source they have absolved themselves from the duty of acknowledging any.

There was, however, or seems to have been, another aspect of Mrs Cole's character that deserves mention. The subtitle of her book, which – as was normal in the period – is long, contains references to a number of 'Cooks of Eminence who have published in France' and says that some of Mrs Cole's recipes are translated from them. These French cooks include the Duke de Nivernois, M. Disang (said to be the author of a book called *Le Maître d'Hôtel*), M. Valois and M. Delatour. As Oxford remarked, it is odd that these authors do not appear in the bibliography of (mainly) French cookery books by Georges Vicaire or, indeed, in any other works of reference. Until recently I had assumed that they must have been obscure works that had not survived, although a little reflection should have made me realise that this was hardly credible. Recently my eyes have been opened to the truth: the names are printed in jest, and by way of mocking those English authors who made a great to-do about following French authors. Those cited by Mrs Cole were men of straw, invented by herself. So we must credit her also with wit and a pleasing capacity for innocent deception.

Before leaving the eighteenth century, I wish to mention one other highly original writer, W. Ellis, author of *The Country Housewife's Family Companion* (1750). His work appeared very soon after the first edition of Mrs Glasse, but there is a world of difference between them. Mrs Glasse, for all her merits of clear presentation, is not a very inspiring author to read. W. Ellis is. His book abounds in anecdotal material, based on his own experience as a farmer in Essex (he, too, 'came in from the fields' to the kitchen) and his travels and correspondence with people elsewhere in England, and provides the fullest collection published up to that time (and indeed until much later) of English regional recipes. There is also an earthy quality to his book, even in his recipe titles, which invests it with that aura of direct communication across the centuries that I noted in connection with Richard Bradley: 'An Oatmeal Pudding made constantly, as part of a Milk Diet, for a gouty Man'; 'A Letter from a worthy Gentleman to this Author concerning the Improvement of baked Pears'; 'How a Cow's Life was saved that was hoved in Clover, when internal Remedies failed, shewn by a Case of my Neighbour's Cow' (the unfortunate cow was stabbed with a penknife, whereupon 'out came Dung and Wind in a very violent Manner', and the wound was then tarred and pitched); 'How the Guts or Chauldron of a Calf is to be made into a Pye'. These are arresting headings, and the reader who is thereby tempted to read the recipes in full will not be disappointed. He will, incidentally, also find that sources are frequently quoted and that among them are several of the most-favoured-by-Davidson writers, such as Sir Kenelme Digbie and William Rabisha.

While Mrs Cole was chastising the plagiarists, a whole new branch of writing on cookery was emerging, in which plagiarism was to be much less easy. I refer to books treating cookery from the scientific point of view. Hitherto cookery had been regarded as an art or skill. True, the medieval followers of Galen had thought that they were practising a kind of science when they rambled away about the four humours; but their approach had little connection with cooking as opposed to foodstuffs. Now, in 1792, we find Francis Collingwood and John Woollams, 'Principal Cooks at the Crown and Anchor Tavern in the Strand', announcing in the preface to their book, *The Universal Cook*, that 'cookery is become a science'. Admittedly they go on to say, 'Every age has contributed its mite to the improvement of this art', thus retaining the earlier concept (and quite rightly, in my view, for it seems plain to me that cookery is a science, an art and a skill, and that the choice between the three descriptive terms must on any given occasion be determined by the question, 'Who is cooking what and how?').

The new approach was further exhibited when William Nisbet, in his *Practical Treatise on Diet* (1801), made a valiant attempt to preserve something of the doctrine of the four humours, while applying to it so many sensible qualifications that it was thoroughly attenuated. He concluded his book with a section entitled 'The Application of Modern

A
BOOK
OF
Fruits & Flovvers.

SHEWING
The Nature and Use of them, either
for Meat or Medicine.

AS ALSO:
**To Preferve, Conferve, Candy, and in Wedges,
or Dry them. To make Powders, Civet bagges,**
all forts of Sugar-works, turn'd works in Sugar,
Hollow, or Frutages ; and to Pickell them.

And for Meat.
**To make Pyes, Bifcat, Maid Difhes, Marchpanes, Leeches,
and Snow, Craknels, Caudels, Cakes, Broths, Fritter-**
ftuffe, Puddings, Tarts, Syrupes, and Sallets.

For Medicines.
To make all forts of Poultiffes, and Serecloaths for any member
fwell'd or inflamed, Ointments, Waters for all Wounds, and Cancers, Salves
for Aches, to take the Ague out of any place Burning or Scalding ;
For the ftopping of fuddain Bleeding, curing the Piles,
Ulcers, Ruptures, Coughs, Confumptions, and killing
of Warts, to diffolve the Stone, killing the
Ring-worme, Emroids, and Dropfie,
Paine in the Ears and Teeth,
Deafneffe.

Contra vim mortis, non eft Medicamen in hortis.

LONDON:
Printed by *M. S.* for *Tho: Jenner* at the South entrance of the *Royall
Exchange*, London. 1653.

Chemistry to the Culinary Preparation of Food', in which he stated roundly that 'the art of cookery is a branch of chemistry'. Meanwhile, the celebrated Count Rumford, a former American and a man of many talents, had been approaching the matter from a different angle. To cut a long and fascinating story short, he found himself on New Year's Day, 1790, taking charge of a carefully planned operation by the military and civilian authorities of Bavaria to capture peaceably and install in workhouses the notorious beggars of that country, who had been terrorising the inhabitants. The operation was a complete success, achieved with great economy. One aspect of the economy of the plan was that it included provision for feeding the surprised and incarcerated beggars a nutritious and adequate diet at the lowest possible cost. It was this requirement that enabled Count Rumford to exhibit his skill in the physics of cookery and his (perhaps dubious) prowess in the science of nutrition. Rumford was indeed the first scientist after Papin to apply scientific principles and practice to the construction of cookery apparatus, including ovens, pots and pans, and even coffee pots. His approach was truly scientific in that he did not merely advocate the use of the apparatus that he designed, or demonstrate its advantages in matters such as economy of fuel, but reached his results by means of careful experiments and explained *why* his inventions worked better than what had hitherto been available.

This irruption of science into the kitchen was a noticeable feature of writing on food and cookery throughout the nineteenth century. There were, of course, many cookery books published that took no account of this. But many authors adapted their work to the fashion and furnished their readers with elaborate explanations of what happens to a piece of beef when it is boiled, and so on. The German scientist Liebig was perhaps the most influential figure in this field during the latter part of the century, and a work such as *The Chemistry of Cookery* by W. Mattieu Williams (second edition, 1892) is generously seasoned with references to him. But England had produced, earlier in the century, one classic work on the subject, *Culinary Chemistry* by Fredrick Accum (1821), of which the first page is boldly headed 'Cookery is a Branch of Chemical Science'. It was this same Accum who introduced his other work, on the adulteration of foods, with the arresting pronouncement: 'There is Death in the Pot'.

Reviewing other books of the nineteenth century, I bypass the well-known figures Eliza Acton and Mrs Isabella Beeton, pausing only to remark that the former author's *Modern Cookery* (1845) is among the most elegantly written (and practical) cookery books ever published and that Mrs Beeton should be judged, and favourably judged, by her first edition (1861) of *Beeton's Book of Household Management* rather than by later versions, published after her death at the age of twenty-eight, in which many changes were made, often for the worse.

I would rather draw attention to the emergence in the nineteenth century of certain new kinds of cookery books. One such was the work of William Hughes, a lawyer who was an enthusiast for fish. Under the pen name Piscator he published in 1843 a book entitled *Fish: how to choose and how to dress*, which was, as far as I can discover, the first book published in Great Britain – possibly the first in the world – devoted to fish cookery. It came out in a second edition in 1854 and is a work of high quality, suffused throughout by first-hand knowledge and genuine enthusiasm. It can be regarded as the prototype of all those books on Meat Cookery, Seafood Cookery, Game Cookery, etc., that we can now count on finding in any bookshop. I suppose that it could also be described as archetypal, since it is much better than most later publications.

It was also during Victorian times that British writers began to treat foreign cuisines more seriously and to write about them on the basis of personal experience. The increasingly good facilities for travel no doubt had something to do with this. There was, naturally, no lack of books about French cookery or translations of French cookery books or books written by French chefs who had been uprooted by the political disturbances inaugurated by the French Revolution and who had migrated to England. This interest in French cuisine is not surprising, given the propinquity of France and the general belief, right or wrong, that the French were the most advanced nation, gastronomically, in the world. It is of greater interest to note that as long ago as 1827 a book called *Domestic Economy and Cookery*, by 'A Lady', had included a fairly wide range of exotic recipes. The author stated in her preface that long residence abroad had made her familiar with European cooking, and that 'the mullakatanies and curries of India, the sweet pillaus, yahourt, and cold soups of Persia; the cubbubs, sweet yaughs and sherbets of Egypt; the cold soups and mixed meats of Russia, the cucussous and honeyed paste of Africa, have been inserted with the view of introducing a less expensive and more wholesome and a more delicate mode of cookery.' (See also pages 132–4.)

The appearance in 1846 of *The Jewish Manual*, a work that contained much material about Jewish cookery, marked a further innovation: writing about ethnic cookery.

Moreover, it was during this period that the existence and global extent of the British Empire began, gradually and rather belatedly, to exert important influences on British cookery and cookery writing.

Recipes for curries and for such dishes as kedgeree and sea turtle dressed in the West Indian manner had appeared in the earlier English cookery books; but, as far as I have been able to discover, no book of the eighteenth century or earlier had a special chapter devoted to, say, Indian cookery. A volume called *Indian Domestic Cookery* was published in the middle of the nineteenth century and ran to six editions. But all other achievement in this field is, to my mind, overshadowed by the work of an army officer, Colonel Kenney Herbert, whose first publications came out under the pen name 'Wyvern'. Stationed in India, he contributed articles to the *Madras Athenaeum and Daily News* and then built around this material a book called *Culinary Jottings for Madras*. This is a splendid volume. The colonel believed in surrounding his recipes with historical material, etymological explanations, amusing anecdotes and, above all, every detail that seemed relevant to him about the choice and purchase of ingredients as well as the preparation of the dish itself. He went on to write other cookery books, including a series that began with *Fifty Breakfasts* and ended with *Fifty Dinners* – another new genre of cookery writing. But his idiosyncratic character is exhibited best in his first work.

So far I have been dealing with English cookery books – books not merely in the English language but written and published in England. The title of my article, though, refers to *British* rather than to *English* cookery books, for I was unwilling, as a Scot, to see Scotland neglected. (Ireland and Wales, unfortunately, have to be; for it is only recently that they have produced cookery books, and I shall be stopping this survey short at the beginning of the present century.)

Scotland has a fine tradition of cookery books, well written and of interesting content. I used to think that one of the earliest was that of Mrs Maciver, entitled *Cookery and Pastry: as taught and practised by Mrs. Maciver, teacher of those Arts in Edinburgh* and first published in Edinburgh in 1773. But, alas, I have discovered that she was the English wife of a Scotsman, and although she used Scottish liquid measures, there is very little else Scottish in her book. There is rather more in what was the very first Scottish cookery book, a slim affair entitled Mrs. McLintock's Receipts for Cookery and Pastry-Work (1736, and now reprinted by the Aberdeen University Press).

For something really Scottish, read *The Cook and Housewife's Manual* by Mistress Margaret Dods of the Cleikum Inn, Saint Ronan's (1826). This book, purporting to be by a character in Sir Walter Scott's novel *St Ronan's Well*, is prefaced by a diverting and sometimes incomprehensible introduction in which another character from the novel, Peregrine Touchwood, Esquire, more commonly styled 'the

Cleikum Nabob', descends on Mistress Margaret Dods and becomes involved with 'the celebrated Dr. Redgill' in a curious farrago of horseplay (as when the doctor is charged by a porker and turns 'a somerset') and gastronomic philosophy, punctuated by dour Scottish comments from Mistress Margaret Dods. Thereafter it sobers up and constitutes an excellent manual for the cook, embracing Scottish, English and French dishes in its scope. The old connection between Scotland and France peeps through from time to time, as when we read of a 'howtowdie', which was originally a *hetoudeau*, or young caponised chicken.

Another good Scottish book of the period was *The Practice of Cookery* by Mrs Dalgairns (1829); but this was lacking in zaniness and had a smaller number of Scots recipes. I prefer *Modern Domestic Cookery* by Jenny Wren (Paisley, 1880), whose introductory material contains much earnest reflection on economy and value for money. She dismisses any thought that she is writing for the well-to-do or the profligates of this life and declares her intended audience to be 'the classes who . . . like to look at both sides of a shilling before it departs from them for ever.'

The enormous mass of cookery books published in recent decades calls for rather different treatment; anyway it is harder to see recent books in a historical perspective. I hope, however, that I have said enough here to demonstrate that all the main genres of cookery books had emerged by the end of the nineteenth century, and that the evolution of British cookery books up to that point had followed what might be described as a natural course, although nudged from time to time by amiably eccentric writers, whose works punctuated its route much as architectural follies, usually of great charm, dot the English landscape.

1982

Feeling Hectic? Try Prune Gruel

What would a seventeenth-century book called *Kitchin Physick* contain? This question used to nag me when noticing in the bibliographies that there was such a book.

Now I know the answer, having procured a reconstructed xerox text, all neatly bound and handling like a book.*

The author of the work, Thom. Cocke, exposes his credentials clearly enough:

> However, that I may a little comply with the mode and humour of times, and swagger in print as well as others; give me leave (Good Reader) to tell thee, that having been beholden to both Universities for my Education and spent in this City almost twenty years in the practice of Physick; I may I hope, among the croud and crew of votaries that daily attend the shrine of *Aesculapius,* be allow'd, *Locum Philosophandi* . . .

And his main message, also clearly expressed, is one which would not sound out of place today: '. . . *meddle not with Physick, or very little: but let nature alone* with a peculiar *Diet,* or only some well prepared *Cordials* proper for your distemper . . .' It is evident that this message was not likely to win general acclaim in the 1670s, for Cocke takes considerable pains to anticipate criticism. A kind of introduction, headed 'N.B.', begins: 'Now I am lanch'd, I expect nothing but storm and tempest . . .'

He identifies one such storm as coming from those who think it beneath the dignity of a physician to treat the subject of diet as a means of averting or curing disease, and gives that view short shrift ('it stinks alive'). He lists with relish and scorn the alternative sources of advice and treatment which are to be supplanted by his own precepts: 'Mountebanks, silly Women, Mechanicks, Pseudo-Chymists', and,

---

* Produced by University Microfilms, Ann Arbor, Mich.

more obscurely, '*Logo-Daedali*, Gin-cracks, Windmills, and Chymical *Camaeras*', and takes a swipe at '*Paracelsus* and almost all that Phantastick gang' who, he avers, 'dyed young' and thus disproved their own doctrines.

Cocke also shows himself to be a rapid operator:

> All that I have else to add in favour of my self, and for the Errata's of the Printer, is, that from my first perusing a late Book, entituled all in Greek *A Direct* (though in truth an indirect) *method of curing Chymically*; to the time of fitting this for the press, was not above eight or nine days; so that I may hope all my own, and with the errors of the Press, will at most amount to no more than a nine days wonder.

There is indeed an air of hasty compilation about the book, but it nonetheless has a tidy structure. It takes the form of dialogues between Philanthropus (a physician), Eugenius (an apothecary) and Lazarus (a patient).

Philanthropus is, naturally, the dominant speaker. When Lazarus timidly offers him a sample of urine, and explains that this is what doctors seem to expect, he is blasted by a sentence that runs for nearly two pages: '. . . impudent lyes . . . contriv'd stories to drive on some design and interest . . . silly illiterate persons . . .' The familiar list of silly Women etc. is expanded to include 'Highwaymen, Bauds, and common Strumpets, Gypsies, Witches, and Conjurors'. Squash! Lazarus has only enough strength left to give Philanthropus his cue for a further tirade: 'If Urine be thus uncertain, and insignificant; I Pray, Sir, then how came this custom into such request . . .' Philanthropus does not fail to explain; but he then adds, as if half-repenting his vehemence, that it may after all be a good idea to take a urine sample to the doctor 'only that it may be in readiness, if the Physician sees occasion to require it'.

Thereafter, Philanthropus does almost all the talking; and what he has to say, after more preambular matter, is divided into chapters on (1) a cooling diet for hot diseases and constitutions, (2) a hot diet for cold ones, (3) a moist diet for dry ones, and (4) a drying diet for moist ones.

As though his initial enthusiasm could not be maintained, Philanthropus gives more space to (1) than to the others, and it is in (1) that he offers real recipes. So (1) is what I reproduce, following the author's eccentric spellings and punctuation but interrupting the uniform flow of his prose with a few square-bracketed interpolations of my own – mainly recipe titles (which he did not provide), so as to bring the recipes into greater prominence.

There is nothing that we can think on, that belongs to Alimens so absolutely necessary, so good, cheap, and easie to be attain'd, as *water*, without which the whole Universe must stand still, or run into immediate confusion.

Its peculiar prerogative is, to moisten, cool, relax, relieve, ease pain, evacuate, thicken, thin, and contributes something to all the active and passive Qualities, Dryness, only excepted . . .

A glass of good spring Water, with a little toast, and a little loaf-sugar mix'd, is a very good mornings draught, for all hot, lean, sanguine, cholerick and hectick persons. So is Water-Caudle made thus:

[WATER-CAUDLE]

Take three pints of Water, boil in it a little Rosemary or Mace, till it comes to a quart, then beat up an Egg and put some of the scalding hot water to it, then give it a wame or two; and with a little Sugar, drink it hot or cold;

[ANOTHER]

three pints of Spring Water put to one pint of Milk with Sugar-candy, or double refin'd Sugar, is a drink that Princes may, and do often refresh themselves with.

[AND TWO OTHERS]

So also is running Water with a Lemon, and some part of the Rine slit into it thin, and a little Sugar and Wine put to it; or Syrup of Rasberries, Baum, Violets, Mint, or Clove-gilly-flowers; you cannot take too much of it, in ardent Fevers out of a bottle cork'd close, and a quill run through the cork to drink out of:

[WITH A WARNING NOTE]

Note, that raw cold Water, in Fevers, Inflamations, and Cholerick Thirst, being drank at once in great quantity may cause obstructions, and many dangerous Diseases, as Dropsies, &c.

[AND REMEDIAL ACTION]

But if you first boil well the water, and use it after it is again perfectly cold, instead of obstructing it will deobstruate, or open obstructions, and may thus be given at any time, in all sorts of Fevers, either malignant or ardent, especially if a little White-wine Vinegar be mix'd with it.

That Water is best, which is insipid, or without taste, clean, light and bright; but to make bad water good, and good water better, boil it well, and then let it cool again before you use it.

Of Water is made Water-gruel (the sick man's Food and Physick) when the *Archeus* abhors all *Cordials* and high Diet: this is ever very acceptable and pleasing, and consequently, not to be neglected by *Memphis* himself, there are these several ways of making it:

[WATER-GRUEL]

Take two pints of River or Spring Water, boil it first, and then let it cool again; then put to it a due proportion of Oat-meal, a handful of Sorrel, and a good quantity of pick'd and well wash'd Currants, (eston'd Raisins of the Sun, and other ingredients, as the Disease will permit, may also be added) tye up these ingredients loosely in a fine thin linnen cloth or bag: boil them all well together (with or without a little Mace, Nutmeg, Rosemary, &c. as occasion offers) when 'tis sufficiently boil'd strain the Oat-meal, and press out all the juyce or moisture of the Currants and Herbs; throwing away the husks; as you eat it, sweeten it with a very little Sugar, Salt, Butter, and fine Manchet may be added, unless the Disease be very acute: Or,

[ANOTHER WAY]

Take a quart of water, put to it a spoonful or two of Oat-meal, and a little Mace, when it is sufficiently boil'd, put in it seven or eight spoonfuls of white, or Rhenish-wine, to make it more nourishing (if the Disease will bear it) beat up an Egg with a little Sugar, and put some of the hot liquor to it, and then give it a walm or two: Or,

[A THIRD WAY]

Take Tamarinds, or Pruens, wash them in several Waters, then stone them, and cut them small; boil them in a sufficient quantity of Water and Oatmeal, and strain the juyce from the flesh, as you did the Currants, and add to it a little Sugar when you eat it.

All sorts of Broths, Ptisans, and Suppings made of Barley clean pick'd, hul'd, and wash'd in many waters, is very pleasing to persons sick of hot Diseases; So are all tart, sharp and sowre things, as Verjuyce, Barberries, Vinegar, Gooseberries, Cervices, Oranges, Lemons, dryed Grapes, or our common red Cherries dryed, quench thirst, cool, cause appetite, and please most sick Pallats, Sorrel, is a most noble and useful plant; Possets made of it, are excellent in ardent or malignant Fevers, the Green-sauce made of it, is the best of all Sauces for Flesh, Gooseberries not full ripe, scalded, and eaten with good Water, a little Sugar and Rose-water, Marmalade of Gooseberries is also a dainty repast for weak and sickly persons, so is their Quideny, the Quideny of Currants, both white and red, do the like; so do Barberries either preserved, or in the conserve, and many such like dainties made by ingenuous Gentlewomen; Tamrind Possets are also very pleasing, and profitable in all hot Diseases: 'Tis made thus:

[TAMARIND POSSET]

Take three pints, or two quarts of Milk, boil in it about two peny worth of Tamarinds (which you may buy at the Apothecaries) until it turn the Milk, then strain it from its Curds: Thus is made White-wine, Rhenish, Lemon, Orange, Sorrel, Pippin, and all Possets made of sowre things, which are excellent in Fevers, and all Diseases coming of Choler; Vinegar Possets will do as well as any.

Apples quodled, and eaten with Water, Sugar and Verjuyce, are grateful to a hot and dry constitution: So Pruens stew'd with Sorrel, Verjuyce or Juyce of Lemon, Endive, Succory, Dandelyon, Spinage, Beets, Purslain, Borrage, Bugloss, Violet, Strawberries, Cynquefoyl, Raspeberries, Mulberries, Burnet, Quince, Plantain, Dampsons, Lettice, Cucumbers, Eggs potch'd into Water, Vinegar or Verjuyce, and eaten with Sorrel sipits or Vinegar, and fine

Sugar may be permitted persons, whose Disease is not acute, or Eggs beaten in a Platter with Butter-milk to a moderate thickness, and sugar'd is also excellent.

[TWO-MILK POSSET]

Two-Milk Posset: that is, boil a quart of Milk, to this put a pint of Butter-milk, take off the Curd, and you have a pleasant Posset: This Bocheet made of Ivory is also excellent.

[IVORY POSSET]

Take Spring-water three pints, boil it away to two; when it is cold, put to it one ounce of shavings of Ivory, a few Coriander, or Carryway-Seeds; you may add also as many bruised Currants as Ivory, put them all in a tin Cofee-pot, adding as you think fit, a little liquorish, and let them stand simpering by the fire, four or five hours, then strain them, and keep the liquor in the pot to drink when you will as Coffee; to make it a more pleasant repast, you may put a little Rhenish-wine to it, and dulcifie it with a little powder of white Sugar candy.

Cullis, and Jelly of Ivory and Harts-horn is a good Restorative Diet; for hot maciated persons, make it thus:

[CULLIS, AND JELLY OF IVORY AND HARTS-HORN]

Take a Chicken or young Cockerel, Pheasant, Snipe, or Wood-cock; those that have not too much money, may take Hogs feet, Lambs, Calves, Pigs-pettitoes or Trotters; or take the bones of Veal, Mutton, Hens, Pullets, Capons, &c. which have sinews sticking to them; Boil all, or any of these in the water wherein French Barley has first been boiled, throw away the Barley, and add to the Water some shavings of Ivory, and a few Currants, or estoned Raisins; when the broth is thoroughly boiled, strain it, and when it is cold it will Jelly; take from it when 'tis cold all the fat from the top, and dregs at bottom; and to a Porenger of this melted, put the yolk of a new laid Egg beaten up with the Juyce of an Orange, and a little Sugar and let it stew gently a little while and so drink it.

These are interesting recipes. Some of them, so far as I know, do not appear in other works – not, anyway, in the same form and with the same detail.

In taking leave of the good doctor, I draw on another part of his dialogue to show how he addressed a specific problem.

Philanthropos (the physician) asks Eugenius (the apothecary) to tell him about some recent patient; and the example given by Eugenius is desperate indeed: a Lazar afflicted with the bloody flux and completely indigent, homeless and friendless. Philanthropos at once prescribes a potion of medical drops in mulled sack or the like.

Eugenius expostulates: 'But, Sir! the man is almost dead . . . and has no two or three shillings, nor farthings to buy the Doctor's drops, or a bit of bread!'

Keeping us in suspense, Philanthropos observes coolly that in the absence of a solution to his predicament the patient must die. Eugenius asks whether he, Eugenius, must then ruin himself by paying for the medicines. This is the cue for Philanthropos to ram home his message. No, there is no need for costly medicines (even though he had just suggested some!). Food, simple food, food 'contrary' to the disease, is all that is required. RICE!

[A LIFE-SAVING RICE DISH]

[Bid the Lazar] buy himself [at the apothecary's trifling expense] a pound or two of Rice, and let him *torrifie*, or parch it a little, as he is to use it, in a hot fire-shovel or frying-pan; or bake it for bread with a few Seeds, Nutmeg, Pepper or Cynamon, and eat nor drink anything but Rice, thus prepared with scalded Milk, or Milk and Water, for seven or eight days . . .

Eugenius, as diligent as a tame MP in asking the right questions ('Would the Prime Minister agree that during her term of office the real income of authors has risen by an average of 37 per cent'), protests that rice is no medicine: ''tis so common a food, that I wonder you should count it for Physick any more than Bread.'

Philanthropos then solemnly declares that he counts 'Bread, and everything we eat and drink' to be Physick. The traditional four qualities (hot, cold, dry, moist) apply to people, foods and diseases. A healthy person requires foods with the same qualities as he himself possesses. A sick person needs foods with qualities contrary to the disease.

It was as simple as that. And there are Cocksians among us today, although, being probably unacquainted with *Kitchin Physick*, they do not so style themselves.

1985

Dumas Père, Chef Extraordinaire

Even among the literary giants of the nineteenth century, Alexandre Dumas père stands out as a writer of astonishing fecundity. His collected works* occupy 303 volumes. Nor is this collection complete. Among the works missing from it is the very last which Dumas wrote, *Le Grand Dictionnaire de Cuisine*. The omission is poignant, for it was precisely this book on which the dying author, beset by doubts about the future standing of his plays and novels, thought that his reputation would ultimately rest.

Dumas died in 1870. Now, more than a century later, one may well ask why he should have doubted the permanence of his literary fame; how he could have supposed that such works as *The Three Musketeers* and *The Count of Monte Cristo* might fall into oblivion; and what prompted him to think that his dictionary of cookery would prove to be the immortal among his works?

The explanation emerges from the pattern of his life. This began in relative obscurity. Alexandre was the son of a French general, a mulatto with roots in Santo Domingo, who performed brilliantly under the Emperor Napoleon but then incurred the imperial displeasure and died in disgrace and penury. The young Alexandre had to make his own way in the world, aided only by his own remarkable vigour and ambition and by the favour of some few people whose esteem for his late father survived. He moved in his late teens from his native town of Villers-Cotterêts to Paris and quickly achieved a reputation as a dramatist, which was enlarged and consolidated by a series of novels, historical works and travel books. At the zenith of his fame he built a fantastic mansion, called Monte Cristo, at Port-Marly outside Paris, where he entertained in a style which was almost regal. This building still stands, although empty and visibly crumbling. And nearby, in the process of being restored by the Association des Amis de Dumas, is the small and Gothic Château d'If, which Dumas built as a literary workshop and

* Collection Michel Levy Frères, Calmann-Levy.

which, by its proximity to the main house, symbolises the two sides to its owner's character: the extravaganza which made him the talk of Paris, even of Europe, and the hard work and technical skill which enabled him to produce such prodigious quantities of writing.

This zenith was reached in the middle of the nineteenth century. As the later decades rolled past, Dumas found that he had lost both his touch with the public and the favour of the literary critics. Even his love affairs, once legendary, sank into ridicule. His last such affair was with Adah Menken, an American Jewess from Louisiana who performed daring deeds on horseback in an international circus. His conquest of her, or hers of him, took place when he was sixty-five and provoked some extremely unkind comments, both in prose and in cartoons. The dashing young lion of Paris society had become a corpulent and ill old man, whose final antics excited, at best, pity.

Thus, when Dumas retreated to the coast of Brittany, near Roscoff, in 1869 to fulfil his long-standing wish to write a major work of gastronomy, he had reason to despair for the fate of his other works and to pin his hopes on this last one, his first in a genre which had been firmly established by Brillat-Savarin and Grimod de la Reynière and which was, patently, capable of securing undying fame for an author who could handle it with sufficient skill. Dumas, in his old age, was not such an author; but the book which he produced remains of great interest.

The book, in its original form, contained two illustrations (one of Dumas himself and one of Vuillemot, the chef who was his principal culinary adviser) and about 600,000 words. Almost a tenth of the prose was taken up by introductory material, in the course of which Dumas described wittily how he settled down on Cape Finisterre to write the book, how he was speedily deserted by the cook who had accompanied him, and how he was 'adopted', with equal speed, by the local population. He observes that he was ill and that he had been worn out by the effort of writing huge quantities of prose to work off his debts. He states that he took with him very few reference works and that he intended to rely mainly on his memory. He hoped to find, in a quiet place where he could breathe the sea air, the rest and the peace which he needed for the composition of the work which was to be, as he put it, 'the crowning achievement' of his literary career.

Dumas died in the following year, in a house owned by his son near Dieppe and at the very time when invading German troops were marching into that port. He had already delivered the manuscript of the dictionary to the publisher, Alphonse Lemerre. However, the book was not published until 1873 (although the copy in the Bibliothèque

Nationale in Paris, which I have inspected, was received there in 1872), and there is some evidence that editorial work was carried out on it before publication. On the other hand, the Preface to the book, by 'L.T.', states that typesetting had begun before Dumas died and that it was the outbreak of the Franco-Prussian War which caused an interruption in the work of the printers. This would suggest that there had been little time for editorial work. The contents of the book point to the same conclusion. The coordination between entries is poor; there are several instances of needless repetition; and the punctuation, paragraphing and spelling are all in a state which cries out for the work of what we would now call a 'copy-editor'.

The explanation of this small mystery seems to be that some work was done on the book after it reached Lemerre but by unskilled hands. Lemerre had some young poets on his premises, and André Maurois (one of Dumas's best biographers) states clearly that two of them, Leconte de Lisle and Anatole France, were charged with the task of reorganising and completing the book. It was not a task for which they had any obvious qualifications, and it is reasonable to suppose that they took the task lightly. Maurois himself records that Mme Maurois, when a young girl, had visited Anatole France, by then an old man, and had asked him about his part in the composition of the dictionary. Anatole France replied: 'I should have been proud to have written the book. But one must leave to the credit of Dumas what belonged to him. I was only a corrector of proofs – and sometimes a *commentateur*.' The last word is ambiguous, but may help to explain why the book is larded (to use a culinary metaphor) with little pieces of prose which have the air of additions made at the last moment by someone who was not familiar with the book as a whole and who had no particular concern for the logical sequence of the information presented in it.

When the first edition did finally appear, it stayed in print for a phenomenally long time. The house of Lemerre was wound up in the 1950s. At that time, so I have been informed, there were still unbound copies of the first edition in the cellars. (These copies were then destroyed; an act which paved the way for a series of coffee-table editions of the book, most of which have been shorn of the introductory material and embellished with numerous illustrations.) Lemerre had brought out, in 1885, a shorter version of the book, called *Le petit Dictionnaire de Cuisine* and now extremely rare; but otherwise the book was left in its original state for seventy years or more.

Criticism of the dictionary has been conspicuously lacking. French literary critics have ignored the book, since they regard it as a cookery book rather than a piece of literature. French gastronomic writers have made reverent references to it, but none has analysed its contents or drawn attention to its mistakes and other imperfections. The nearest approach to criticism in France is to be found in a series of comments appended to one of the coffee-table editions by Jean Arnaboldi. However, his comments are generally obsequious in tone ('Is it possible, dear Master, that you have here overlooked . . .?'); and he has managed, by some miracle, to aim several of his 'corrections' at passages where Dumas was in fact right!

Writers outside France have paid some attention to the book. Many references to it can be found in English books on cookery and food in the period from 1875 to the end of the century. Most of these are based on the assumption that Dumas was a great gastronome and that his work should be treated as an authoritative source rather than subjected to critical scrutiny. However, one writer, the highly idiosyncratic Dr J. L. W. Thudichum, went further in his book *The Spirit of Cookery*, subtitled 'A Popular Treatise on the History, Science, Practice, and Ethical and Medical Import of Culinary Art', published in 1895. He cites Dumas frequently and applies the adjective 'great' to the dictionary. But it is clear that he has actually read it from beginning to end (an unusual feat) and his judgement of it is a balanced one.

> This work contains much excellent matter, and owing to the technical supervision extended to it by D. F. Vuillemot, a pupil of Carême's, is in the main reliable; but it also contains much irrelevant matter in the shape of inventions of the nominal author, flat anecdotes and shallow observations. Much of this short-coming is no doubt due to the alleged circumstance of Dumas having availed himself of the assistance of subordinate contributors, whose performance, consisting mainly in abstracting older authors, he did not take the trouble to control. This circumstance also led to many repetitions; but leaving these out of sight, the work is an admirable compilation, and in many parts an enthusiastic picture of French cookery at the beginning of the last quarter of the century now drawing to its close.

It may be that the dictionary, which, by the sheer weight of its recipes and the tidal flow of Dumas's own prose, not to mention the weight of his reputation, is apt to have a hypnotic effect on French readers, lulling their critical faculties to a state of complete quiescence; whereas a foreigner, who has to translate the prose mentally as he reads the book, is more likely to reflect on what is actually being said and to spot at least the most glaring errors. Thus Dr Thudichum and I were both, independently, startled by Dumas's recipe for Norfolk dumplings, which reads as follows in English:

> This dish, which owes its name to the Duke of Norfolk, who had a great affection for it, is made in the following way. You add to a fairly thick dough a big glass of milk, two eggs and a little salt. Cook it for two or three minutes in quickly boiling water. Discard the water, drain the dumpling in a sieve and serve it with slightly salted butter.

Only a moment's reflection is needed to realise that there is something radically wrong here. A dumpling of the size indicated could not possibly be cooked in two or three minutes. In fact, Dumas has got everything wrong except the title of the recipe. There are indeed such things as Norfolk dumplings; but they are an ancient tradition of the people of Norfolk, and their name has nothing to do with any duke. They are made as follows, according to the careful observations of Mrs Arthur Webb:*

> The farmer's wife very skilfully divided a pound of dough (remember, just ordinary bread dough) into four pieces. These she weighed, and so cleverly had she gauged the size that they weighed approximately 4 oz. each. She kneaded, and rolled them in a very little flour until they were quite round, then put them on a plate and slipped them into a large saucepan containing fast-boiling water. The saucepan lid was put back immediately, and then, when the water came to the boil once more, 15 minutes' rapid boiling was allowed for the dumplings . . .
>   Dumplings in Norfolk are not a sweet. They are a very substantial part of what might be the meat course, or they might serve as a meat substitute. In the villages I found that they were sometimes put into very large pots and boiled on top of the greens; then they are called 'swimmers'.

When this sort of comparison is made, the reader is left musing over André Maurois's statement that foreign cookery held no more secrets for Dumas than the cuisine of his own mother and grandmother; he is indeed led to speculate about the extent to which Dumas really practised the art of which he wrote so confidently.

In searching for evidence, other than that provided by his own

---

* *Farmhouse Cookery*, London, *c*. 1930.

assertions of enthusiasm for cookery, that Dumas really was a cook, I soon realised that a prior question posed itself; namely, how much evidence could one expect to find? The answer seemed to be that there might be very little, even if Dumas had done a lot of cooking. In default of any formal appraisal of his prowess in the kitchen – and why should anyone have undertaken that? – one could only expect occasional references in diaries or correspondence. And this is what one does find. George Sand, for example, recorded in her diary for 3 February 1866 that she had been to dine with the Jauberts and that Alexandre Dumas père and fils were both present. She said that: 'Dumas père had cooked the whole meal, from soup to salad! Eight or ten wonderful courses . . .'

More details are known of a lunch which Dumas cooked two years previously, when he was living in a villa outside Paris with a female opera singer from Naples, a temperamental young woman who made a habit of firing the household staff at inconvenient moments. She did this on Saturday, leaving the house without servants on the eve of a sunny Sabbath which lured many of Dumas's friends to come out of Paris and visit him, in the confident expectation of a good lunch. Gabriel Ferry, in his *Les dernières années d'Alexandre Dumas* (1883) describes in detail how Dumas coped with the problem. Although the departing servants had left the kitchen almost bare, he managed to find some rice, butter and fresh tomatoes. With these he confected a dish which fully satisfied the expectations and appetites of his friends.

This last episode seems rather thin as evidence of culinary genius. But Ferry also gives us a glimpse of Dumas acting as the earnest student of cooking techniques. Although he had lived in Italy for a number of years, Dumas had not acquired a taste for macaroni and had never bothered to find out how it was cooked. Later, when he was running a sort of gastronomic column in one of the numerous periodicals which he sponsored, he was embarrassed by his inability to answer questions about macaroni. The result was that he spent some time, with notebook and pencil, in the kitchen of Mme Ristori, observing in detail how her cook prepared macaroni. This rather simple discovery is presented as a piece of impressive research on his part.

More convincing evidence comes from a book called *An Englishman in Paris*.* Vandam devotes a whole chapter of his book to Dumas, whom he knew well and admired greatly; and this chapter includes an account of how Dumas dealt with a rumour, put into circulation by the cook of Dr Véron, that his vaunted knowledge of cookery was pure sham. The matter hinged on a certain recipe for carp, and Dumas undertook to cook a dinner for Dr Véron, including the carp dish, himself; and that he would do so in the presence of an impartial witness. Vandam was selected as the witness and went to attend on the writer-chef in this capacity.

At three o'clock next day I was at the Chaussée d'Antin, and was taken there by the servant into the kitchen, where the great novelist stood surrounded by his utensils, some of silver, and all of them glistening like silver. With the exception of a soupe aux choux, at which, by his own confession, he had been at work since the morning, all the ingredients for the dinner were in their natural state – of course, washed and peeled, but nothing more. He was assisted by his own cook and a kitchen-maid, but he himself, with his sleeves rolled up to the elbows, a large apron round his waist, and bare chest, conducted the operations. I do not think I have ever seen anything more entertaining . . . At half-past six the guests began to arrive; at a quarter to seven Dumas retired to his dressing room; at seven punctually the servant announced that 'monsieur était servi'. The dinner consisted of the aforenamed soupe aux choux, the carp that had led to the

* Published anonymously, but written by A. D. Vandam, 3rd ed., London, 1892.

invitation, a ragoût de mouton à la Hongroise, rôti de faisans, and a salade Japonaise. The sweets and ices had been sent by the pâtissier. I never dined like that before or after.

It could be argued that this was a single *tour de force*, rehearsed by Dumas beforehand. Such an argument can be countered by turning to some hitherto unpublished material* in the possession of M. Robert Landru of Villers-Cotterêt. This takes the form of manuscript notes, entitled *Souvenirs sur Alexandre Dumas père*, by Henri-François Lhote, son of a close friend of the novelist. The notes include not only an account of a specific dish prepared by Dumas (a confection of crayfish, for which he used so much cognac that one of the lady guests, who ate plentifully, became intoxicated and had to be helped from the table) but also a convincing account of how Dumas interested himself in cookery when he came to stay with the family, as he often did, for a week or more at a time. 'Once installed, Dumas would set off into town with the maid, buying in this shop and that the things which he was planning to cook with her in the evening; for he was a discriminating gourmet and an excellent cook.'

Other scraps of evidence are to be found, such as the description given by Gustave Geffroy in his book on the life of *Claude Monet** of how Dumas and the painter Courbet spent some time singing and cooking together at Etretat in 1868; but perhaps enough has been given already to show that there was some real substance to Dumas's reputation as a cook.

Dumas's ability as a writer of eloquence and verve is legendary and unquestioned. His credentials as a cook, although open to question, have been shown to be plausible. The combination should have produced a great book; and there is no doubt but that Dumas intended it to be a great book. Yet it is not. There are good things in it, but they are embedded in too much padding and flawed by too many errors. What went wrong?

The first thing to be said is that Dumas was an old man and an ill one when he wrote the dictionary. Sparks of brilliance still flashed forth, but intermittently; and the writer lacked the stamina and powers of application which would have enabled him to bring his unruly mass of recollections and other material into proper order. Even a day's work on his ascription of recipes and other material to their sources would have put right many omissions. (One of these had amusing consequences. The Association des Amis de Dumas resolved not so long

* Extracts from this are quoted in *Dumas on Food*, London, 1978.
† Paris, 1922.

ago to have a lunch consisting of recipes which the master had bequeathed to the world in his *Dictionnaire*. One of these was his recipe for kedgeree made with turbot. Alas, it should have been the Amis d'Urbain Dubois who ate and enthused over this dish, for the recipe came straight from a book by the other author, and Dumas forgot to say so!)

However, what is more important in my view is that Dumas was not as well equipped as he fancied to write this particular book. His knowledge of foodstuffs was patchy, his knowledge of foreign cuisines superficial and his command of the associated disciplines of natural history, chemistry and nutrition elementary or non-existent. His engaging enthusiasm, the extent of his travels and the fact that a largely unjustified but impressive reputation for gastronomic expertise had become attached to him, all conspired to give him false confidence. He made little use of reference books because he did not feel the need to do so. Yet even some casual checking would have told him, for example, that the anchovy *does* have scales, which he denies. Even a few minutes' thought would have made him hesitate to retail as fact the (undocumented) story of the whale which found and traversed an underground waterway between the Atlantic and the Pacific in the Isthmus of Panama, before the Panama Canal was built.

Yet, criticise the book as one may, one must admit, even announce with pleasure, that it contains some pure gold, that many of the anecdotes in it have never been more wittily related, that the enthusiasm of the author and the magnetism of his personality still shine through the pages a hundred years later, and that the book he produced, although overshadowed in his own œuvre by others of more consistent brilliance and overshadowed in the genre of gastronomic writing by better books written both before and after his, does and will remain one enduring monument to his fame.

I allow myself to conclude this essay by quoting from one of the best and most happily phrased entries in the book, that on the hermit crab.

A species of crab of which the meat is regarded as a delicious morsel. It is usually grilled in its shell before being eaten.

There is nothing more comical than this little crustacean. Nature has furnished him with armour as far as the waist – cuirass, gauntlets and visor of iron, this half of him has everything. But from the waist to the other end there is nothing, not even a shirt. The result of this is that the hermit crab stuffs this extremity of himself into whatever refuge he can find.

The Creator, who had begun to dress the creature as a lobster, was disturbed or distracted in the middle of the operation and finished him off as a slug.

This part of the hermit crab, so poorly defended and so tempting to an enemy, is his great preoccupation; a preoccupation which can at times make him fierce. If he sees a shell which suits him, he eats the owner of the shell and takes his place while it is still warm – the history of the world in microscopic form. But since, when all is said and done, the house was not made for him, he staggers about like a drunkard instead of having the serious air of a snail; and so far as possible he avoids going out, except in the evening, for fear of being recognised.

1979

English Perceptions of Turkish Cookery in the Eighteenth and Nineteenth Centuries*

This study is based on the cookery books published in England (hence English rather than British) during the period, and on those recipes in them whose titles proclaimed some connection with Turkey. It does not examine what British travellers in Turkey wrote about the food which they had there: this would be an interesting resource to explore, but would yield more information about Turkish meals than about Turkish cookery.

Occasional 'Turkish' recipes had appeared in English cookery books of the seventeenth century; but we find no hint of Turkey in the book of recipes (published in 1710, after his death) of Patrick Lamb, who had been a royal cook under many monarchs. Nor do we find any Turkish dishes in the very extensive compilation of recipes by John Nott in 1726, although he cast his net widely, including recipes for dishes in the French, German, Dutch, Italian, Spanish and Portuguese manner.

The Country Housewife and Lady's Director (also 1726) by Richard Bradley (see page 101) was a work of originality, reflecting keen interest in new fruits and vegetables. Bradley recorded some English regional recipes and also exotic recipes from abroad. But nothing Turkish.

In the 1740s we begin to find what we are looking for. A very large compendium of recipes which had first come out in 1737 under the title *The Whole Duty of a Woman*, was republished shortly afterwards as *The Lady's Companion*. In this form, and in the edition of 1743, occurs this recipe:

---

* This paper, by Alan and Jane Davidson, was given at an international congress on culinary history at Konya, 1986.

TO DRESS MUTTON THE TURKISH WAY

Cut your Meat into thin Slices; then wash it in Vinegar, and put it into a Pot or Sauce-pan that has a close Cover to it, then put in some Rice, whole Pepper, and two or three Onions; let all these stew together, skimming it frequently; when it is enough, take out the Onions, and dish it with Sippets, and serve it up.

This work is obscure and the recipe might have languished in its pages unseen; but in 1747 Hannah Glasse chose it as one of more than 250 which she shamelessly took from the earlier work; and Hannah's book, *The Art of Cookery Made Plain and Easy*, was a great success, passing through numerous authorised and pirated editions until well unto the nineteenth century. As a result, this recipe acquired considerable currency. But, as a solitary peep-hole into the mysteries (as they then were) of Turkish cuisine, it was quite outstandingly inadequate; and it was not echoed in the other great cookery book of the century, that by Mrs Raffald (1769). This had no reference to Turkey. Nor had the big cookery book by Richard Briggs (1788). Thus by the end of the century there was virtually no sign of any informed interest in Turkish dishes.

Two of the best known nineteenth-century cookery books were first published early in that century: *Domestic Cookery* by 'a Lady' [Mrs Rundell] and *The Cook's Oracle* by the eccentric Dr Kitchener. The latter was adventurous in its selection of dishes, but contained nothing Turkish. The former was less adventurous, and it is no surprise to find that the rare first edition (1806) has no mention of Turkey. However, Mrs Rundell's book came out in many subsequent editions and, jumping ahead in our survey, we find that that of 1847, which was edited and enlarged by Emma Roberts, had a substantial section on oriental cookery. This turns out to be mainly Indian, but does include two 'Turkish' recipes, each identified as an addition by Miss Roberts. They are reproduced below; and are conspicuously feeble efforts to exemplify Turkish cuisine.

TURKISH SOUP – E.R.

Take some good gravy from a leg of beef, all sorts of vegetables, and a little spice; stew all together, and when strained and cleared from fat set it on the fire, and when it boils add half a pound of rice to three quarts of soup with a quarter of a pint of cream, stir it into the soup, when the rice is tender, taking care not to let the soup boil, and stirring the same way until the soup is served.

D'ALMOY'S – A TURKISH DISH – E.R.

Take equal quantities of cold dressed veal, minced very fine, fat, and crumbs of bread, and season it well; add chopped onions, parsley, salt, and cayenne pepper. Wet it with one or two eggs, according to the quantity, adding, if necessary, a little cold melted butter; make the mixture into balls or egg-shapes, and roll them in as much boiled rice as they will take round them. Stew then for an hour and a half in good gravy, well seasoned, and serve them up in it.

Back in our chronological sequence, we come to a large but relatively obscure compilation, *The Family Receipt-Book* (undated, our copy inscribed with the date 1810) which contained two Turkish recipes. One, for Turkish Pilau, consists in a lengthy quotation from Grimod de la Reynière. The other, given below, is for Turkish dolmas, which perhaps explains Emma Roberts's curious title 'd'Almoy's' above.

TURKISH DOLMAS

Cut the meat, both fat and lean, from about two pounds of the best part of a loin of mutton; and, chopping it as small as for forcemeat, add an onion, parsley, salt, spices, and a tea-cupful of rice. Mix the whole well together; and, scalding some cabbage leaves till they are quite flexible, take a little of the mixed meat, not more than the size of a large walnut at a time, and wrap or envelope it in part of the scalded cabbage leaf, so as to form it all into balls, without squeezing them hard. Then, laying the bones from which the meat is cut at the bottom of the stewpan, and the dolmas over them, pour in as much boiling water as will cover them; and keep shaking, but not stirring them, over a gentle fire, till they are done. When they are ready to dish, beat up the yolk of an egg, mix it with the liquor and lemon juice, and pour the whole over them. Dolmas are frequently made after the same manner with cucumbers instead of cabbage; in which case, the cucumbers, being well pared and scraped, have a small piece cut out, to take away their seeds, &c. when they are filled with the prepared meat, and have the pieces replaced and tied on, after which they are treated in all respects the same as the other dolmas.

This recipe is more impressive than Emma Roberts's later contributions. But something more impressive still had also been published well before her, in 1827. The book in question, entitled *Domestic Economy and Cookery for Rich and Poor; containing an account of the best English, Scotch, French, Oriental and Other Foreign Dishes* . . ., was described as having been 'composed with the utmost attention to Health, Economy and Elegance, by A Lady'. It is a very substantial book, of almost 700 pages; little known; but distinguished by a vigorous style and a profusion of knowledgeable footnotes. We wish we knew who the 'Lady' was, and how she acquired her arresting ideas and information; for example, recommending the making of bread as the Laplanders make it, from pine bark, and the statement that a physician of one of the Embassies to China had told her of seeing very small children 'lying upon the sides of tanks, gathering every thing that had life, and putting what they had collected into little boxes formed like mouse-traps, to prevent their escape. The produce was put into the rice-pot.'

However, here we are more concerned with her chapter on Oriental Cookery and the eight Turkish recipes included in it; one from an earlier author, who is rebuked for having failed so to identify it. This recipe, with some of her general comments on Turkish cookery, is reproduced below, followed by two of the other recipes.

A DELICIOUS DISH

Take good cow's milk and put it into a pot; take parsley, sage, hyssop, savory, and other good herbs; chop them and stew them in the milk; take capons, and after half roasting them, cut them in pieces, and add to them pines, clarified honey, and salt; colour with saffron, and serve up.

[COMMENTS] This dish is completely Turkish. The sweet herbs (the milk is in the Arab style), the saffron, the capons, the making of which is a constant practice in the East, and of which we have no trace among our nations anterior to the time of the Crusades; but, above all, the sweets, the honey, and the pine kernels, which are richer and stronger than almonds, and must have been imported . . . [There follows a passage drawing attention to the existence of this recipe in the *Forme of Cury*, a medieval compilation of recipes by the cooks of King Richard II, and leading into remarks about Turkish food and cookery.]

. . . The Turks use the finest spices, rice, saffron, and sweets, profusely, in most of their meat dishes. Every sort of food that is presented to women is invariably sweet; and the men keep them always supplied in their harems with confections, and all sorts of nuts, &c., to prevent them as much as possible from contentions. Dr. Clark, when he saw labels scattered about in the seraglio, thought that they were for liquors prepared in secret; but they were for different compounds of *eau-sucrée*, flavoured with various fruits and flowers, the manufacture and consumption of which is one of their chief employments. . . .

The Turks, like the Jews, have been forbidden pork, probably from the same reason. The Levantines far surpass us in the healthiness and excellence in dressing meats, though their unceremonious manner in presenting it, the way they squeeze it in their hand, &c. is at first not very agreeable to strangers, who do not take into consideration their frequent ablutions: besides, the true amateur of good living knows how much higher flavoured meats are from the hand than in any other mode. We, from prejudice, go into other countries in the proud superiority of our own customs and manners; and as the vulgar first attract our notice, we generally mistake their manners for those of the country. Were one of our fashionables to go down into one of our remote counties, and see a boor stuff a large wooden or horn spoon, full of some coarse food, into his wide open mouth, with his eyes shut, it were odds if he ever again ate with a spoon; declaring, perhaps, that pretty tapering fingers were expressly made to feed man more delicately.

TURKISH YAUGH, WITH ONIONS OR APRICOTS

Brown the onions in a stew-pan with butter, cut three pounds of lamb into steaks, and add them; cover very close, and leave it ten minutes. Prepare the following spices: cayenne, black pepper, cloves, and cinnamon; mix and rub them together into a fine powder, put it into the sauce with a little salt, shake and cover it very close, and leave it to simmer for an hour; add two table-spoonfuls of vinegar, let it incorporate, and serve it hot.

The same dish may be dressed with apricots (which are kept in dried cakes), without the onions. Slices of sheep's tails, which are very fine in the East (the fat being a rich gristly jelly), are often dressed in this way. Serve boiled rice with either.

TURKISH SHERBETS

Extract by pressure or infusion the rich juice and fine perfume of any of the odoriferous flowers or fruits; mix them in any number and quantity to taste.

When these essences, extracts, or infusions are prepared, they may be immediately used, by mixing in proper proportions of sugar, or syrup and water, some acid fruit, such as lemon, pomegranate, tamarind, &c., are added to raise the flavour, but not to overpower the perfume, or taste of what the sherbet is made.

These sherbets are very healthy, having all that is exhilarating, with the additional refreshing and cooling qualities so requisite in hot countries, and free from fermentation, which is destructive in certain degrees to health, however satisfying for the moment.

These preparations are beautifully clear, and much more delicate than if they were preserved with sugar.

This author's Turkish recipes form a substantial element in a chapter which can rightly be described as the first serious attempt – and a good one – to introduce the subject to the British public. It is of interest that the author states at the beginning of the book that 'long residence abroad' has made her familiar with foreign dishes. Unfortunately, she does not amplify this statement by indicating where she had lived. The omission entitles us to speculate; it seems possible that she spent time in India, and that in travelling to and fro she visited Russia, Turkey, Persia and Egypt.

But her book seems to have made no impact. We have not come across any mention of it at all; it may be that the level of sophistication which she displayed was too great for the 1820s.

Eliza Acton's *Modern Cookery* (1845) has been described by Elizabeth David as the greatest cookery book in the English language. It is essentially English, but Miss Acton included a chapter on Foreign and Jewish Cookery. This contains only one recipe of interest here, which reads as follows:

SIMPLE TURKISH OR ARABIAN PILAW
(From Mr. Lane, the Oriental Traveller.)

'*Piláw* or *Piláu* is made by boiling rice in plenty of water for about twenty minutes, so that the water drains off easily, leaving the grains whole, and with some degree of hardness; then stirring it up with a little butter, just enough to make the grains separate easily, and seasoning it with salt and pepper. Often a fowl, boiled almost to rags, is laid upon the top. Sometimes small morsels of fried or roasted mutton or lamb are mixed up with it; and there are many other additions; but generally the Turks and Arabs add nothing to the rice but the butter, and salt, and pepper.'

Obs. – We are indebted to the courtesy of Mr. Lane for this receipt, which was procured from him for us by one of his friends.

It is curious that Alexis Soyer, the flamboyant chef whose exploits at the Reform Club, in Ireland, and also in the Crimea, attracted so much attention, and whose natural curiosity was considerable, did not explore Turkish cookery as much as he explored the kitchens of the British Army in the Crimea. But the only trace we have found of this is a recipe in an appendix of 'Army Receipts' to his book *Soyer's Culinary Campaigns* (1857), for 'Turkish Pilaf for one hundred Men'. This ends with the laconic observation: 'Any kind of vegetable can be frizzled with the onions.'

Mrs Beeton's *Book of Household Management* (1859–61), which has eclipsed all other English cookery books in fame, has no recipe connected with Turkey. But the light kindled by our anonymous 'Lady' in 1827 was about to shine forth in full splendour. The year 1864 saw the publication of the first Turkish cookery book in the English language, the *Turkish Cookery Book* by Turabi Effendi.

The title-page and preface of the book* show that its immediate inspiration was the banquet held by the Viceroy of Egypt aboard his yacht, during a visit to England in 1862; but suggest that this occasion merely provided a stimulus for a project which was already under way. Turabi Effendi describes himself as the 'Compiler' and states that the recipes come from 'the best Turkish authorities'. He does not identify these. However, thanks to Turgut Kut (see page 12), we learned that the book was in fact a translation of the first Turkish cookery book, by Mehmed Kâmil, which had come out in 1844.

Turabi Effendi himself was still a mystery so far as we were

---

* Now reprinted in facsimile by Cooks Books, Rottingdean, 1987.

concerned. *The Times* and the *Illustrated London News* carried reports of the Viceroy's banquet, listing the 48 guests, but there is no mention of Turabi Effendi. (The *Times* report said crossly that the menu had not been made available to the press, so it could only reveal that fresh fruits were on the table.)

However, Jill Tilsley-Benham has now unearthed some information from *Recollections of an Egyptian Princess by her English Governess*, by Ellen Chennells, 1893. This author, who went to Egypt in 1871 writes: 'We had a visit one day from an English lady who had married a Turk some years previously, when the latter was Attaché to the Turkish Embassy in England. Mrs Turabi was accompanied by two ladies . . .' So it looks as though Turabi was at the Egyptian Embassy in London around the time of the Viceroy's banquet; and we may speculate that it was having an English wife which prompted him to do his translation.

Turabi Effendi's worthy book had no noticeable impact. One might, for example, have expected his recipes to be reflected in George Augustus Sala's *The Thorough Good Cook* (1895), since Sala proclaimed that he had made his book 'as cosmopolitan as possible' and that he himself had 'seen and essayed the cookery of two generations all over the globe'. However, his few references to Turkey are disappointing. He attributes to Turks a liking for sour cream, and states that the use of honey in Greek sweet dishes, and even in some savoury ones, was a practice learned from Turkish confectioners. Otherwise, he gives short recipes for *Capon à la Turque* and for Turkish sherbet. The former calls for the use of bacon. The latter is a concoction of sugar, water, lemon juice and veal stock.

The conclusion must be that English perceptions of Turkish cookery in the eighteenth and nineteenth centuries were nugatory. The 'Lady' of 1827 offered a serious, but partial, contribution of knowledge. Turabi Effendi gave an excellent conspectus. Neither seems to have had a noticeable audience, or any influence, at the time.

The situation in the second half of the twentieth century is better. Historical studies now acknowledge the influence of Ottoman cuisine on Western Europe. The number of cooks in Britain who desire authentic information about foreign, including Turkish, foods and dishes has increased enormously, and such information is now more accessible. In short, progress is being made. But just think: what astonishing ignorance prevailed until recently!

1986

Managing Your Dwarfs

Staying the night on the Delaware coast in 1950, I found a bookcase of books that no one reads and checked through them. A battered volume (no title-page, many leaves loose) called *Yourself and Your House Wonderful* beckoned irresistibly. It left with me, and in its place stood a discarded book of mine, such as would interest other visitors, and in better condition. I quieted my conscience at the time (but only temporarily – I still worry over what I did) with the thought that the landlady would not have understood if I had proposed the exchange, and that I might as well act in her interests as well as my own.

The book, *circa* 1920, was an attempt to explain to children how their bodies work, with emphasis on what happens to food when we ingest it. The author was H. A. Guerber, already responsible for thirty-two other books; and the publisher was the Uplift Publishing Company. The technique was to explain the mysterious in terms of the familiar. So the body becomes a house; and its inhabitants, who are all dwarfs, represent the organs of digestion. Guerber portrays in vivid terms how they could become tired or irritated, or alternatively maintained on top form. Each chapter ends with a series of questions, often disconcerting. 'Do you know that you are like a snail?' 'When you have visitors, do you show them what is in your garbage can?'

The dwarfs only exist beyond the boundary of visibility. Thus the Tongue and the Spittle Bucket are merely capitalised, not micropersonified.

The principal dwarf is the Stomach Dwarf. He waits down in his room for signals that food is coming, then runs to the bottom of the stairway until the Spittle Bucket has doused the food and the Tongue has kicked it downstairs. 'If it is good, wholesome food, the Dwarf is greatly pleased.' He is also pleased if chomping and spittling have been carried out satisfactorily; but very cross if what thuds down the stairs still needs cutting up. There is no cutting equipment in his domain. But we are left to assume that the buckets of 'special' juice which he has available will eventually reduce everything and anything to a watery pulp; for his next act is to open a little back door and permit all this to go on its way towards the next Dwarf.

With a fine sense of drama, Guerber does not take us through the back door at once, but lingers to explain how the Stomach Dwarf now has to mop up, clean and tidy his juice buckets, and have a rest. He will fly into a rage if during this time a new signal of 'Food coming' is sent down. (So, no snacks between meals.) The rage can reach such proportions that unwanted food may be hurled back up the stairs. The remedy then is a little hot water with a pinch of salt, 'which the Dwarf is glad to use to wash out his little room and make it sweet and clean once more.'

The thought that thorough chewing makes the task of the Stomach Dwarf easier is expressed with almost frantic frequency, and buttressed, for the benefit of those with babies, by an assurance that proper chewing is impossible until the child has *all* its teeth. 'This is so well known by wise doctors, that there is a law in France, to forbid giving any solid food to children under two years of age. Any person caught doing so, is therefore arrested, put in prison, or fined . . .'

Now can we see beyond the little door? Not quite yet. We first have a lecture on subjects suitable for conversation and subjects not. The bowels are in the 'not' category, but we are particularly advised not to 'snicker' if any allusion is made to them, but just to reflect that the speaker has made a social error equivalent to bringing the garbage can into the drawing room.

Thus is heralded the appearance of the Garbage Can Dwarf, a servant potentially as devoted as the Stomach Dwarf, but no less demanding of considerate treatment. What particularly upsets him is a situation in which he sends a message saying 'Ready' and gets one back saying 'Not now, wait.' If this happens often, he may go on strike and send no messages, even though his Garbage Can is full and filling the inside of the house with bad smells. This means trouble. How easily avoided by a child who trains his little servant to empty the can at the same time each day, preferably very early in the morning!

There is still the kitchen sink to consider. This is the domain of the Bladder Dwarf, who is remarkably like the Garbage Can Dwarf, but for whom thrice-daily activity (on rising, at noon and on going to bed) is recommended.

So far so good. These Dwarfs are comprehensible. But Guerber, his own dwarfs doubtless managed to perfection and over-stimulating him by the adulatory messages they send upstairs, now becomes over-confident in his technique and introduces the Twin Pumping Dwarfs. These two reside in the heart and are pictured as pulling on tiny ropes to send the Blood Boats on their way. Here inconsistency creeps in. The Twins, obviously, must never stop working; yet their common complaint is that they need a 'wee rest'. Perhaps Guerber realised that this wasn't plausible for, in a frantic effort to recapture his audience, he starts pouring tiny red beads into a bottle of water. The manœuvre fails. Shrugging at these demented antics, our children always asked us to turn back to the Garbage Can Dwarfs. Guerber should have stuck to food.

1987

THE STOMACH DWARF

Part Five
Seafood

The Giant of the Mekong

'Alan? Hi! Listen, the Tasseng caught one this afternoon. We're keeping the head for you. When can you get up here?'

The voice crackled so that I could hardly hear. It was coming over a radio-telephone link from the remote village of Ban Houei Sai, way up in the north-west corner of Laos, right beside the notorious Golden Triangle where Laos, Thailand and Burma meet and the opium warlords hold sway. I was about to have dinner in the British Embassy in Vientiane, capital of Laos, hundreds of miles downstream from Ban Houei Sai but on the same mighty, brown, River Mekong.

The telephone was in the hall, which looked like the entrance to a bank or hotel of London in the 1960s. It had been designed by a British architect, a child of his times, to house the first British Ambassador to

Laos. I was the fifth. The first had been interested in orchids, but my enthusiasm was fish. Both these subjects had appeal, because no one had previously made catalogues. Indeed Laos was a country without inventories. The Americans (and the Russians and the Chinese and the Vietnamese) knew where all the airstrips were, but not much else had been counted and identified.

Dinner had to be delayed for five minutes. The news about the Tasseng, a village elder of Ban Houei Sai and an expert fisherman, caused an instant rescrambling of plans. What he had caught was a *pa beuk*, as the Laotians call it, a member of the rare species *Pangasianodon gigas* Chevey, which exists only in the Mekong River and its main tributaries and for which the fishing season at Ban Houei Sai lasts only a month. The pa beuk is probably the biggest freshwater fish in the world, but fewer and fewer were being caught each year. This might be the last chance to secure the head of one for the British Museum.

I busied myself making some local calls. I never really understood who did what in the huge American Embassy and their even larger Aid Mission, but I did know the man who scheduled their numerous daily flights in Laos (ten times more numerous than the flights of Royal Air Laos, the national carrier). He said that there was room for me in a rice-dropping flight which was due to take off at 0600 next day for Sayaboury and Ban Houei Sai. I told my number two that I would be away. I told my driver that I would be leaving at 0530. And I told my wife over dinner. None of them was surprised. They all knew about the pa beuk.

Rice-dropping planes fly with their doors open and they don't cut their engines on the airstrips where they call. So it's easy to get out of them but you may be half blown away when you do. At Ban Houei Sai I staggered out of the slipstream and greeted Jack Huxtable, USAID Coordinator for that area. (Those were the days when the United States Government still had an Aid Mission in Laos, and half the country, including Ban Houei Sai, was under the control of a non-Communist government in Vientiane.) Jack gave me a real American breakfast on the verandah of his house, overlooking the Mekong. We were also overlooking the head of the pa beuk, which was sitting right beside us on the floor. Jack said that the fish had been kept captive, tied to bamboo poles at the side of the river during the night, in order to keep it fresh; and that it had been expertly cut up at dawn. He figured that except for the head everything had by now been sold in the market.

Jack also told me that the fish had measured just over 2 metres. So it was a middle-sized specimen. I knew off by heart the dimensions of the fish caught in the previous season (1973). A record, apparently the first of its kind in the history of Laos, had been made for me by a young Lao mechanic at Ban Houei Sai. But I had also studied such fragmentary earlier records as were available, and I knew that there were authenticated reports of pa beuk measuring 3 metres and weighing over 250 kilos.

After breakfast we drove down to the tiny office of Royal Air Lao, to weigh the head on their baggage scales. It registered 49½ kilos. So I could pay the Tasseng (the cost being reckoned per kilo, and quite high, since many Laotians think that the choicest bits of flesh are in the head). A chopper was flying back to Vientiane almost immediately and the pilot cheerfully agreed to give a lift to myself and my precious head. I had it in the Embassy freezer by the middle of the afternoon.

We washed it before we froze it. It looked kind of dignified, grey-brown in colour with the characteristic little white star on its brow and the relatively small eyes set low down by the mouth.

Late that evening I sat down to list the mysteries surrounding this huge fish, mysteries which I hoped the British Museum could help to unravel by studying the head. I knew that this would be the first time that a substantial piece of a pa beuk had reached the western hemisphere, for detailed examination.

Here are the mysteries:

1 Why does nobody ever catch a baby pa beuk? They start at 1.4 metres. Obviously, there are smaller ones. But Laotian and Thai fishermen never find them.
2 How old is an adult pa beuk? A Thai expert had calculated that a fish 2 metres long would be in its sixth year. But this rate of growth would be surprising.
3 How does spawning take place? Nobody knows. But the same Thai expert (Mr Tiraphan Pookaswan) had obtained information from a fisherman that a female fish, 2.3 metres long, contained ovaries weighing 16 kilos, comprising millions of eggs 5 mm in diameter. He had himself recorded that a male of the same length had testes 43 cm long which weighed 140 grams.
4 Where does spawning take place? Laotians traditionally believe that it happens in a lake in China, through which the Mekong flows. But there are difficult falls on the Mekong, just before the Chinese frontier. Could the pa beuk negotiate these? No one knows.
5 Could the pa beuk come upstream from Cambodia to Laos? There certainly were pa beuk in Cambodia until recently. But opinions differ on whether they could pass the Falls of Khong, on the Laotian

side of the frontier. The main fall looks quite impassable; but there
are scores of subsidiary passages.

6 Is there one population of pa beuk, with its headquarters in some
favoured part of the Mekong; or are there a number of separate
populations? The evidence is inconclusive.

7 Why was it that the pa beuk taken in Cambodia and the south of Laos
were reputedly not very good to eat, being rather fat, whereas those
taken upstream were delicious? Could this be the beneficial effect of a
long spawning migration?

8 Is it true that the pa beuk eat nothing but the vegetation in the river?
One which survived for a while in captivity is said to have accepted
other foods.

9 Why does the pa beuk have no teeth? There are some other catfish
which have teeth when they are young, but lose them in old age.
Could the pa beuk be simply the elderly form of a catfish which is
familiar to us under another name, and has teeth, in earlier life?

In preparing my brief for the British Museum, I took the last question
first. The theory that the pa beuk is not really a separate species but just
the full-grown form of another species is tempting. It explains at once
why small pa beuk are not caught. But there are serious objections to it.
First, there simply are no other catfish in the Mekong which could
plausibly be supposed to be the young version of the pa beuk. A
Japanese expert, Dr Taki, recently made an exhaustive study of the
fishes of lowland Laos. In my amateur way, I did too. We looked at all
the other pangasid catfish. None of them fits.

The second objection is that the theory flies in the face of all popular
traditions in Laos. To say this is not to disprove it. But the traditions are
so strong and the interest of the Laotians in the pa beuk so intense that it
seems scarcely credible that the whole nation should have made such a
fundamental mistake. The people who do the fishing usually know the
fish; and the Laotians are all fishermen.

But few of them have actually fished for the pa beuk. To do this you
need four men and a boat; and a net which weighs about 150 pounds
and is nearly a quarter of a mile long. This is a lot of capital equipment
for Laotians, especially so when you take into account the shortness of
the season and the possibility that you can fish hard, day and night,
throughout the four or five weeks without catching a single pa beuk.

All this I had learned the previous year, when I was able to go out
fishing for the pa beuk with the Tasseng mentioned above, who is the
most experienced fisherman at Ban Houei Sai. The stretch of the
Mekong immediately south of the village is uniquely suited to the

fishery. The river is about a quarter of a mile broad and uniform in depth. We put one end of the net, with a marker-float, over the side near the Laotian bank of the river, then paddled across almost to the Thai bank, paying out the net as we went so that it stretched right across the river. Then we floated downstream with it for two miles before gathering it all in again and repeating the whole process. If a pa beuk had been coming upstream, cleaving the water just below the surface with its powerful grey body, it would certainly have caught its head in the net and been taken. But we had no luck.

The fishing was tedious work, but completely businesslike. The effort involved was considerable, but it was precisely what was required and no more. Until twenty or thirty years ago the practice was much more complicated.

It was at a place called the Golden Basin, not far upstream from Vientiane itself, that the maximum ceremonial attended the fishery. In those days pa beuk were to be had there, in the vicinity of a very deep pool. But the manner of fishing for them was so complicated and so inhibited by regulations of a magic nature that it is a wonder that any of the fishermen ever caught one. To begin with, the period of fishing was dictated by the waxing of the moon rather than by the state of the Mekong, which would have been more relevant. Then, before any fishing began, those who were taking part had to spend almost a week propitiating the various important Spirit Chiefs who looked after that part of the river. (These spirits had names such as the Spirit of Siri Mangala, the Golden Swan and the Spirit of the Golden Basin itself. The Spirit of the Golden Basin required a procession of boats conveying swords, water gourds, trays of betel-nuts and leaves, pieces of silver and of beeswax, green coconuts, sweetmeats, candles, incense tapers, sandalwood flowers and a gong and two flutes, all to be offered to it with suitable music and incantations.)

After all these rules had been obeyed, and all the offerings made, the fishermen were allowed to start fishing. Even then, they were further distracted by the requirement that they should hurl abuse at each other throughout the fishing. They had to call each other 'bald-headed fool' and other even more uncomplimentary names; and they exchanged sexual insults in the most liberal manner. However, despite all this, they did catch some pa beuk. Local people believe that the fishery ceased to be successful – and therefore died out – because the appearance of motor-boats on the river disturbed the conditions which had previously encouraged the pa beuk to use the Golden Basin as a sort of headquarters.

There was also a fishery for the pa beuk, until quite recently, near the royal capital, Luang Prabang; and it too was hedged with magic restrictions. One Laotian told me of an incident which befell the then Crown Prince of Laos, long ago. The Crown Prince had been out fishing and had caught a pa beuk. Villagers gathered round and advised him to cut it up on the spot so that the local *phi* (spirit) could have some as an offering. The Crown Prince preferred to take it first to the village, where there were better facilities and whence it would have been easier to take most of the delicious meat back to the palace in good condition. But the engine of his boat caught fire on the way . . . Nobody was surprised.

The Crown Prince's interest was understandable. The pa beuk is a fish of superlative quality. Its flesh has admirable texture and unmatched flavour. Like that of the sturgeon, it bears some resemblance to veal; and some people, tasting it for the first time, mistake it for meat. But it is fishy in a subtle and majestic way, and in my opinion there is no other fish which has quite the same qualities. All Laotians would agree with this. Many of them believe that it is advisable to eat at least one portion of pa beuk every year to ensure a long life and active old age. But nowadays fewer and fewer of them have the chance to follow this precept, since the number of pa beuk being caught has greatly diminished.

I should like to say that the pa beuk will survive. But I don't know. Nobody knows. There is simply not enough information available about this wonderful fish to form the basis of a serious judgement about its future.*

All one can say is that the evidence is overwhelming that the numbers of pa beuk have shrunk dramatically and more or less steadily over the last few decades; that it is now one of the rarest fish in the Mekong; and that fishing for it has stopped in many places where it used to be caught. However, this last point is not conclusive. It only means that the heavy investment of equipment and time by the fishermen ceased to be justified by the diminishing chance of catching a pa beuk. It may emerge in later years that small colonies of pa beuk survived in these places and that the respite from the attentions of fishermen has helped to ensure the continuation of the species.

I hope so. It would not really be anybody's fault, but it would be everybody's loss if this noble creature vanished from the mighty river in which it has been revered for so many centuries.

1975

---

*But now, hurrah! The news from Thailand is that Thai fishery experts have succeeded in producing young pa beuk from a female laden with eggs.

Not Yogurt with Fish

In a number of countries of south-eastern Europe and the Near East it is considered inappropriate to consume yogurt and fish in the same dish.

In many other parts of the world the combination might seem surprising, but would not seem 'wrong'. In the Indian sub-continent there are well established recipes for cooking fish with yogurt.*

What can be the explanation of the taboo, where it exists?

In one of the countries affected, Bulgaria, I talked to nutritionists and persons interested in food history. They all agreed that Bulgarians would not cook fish and yogurt together, or dress cooked fish with yogurt. But none had a convincing explanation. One nutritionist suggested tentatively that, since both fish and yogurt are good sources of protein, there might formerly have been a feeling that it was wasteful to consume the two together; and that such a feeling, transmitted down through the generations, could have hardened into a taboo. But her earnest eyes transmitted doubt as she spoke. And her hypothesis invites what seem to be unanswerable questions. If not with fish, then why with meat?† Would Indians not have been as frugal with their protein resources as Bulgarians?

It seems possible that, if yogurt originated in Central Asia (where little fish is eaten) and then moved south and west, it would have arrived in the Balkans and Near East with traditions of consumption which did not include use with fish, and that these would eventually have been interpreted as excluding such use. But, again, not in India!

I could not find any discussion of this question in the literature, and remained baffled until Detective J. Tilsley-Benham of the Hippocratic Special Investigations Unit (she who cracked the Mystery of Turabi

---

* The seafood recipes given by Julie Sahni in her *Classic Indian Cooking* (New York, 1980) include several examples. Of Dahi Machi (Fish in Velvet Yogurt Sauce) she says: 'This Bengali preparation of fish fillets poached in a mild onion-rich yogurt sauce is eaten every day by the local people.'

† There are numerous dishes involving meat and yogurt in countries of the Near East. To give one example, Neset Eren, in *The Art of Turkish Cooking* (New York, 1969), gives a recipe for Yogurt Salçasi (Yogurt Sauce) and states that it is for use 'on some meat kebabs, and some meat dolmas'.

Effendi – see page 136) uncovered clues in Iran. What she discovered was that in that country a simplified form of the Hippocratic/Galenic Doctrine of the Humours (reminder: this postulates four basic qualities for everything, including foodstuffs, and these are hot, cold, dry, moist) survives as a basic feature of everyday life.* The simplified belief which Persians hold is that in food there are two basic qualities to consider, hot and cold (*sardi/garmi*), and that a balance must be kept between them. When she asked Iranians about fish and yogurt, they were astonished that anyone would even think it necessary to pose the question, so obvious was the answer: 'Did I not know, they asked, that the Hot and Cold effects of certain foods increase dramatically if they are eaten at the same time? The mixture of honey and sweet melon, for example, is far too Hot, and that of yogurt and water melon disagreeably Cold. But the worst misalliance, and most frigid marriage, is that between yogurt and fish.'

So, problem solved? Yes, but the relentless detective pursued the matter further, figuring that a scientific view from an Iranian chemist would be worth having. The chemist she located, 'a fragile raven-haired beauty' called Shireen,

> talked fluently on the human process of digestion, and leaden words like molecule and metabolism hung on her cherry lips like jewels from the poetry of Hafiz. Both Shireen and her mother (a cancer-specialist, no less) judged sardi garmi to be an antiquated system of small value. Obviously it had evolved from long empirical observations of scientific phenomena – 'Hot' sugars and fats do concentrate the blood and lead to hypertension, and everyone knows that 'Cold' prunes and rhubarb have laxative effects. The concept of balance is admirable, but only when applied to vitamins and hormones – not humours! Take my fish and yogurt as a case in point. It is true that many people suffer if they eat these foods together, so there has to be a logical explanation. I hinted hopefully that they might provide one, but with little time to spare they could do no more than formulate a reasonable-sounding theory. The process of digestion, they said, is dependent on food molecules being broken down to their original states. The more complex the molecule, the more difficult it is to break down. Combinations of certain foods do indeed result in Gordian Knots

* Jill Tilsley-Benham argues that the doctrine surviving in Iran is not a simplified left-over from the classical world, but a direct offshoot of more ancient, Asian beliefs. In classical Greece these beliefs were developed into the more complicated theories of Hippocrates and Galen; in Iran they still live on in something very close to their original shape.

of this type. Phosphate ions, for instance, readily form complexes with other ions under suitable conditions. Therefore it is possible that large amounts of intractable molecules result when such high-phosphate foods as fish and yogurt are combined.

The Tilsley-Benham Report was laid before the 1985 Oxford Symposium on Food History,* and no one questioned either of the alternative solutions proposed in Iran. There the matter rests, so far as I am concerned; but I still go round asking people from the Balkans, the eastern Mediterranean and the west of Asia how they feel about yogurt with fish, and whether they can say why.

1985/7

* See Jill Tilsley-Benham, 'Is that Hippocrates in the Kitchen? – A Look at Sardi/Garma in Iran', in *Oxford Symposium on Food and Cookery, 1984 & 1985: Cookery – Science, Lore and Books*, London, 1986. The quotations towards the end of the present essay are taken from this source, by kind permission of the author.

Fish Livers in Shetland

When I went to Shetland it was with an intention so specific and limited as to border on monomania. I wanted to find out about the traditional dishes of fish livers, often combined with oatmeal, there.

The phenomenal scale of this practice arose because the fishermen gutted their fish ashore before shipping them south, and their families frugally made use of the edible parts thus discarded. But I knew that in recent times North Sea oil had transformed the Shetland economy. Hence doubt: would many Shetlanders still do as their ancestors did in this respect? Indeed, as the ship from Aberdeen drew into the small and bustling harbour of Lerwick, my wife and I wondered whether we would easily find people to tell us anything at all about fish livers.

We needn't have worried. Informants were numerous and communicative. Indeed Mrs Hutchison, who provided us with bed and breakfast in her spotless and spacious bungalow, was herself a prime source.

By way of introducing us to the subject, she explained that the fish livers vary not only with the species of fish but also according to the season and the habitat of the particular fish which have been caught. One variation which is important to cooks is in oiliness. The more oily a liver is, the more oatmeal must be used with it. A Shetland cook has to use her discretion in this, not follow a recipe.

Mrs Hutchison went on to give her view that if you cook the livers in 'muggies' (the fish stomachs) you get the full force of their vitamins; and that if you cook the livers in a fish head the effect is less concentrated. I wondered about this. An expert at the Torry Research Station in Aberdeen had mentioned that the consumption of large quantities of fish liver could be harmful, precisely because one would have an overdose of vitamins. Perhaps 'muggies' would be safer fare.

By this time, however, convinced of our genuine interest, Mrs H was proposing that we make 'krappin' together, in her kitchen. This is the liver-in-a-fish-head dish, and she emphasised that it was supposed to be a *quick* dish for busy Shetland crofters. It should only take five minutes to clean a big fish head under running water, and not much longer to prepare the stuffing. Some people sewed up the back of the head after putting in the stuffing. She had one friend who even sewed up the lips.

But none of this sewing was necessary. One ought to be able to make the dish in under a quarter of an hour, then just leave it to cook for half an hour to an hour, depending on the size of the fish head. We would see.

Indeed we did see; what is more we were not spectators, but served as apprentices, carrying out the whole operation under her directions. (There seemed, incidentally, to be no problem in obtaining fish livers, but it was some time before the small boy who was sent for a suitable fish head came back with one of the right dimensions. Mrs H commented with tolerant disapproval that the fish trade nowadays took less care to keep an array of these in stock for customers such as herself.)

The operation went smoothly, although more slowly than if Mrs H had been doing it herself. As on another occasion, when a Japanese sushi chef invited me to take over from him for a while, I was impressed by the natural, or rather unnatural, stickiness of my fingers, which caused a minor but still deplorable wastage of oatmeal. Anyway, the Krappin Heid (to give the dish its full title) was delicious; and I was able to record the Hutchison recipe in full detail in my *North Atlantic Seafood*.

Fresh from this experience, we met a man who belonged to the sew-up-the-head school. This was Mr J. S. Ross from Out Skerries, whose recipe was that of his mother. It called for a cod's head and cod livers. The livers are mixed with oatmeal and also, if you like (as his mother did), onion, but you must be sure that liver dominates the mixture. You sew up the back of the head, insert the stuffing through the mouth, then sew up the mouth too (I could imagine Mrs H's reactions to this twofold sewing operation). Boil the head for half an hour, then serve it hot on a very hot plate.

Our single-minded quest now brought us to Mrs Mowat of North Roe, another enthusiast for Krappin and a supporter of Mrs H in declining to sew up the head. She allowed that, if a cod's head big enough for several people was not available, several haddock heads (one per person) would do. She added an interesting comment: if no fish heads were to be had, the krappin could be stuffed into a large cabbage leaf. She would use a half-and-half mixture of oatmeal and flour in making the stuffing, which ought to be of about the same consistency as the kind of stuffing which one normally makes for a chicken.

Next, we met Mrs Sinclair, formerly of Sandwick and now of Lerwick. She said that she was particularly fond of Stap, the other of the two famous fish liver dishes, but that fish livers were now hard to come by. Her idea of making Stap seemed to be to stuff a fish head with livers (not mixed with oatmeal or anything like that), cook this, then remove the livers and the fleshy parts of the head and mash all together before adding salt and white pepper and serving. She explained that you could perfectly well cook the livers in a stone jar standing in the same pot which you use for cooking the fish head; the pot is covered and the livers cook by steaming. She also observed that haddock was usually recommended for Stap, though other fish would do quite well.

Mr Willy Fraser, a highly respected Shetland fishmonger, had his own ideas about why fish liver dishes had gone out of fashion. He said that line fishing was what used to be done, and that the fish were then landed ungutted, partly because the fishermen would not have had time to gut them. So the livers were available, and were kept and used. But since the Second World War the general practice had been to fish with nets. The men now had time to gut the fish at sea, and the general demand from wholesale merchants was for gutted fish; so the fish were gutted and the livers thrown overboard with the rest of the offal.

Mr Fraser said that in the old days people would have fish liver in one form or another three or four times a week; it was very rich in protein, he thought, and did them a lot of good. Nowadays, older people would come to his shop and complain that they couldn't get fish livers; but he had noticed that on the rare days when he had some they would make enthusiastic noises but wouldn't actually buy any.

The television show Pebble Mill at One now entered the picture. Mr Fraser had seen an item in this programme which showed the preparation of a fish liver dish on the Isle of Skye. Piltocks (saithe) had been stuffed with a mixture which seemed identical with krappin, and the result was much the same as a dish known as Cuids or Liver Piltocks in Shetland (except that the Pebble Mill at One people had decorated the dish with slices of lemon, a terrible solecism). To make this dish, gut the fish without cutting them open, stuff them with livers (no oatmeal), put a potato in the gullet of each to keep the stuffing in place, and cook them thus.

Talking about Krappin Heid, Mr Fraser said: 'I only had it once, and I wasn't thrilled.' But he had views about the choice of fish livers. He thought haddock best of all, followed by cod. These were soft after being cooked. But some people preferred ling liver, which remains hard enough to be sliced like lamb's liver.

Mr Fraser's brother-in-law told us about a man from Whalsay 'who lived for food, but didn't live very long.' This man used to take a big cod's head, put it in the middle of a large pot, surround it with fish livers, apply heat until the livers melted and then spoon the melted liver over the head as it cooked. He would eat the flesh from the head, with potatoes of course, using the liver oil as a sauce. There was an implication that the appalling richness of this dish contributed to the shortness of his life.

Finally, Mrs Grey told us about making liver piltocks in the island of Yell. The piltocks were laid in a pie dish and covered with fish livers, then put in the oven and baked. The heat melted the livers and the fish were cooked in the liver oil. She also told us about a certain Dr Jamieson, who used to go out and catch piltocks every evening. Then he would gut them and put them in a little wooden tub ('daffick' in dialect) before making Stap with the piltocks and their livers, assuring everyone that this was the most nutritious kind of Stap. Dr Jamieson ate this dish daily; it was reassuring to know that he survived in good health on this regime.

We had, by the time we sailed back to Aberdeen, absorbed a near-surfeit of both information and actual fish liver. But Mrs Sinclair was making sure that we would be all right. Her cottage is on the coast and she made a great point of telling us that she would come out in front of it and wave a sheet in the air as the Aberdeen boat went by, 'to wish you Godspeed and safe home'. So she did, and we were touched by this simple gesture of goodwill towards the inquisitive foreigners, as they headed back towards their own more sophisticated but less civilised part of the world.

1978

Sandals from the Sea

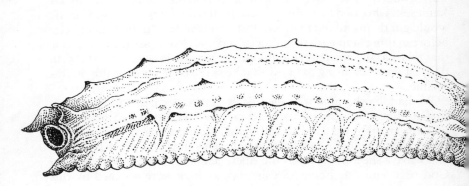

Visitors to Barcelona, including the swarms who will descend on the city for the 1989 Olympics, can have a new seafood delicacy if they know how to ask for it and can afford the high price. The name is *espardenyes*, meaning sandals or slippers. (Warning: the same word can mean a kind of slipper-shaped open sandwich. Having read that a certain restaurant had *espardenyes* as a speciality, I took a taxi right across the city to it, only to be confronted by these unwanted sandwiches. Make sure you go to a real seafood restaurant.)

A Californian student of Catalan cookery told me about these sandals of the sea – more expensive even than lobster, he said – and asked me what they could be. The answer was surprising. They are a species of a seafood which is well known in the Orient, and greatly liked by the Chinese: what are called 'sea cucumbers' or 'sea slugs', or in Malaysia *trepang*. In French they are *bêches de mer*. Not fish, not crustaceans, not molluscs, but in a class of their own (the Holothurians), these are very primitive living creatures, which do indeed look something like a medium cucumber or a giant slug. After arduous preparation they yield rather rubbery 'flesh', prized by the Chinese for its slippery texture and also for its reputation as an aphrodisiac; the shape is vaguely phallic and if one squeezes a live specimen it will eject sticky threads.

Since most kinds of seafood are found all round the world, it would be natural to expect to find these ones in the Mediterranean, but I had never heard of them there. Now I know that they are there, represented by the species *Stichopus regalis*. It seems that local fishermen in Spain and Provence (where the name is *pantuflo*, again meaning sandal or slipper) knew about them, and ate them, but until about ten years ago they were not seen in the markets, nor mentioned in any Mediterranean cookbooks. Who 'discovered' them? Probably an enterprising chef in Barcelona, but to the best of my knowledge no one has claimed credit.

After some practice I had trained myself to take a certain limited pleasure in eating oriental sea slugs, but no training at all is needed for their Mediterranean relations, which are just plain delicious, anyway as served at the restaurant Botafumeiro. This is one of those marvellously professional and busy establishments where everything is good: no unnecessary frills; kitchen and chefs in full view; very fresh seafood on display in lavish variety; knowledgeable customers and knowledgeable waiters.

When asked whether you want your *espardenyes* cooked *a la parrilla* (broiled), say yes. Have no fear that you will be brought a whole one (which might be 9 inches, 23 cm long). What will come will be firm white morsels, looking like tiny, slightly curled, filets of sole, about 1½ inches (3.8 cm) long and 1 inch (2.5 cm) wide when flattened out. As you eat them, you can reflect with satisfaction that this is one treat which gourmets of the past missed through simple ignorance. The 'sandals of the sea' have had to wait until the 1980s for proper appreciation.

1987

A Fishy Tour Round the North Sea

They come at the fish from all sides, do the fishermen of the North Sea. From Boulogne in the south; Lowestoft and Aberdeen in the west; Bergen and Esbjerg in the north; Bremerhaven, Ijmuiden, Scheveningen, Ostend in the east. But they do not all pursue the same fish. Behind the fishermen lie the cooks, whose national and regional preferences in fish help to determine what is landed by whom.

These preferences change in the course of time. In 1911, when Walter Wood's massive volume *North Sea Fishers and Fighters* was published, he could declare roundly that all North Sea fish fell into two categories, 'prime' and 'offal'. 'Naturally enough,' he commented, 'the prime goes to the high and rich community ashore, and the offal to the people.' Prime fish included sole (easily first), turbot, brill, with lemon sole and the best plaice not far behind. Offal comprised haddock, halibut, gurnard, whiting, witches and megrims (two species of flatfish), and – at the very bottom of the scale – skate, ray and the like ('despised at many ports, even by the poorest classes').

What, haddock counted as offal? Wood himself detected a paradox, remarking that, 'properly cooked and served, a choice haddock is a welcome dish at any table'. He also noted that on the other side of the North Sea skate counted almost as prime fish. Nowadays, judging by prices in restaurants and at my local fish and chip shop, skate is almost prime here too.

Particular preferences which I have noted while travelling in the North Sea countries over the last ten years are: turbot in France, Belgium and the Netherlands; plaice in Germany and (especially) Denmark; porbeagle shark for the restaurant trade in Germany; codling, pollack, saithe in Norway.

Why is turbot more appreciated on the Continent than in Britain? Certainly, it is reckoned a good fish in Britain; but we don't really match the enthusiasm and demand for it in, say, Belgium, where a dish of turbot with mousseline sauce is almost a standard feature of restaurant menus. There may be a historical explanation for this, which has eluded me so far; but it does seem possible that turbot are at their best on the east side of the North Sea. An eccentric and learned cookery author, Dr Kitchener, commented in his posthumous work *The Housekeeper's Oracle* (1829): 'The finest turbots that are brought to the London Market, are caught off the Dutch coast . . .'

Tastes in how to cook particular fish also vary from country to country. In Britain herring is a fish to be cooked – fried or grilled. In France it is also cooked, but often in more elaborate ways (for example, the *Gratin de hareng à la crème* of the Pays de Caux in Normandy). In the Netherlands it is something to be eaten raw, as the famous *groene haring*.

Until fairly recent times, *groene haring* was the first herring of the season, landed in April or early May. Pomp surrounded, and still surrounds, its arrival at the great fishing port of Scheveningen. The first pallet-load was for the Queen. In the ensuing weeks the *groene haring* purveyors, with their mobile stalls and garnish of chopped onion, had to make the best of a short season.

That has all changed, and *groene haring* can now be had all the year round. The explanation is that it was discovered that some of the fish harboured tiny worms (nematoids) which were harmful to eat, and that freezing was the best way to kill these. It then dawned on the trade that if the *groene haring* had to be frozen anyway, for reasons of public hygiene, they might as well stay frozen.

Or take plaice. In Britain it is eaten with moderate enthusiasm, usually as fillets, usually frozen. The picture is very different in Denmark, where it is just about number one fish and housewives want it alive. I well remember going with a Danish family at Skagen in the north of the country to the fish quay, and seeing how they chose plaice which were still flapping vigorously, and how they then debated which of various recipes (one of them given below) to use in cooking it.

The Danes are also very keen on their fish balls, *fiskefrikadeller*, but it is in Norway that the use of minced fish – fish forcemeat – is most extensive and remarkable. A special kind of shop, the *fiskemat*, exists just to provide it in the various forms most suited to fish balls or fish puddings. The fish pudding recipe which I give below is no economy dish, but made with very fresh fish and lots of cream. It is rather like what we would call a fish soufflé, but for the Norwegians it is firmly classed as a 'pudding'.

None of the continental countries has the British institution of 'fish and chips', but the Belgians do have their *Mosselen met frieten* (*Moules et frites* in the francophone part of the country: mussels and chips to us), which counts almost as a national dish.

I found that France and to some extent Belgium also have a rich repertoire of fish soups. Why is there no English fish soup? A mystery. We have all the materials that we need. Perhaps a really hearty fish soup doesn't fit into our meal patterns. As it is, I have had to go to Scotland for a seafood soup with respectable credentials, and of real excellence.

While travelling around I looked out for any counterpart to our possessive name of 'Dover sole' for the most esteemed of North Sea fish. None did I find. The sole, *Solea vulgaris*, does not, of course, congregate solely (pun not intended) around Dover, but has a wide distribution from the Mediterranean up to the south of Norway. The 'Dover' bit arose a long time ago when Dover was the main port for landing sole for the London market.

Shrimp, however, attract national and possessive feelings. The Danes think their own best, as do the Germans. Norwegians, who have access to northerly cold-water species, would not exchange them for either of these. In England, Morecambe Bay shrimp are prized, while the same and similar species in France are presented as local specialities.

Surveying this whole area of seafood cookery, I am struck by the wide differences between the countries in the variety and strength of local traditions. To be sure, there are local recipes to be found in all of them. But by far the most are found in France and Denmark. Norway, Germany and Belgium return average scores. Britain and the Netherlands show up less well (though we can point with pride to our kippers and the Dutch excel in smoking eel).

Being a firm believer in the virtues of simple cookery, and ever ready to denounce the fallacy that the more hard work you put into making a

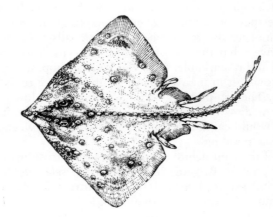

dish the better it will be, I should like to think that the low British score simply reflects realism. No fancy French tricks for us, as Hannah Glasse proclaimed in the eighteenth century. But the truth is that we could benefit considerably from more traffic of recipes across the North Sea, and I hope that the samples which follow may help.

All the recipes give quantities for four. There is one for each of the North Sea countries, going counter-clockwise from France round to England; but Scotland, my own country, has a double ration.

MAQUEREAUX A LA FAÇON DE QUIMPER
Mackerel Quimper Style

1 large or 2 small mackerel
  (total cleaned weight
  1 kg/2 lb)
court-bouillon
1 tbsp Dijon mustard
2 egg-yolks

1–2 tsp vinegar
salt and pepper
2–3 tbsp fines herbes *– use*
  parsley, chives, tarragon
5 tbsp melted butter
a few sprigs of parsley

Cook the mackerel in a strong court-bouillon until they are done (about 10–15 minutes). Take them out, let them cool, then lift the fillets.

Mix the mustard with the egg-yolks, then add the vinegar, salt and pepper to taste, and the herbs, and stir well. Pour the melted butter, which should be lukewarm, into this sauce. It should turn out creamy like mayonnaise, and the flavour of the tarragon should be dominant.

Arrange the fillets of mackerel around a platter, pour the sauce into the middle, and decorate the whole with sprigs of parsley.

ZEEVIS OF ZIJN BRABANTS
Seafish in the Brabant Way

When I had this dish, and the recipe was given to me, in the Ostend restaurant *Au Vigneron* many years ago it was presented as Zeewolf op zijn Brabants, calling for wolf-fish (*Anarhichas lupus*). This is an excellent fish, but easier to find in Belgium or the Netherlands than in Britain. Its cooking characteristics are similar to those of cod or haddock, and the recipe works well for either.

900 g (2 lb) cod or haddock
  fillets
500 g (1 lb) potatoes
500 g (1 lb) chicory (blanched
  endive)

salt and pepper
100 g (3½ oz) butter
1 shallot, finely chopped
400 ml (⅔ pint) fish stock
400 ml (⅔ pint) dry white wine

Peel the potatoes, slice them, season them and fry them until golden in about half the butter. Remove them and give the same treatment to the (chopped) chicory, which needs only a short time in the pan.

Meanwhile, butter an oven dish, stew the chopped shallot in it and sprinkle with salt and pepper. Put the fish in this and pour the fish stock and wine over it. Cover with aluminium foil and leave to cook gently for 10 minutes in a moderate oven (355°F, 180°C, mark 4).

Arrange the fried potato and endive in a fairly deep oven dish, and put the fish on top of them. Reduce the strained fish broth by boiling, uncovered, for 5 minutes or so, then add the remaining butter and seasoning to taste. Cover the fish with the sauce and put the dish in the oven until the sauce is glazed.

SCHELVIS MET MANGO-SAUS
Haddock with Mango (Chutney) Sauce

Dutch fish cookery is fairly conservative, so, contrarily, I have chosen something out of the way, which reflects the influence of the East Indies on Dutch cooking. It is adapted from an enterprising compendium by the Dutch author Ton van Es, who has a historical turn of mind. A similar recipe is found in Germany, and it certainly does great things for haddock. The fish spice mixture called for varies from country to country, but pepper is usually the main ingredient.

750 g (1¾ lb) haddock fillets
juice of ½ lemon
6 tbsp white wine
1 medium onion, thinly sliced
  (optional)
butter
2 tsp fish spice mixture

FOR THE MANGO SAUCE
a jar of mango chutney
  (220 ml/⅓ pint)
300 g (⅔ lb) sour apples
2 chunks of preserved ginger
1 tbsp ginger syrup
1 tbsp lemon juice
½ tsp powdered ginger

Put the haddock fillets, lightly salted, in an oven dish, and sprinkle the lemon juice over them. Then pour over the white wine and cover them (if you wish – I don't) with the thin slices of onion. Add knobs of butter and the fish spices (*viskruiden* in Dutch). Cover with aluminium foil and bake in a moderately hot oven (400°F, 204°C, mark 6) for 25 to 30 minutes.

Meanwhile make the mango sauce. Warm the mango chutney while you peel, core and thinly slice the apples. (I'm slow at dealing with the apples, so I prepare them in advance, keeping the slices in acidulated water until required.) Add these to the chutney, with the chunks of preserved ginger, finely minced; the ginger syrup and lemon juice; and finally a sprinkling of powdered ginger. Let all this cook gently until the apples are soft. Then serve it in a large sauceboat (there will be lots of it) when you bring the haddock to table.

KRABBENBROT
Shrimps on Rye Bread with a Fried Egg

The classic shrimp dish of the German North Sea coast. If you wish to be really authentic, eat it with a cup of strong tea, sweetened with large lumps of sugar candy.

200 g (7 oz) cooked North Sea shrimps
4 slices dark rye bread

60 g (3 oz) butter
4 eggs
salt and pepper to taste

Butter the slices of bread and spread them thickly with shrimps. Heat the remaining butter in a frying pan and fry the eggs in this, sunny side up. Put one fried egg on top of each helping, season with salt and pepper, and serve.

RODSPAETTER SKAWBO
Plaice with Cranberry Sauce

A simple recipe from Skagen in the north of Denmark, which turns plaice into a real treat. Use very fresh fish, as Danes would do. Their cranberry sauce would be made with the small cranberries known as *tranebaer*, but I find that American commercial cranberry sauce (into which I mix a little grated lemon peel) does very well.

1 *large or 2 medium plaice,*
  cleaned, head and tail off
  (save for stock)

flour for dusting the fish
60 g (2 oz) butter
½ cup cranberry sauce

Cut the plaice across into pieces about 3 cm (1¼″) wide and dust them with flour. Heat the butter in a roomy pan and fry the pieces of plaice for several minutes on each side (less for the thin slices from the tail end), turning them frequently, until done.

Serve at once, with the cranberry sauce; and provide also boiled potatoes with brown melted butter to dribble over them.

FISKEPUDDING MED REKASAUS
Norwegian Fish Pudding with Shrimp Sauce

In Norway there is a special kind of shop called *fiskemat*, where you can buy fish forcemeat etc. ready prepared. But it is not difficult, with a blender, to make your own. Once you have it, you can go on to make either fish pudding, as here, or *fiskeboller* (fish balls).

The amount of shrimp sauce provided by Norwegians is generous. You could make less.

2 *cups raw fish flesh, free of*
  skin and bone, e.g. haddock,
  pollack, saithe
1 *tsp salt*
1 *tbsp potato flour*
½ *tsp mace*
¼ *tsp ground ginger*
30 *g (1 oz) butter*
½ *litre (1 pint) single cream,*
  plus
2 *tbsp fish stock (optional)*
more butter for greasing the
  dish

FOR THE SHRIMP SAUCE
450 g (1 lb) cooked shrimp
  meat, chopped in small
  pieces
60 g (2 oz) butter
4 tbsp flour
450 ml (1 pint) milk
3 tbsp single cream
salt and white pepper
1½ tbsp lemon juice
2 tbsp finely chopped dill

Combine all the ingredients for the fish forcemeat, except the cream, and blend them until the butter has 'disappeared'. Continue blending, adding the single cream (with the fish stock if used) in instalments. The result will be very light, and is to be used without delay.

Grease a Pyrex or similar dish of suitable size and pour the forcemeat into it. Tap the sides to help it settle down. Then cover it with greaseproof paper, place it in a baking tin half full of boiling water, put this in a preheated oven (355°F, 180°C, gas mark 4) and leave it for between 45 and 60 minutes. (The water may need to be topped up with more boiling water.) Test with a knitting needle; when it goes into the pudding and comes out dry and clean, the dish is ready. Let it stand for a few minutes after taking it out, and pour off any excess liquid before you serve it. (There is no need to go through the business of inverting it on to a platter if the dish it was cooked in can be brought to table; always a relief, for me anyway.)

Meanwhile, you have made the shrimp sauce, thus. Melt the butter in a pan, remove from the heat and stir in the flour with a whisk. Add the milk and cream, then cook the mixture over a low heat, whisking all the while, until it is smooth and fairly thick. Now season with salt and white pepper, stir in the lemon juice, add the chopped shrimp, and let the whole heat through. Finally, add the dill and serve the sauce with the pudding.

PARTAN BREE
Crab Soup

Partan is the Scots word for crab, and bree means stock, broth or, as here, soup. Recipes vary, but this one is my favourite. It does not stray far in ingredients and method from that in the famous *Cookery Book of Lady Clark of Tillypronie* (1909), but the quantities are reduced and advantage taken of the blender which she did not possess.

If you prefer to use a pack of frozen crabmeat (500 g/1 lb), with the white and brown meat conveniently separated into two sachets, use 120 g (¼ lb) of each, keeping the rest for other purposes.

1 dressed crab	*125 ml (¼ pint) single cream*
75 g (3 oz) rice	*salt and white pepper*
550 ml (1 pint) milk	*a dash of anchovy essence*
550 ml (1 pint) fish or chicken	*chopped parsley*
stock	

Set the rice to cook, until soft, in the milk.

Meanwhile, pick out, chop into fair-sized chunks and reserve the white meat of the crab. Blend the brown meat with the rice and milk until smooth.

Put the blended mixture in a large saucepan over a low heat and gradually stir in the stock and the seasonings (careful with the salt if your stock is already salty), together with the white crabmeat. Bring it almost to a boil, but not quite. Just before serving, stir in the cream.

Strew the chopped parsley in the bottom of the soup tureen, or individual bowls, and pour the soup over it.

FISH CUSTARD FROM SCOTLAND

A dish from high tea at my grandparents' house near Glasgow. A dish – aye, there's the rub; my grandmother had just the right dish, but I don't. Ideally, you would have a baking dish just over 15 by 15 cm and nearly 5 cm deep, assuming that your rolled fillets will be nearly 4 cm in diameter. In practice, they turn out a bit different, and we usually finish by improvising, perhaps with a Pyrex casserole. The amount of custard is generous, so there can be some room to spare in the dish.

4 small fillets of haddock or
whiting
butter
3 beaten eggs

40 ml (¾ pint) milk
salt and pepper
chopped parsley

Cut the fish fillets in two lengthwise, then roll them up and put them in a thoroughly (but not lavishly) buttered baking dish, on their ends. Place a knob of butter ('not a doorknob,' said an aunt, aghast at my first prodigal attempt, 'a *wee* knob') on each; it will later melt and spiral down inside the roll.

Make a custard mixture of the beaten eggs and milk, season it, and pour it over the fillets, which will be amply covered. Bake the dish for about 40 minutes in a slow oven (290°F, 145°C, gas mark 1), then sprinkle a little chopped parsley over it and serve. The rolled fish fillets will be such that each can be lifted out with a tablespoon, bringing with it some of the custard mixture.

FRICASSEED SKATE

An eighteenth-century recipe (the earliest version I have found is in John Farley's *London Art of Cookery*, 1787) which was copied by nineteenth-century writers but then fell out of sight. Many earnest experiments in interpreting Farley's text finally led us to the result below, which makes a superb dish.

1¼ kg (2½ lb) wing of skate
  (ray)
½ tsp mace
a good pinch of grated nutmeg
a bouquet garni
salt

50 g (2 oz) butter
4 tbsp flour
250 ml (almost ½ pint) single
  cream
200 ml (⅓ pint) white wine

If what you have is a section of a large wing of skate, dress it so that you have clean pieces, free of cartilage, about 2.5 cm across and 5 cm long. Don't worry about the exact size or shape. A wing of skate being what it is, you are bound to finish up with some triangles, rhomboids, etc. If you are dealing with a small wing, it will be simpler just to cut it up along the lines of the fibres, from the thick side to the thin side, into strips about 2.5 cm wide – the flesh will slip off the cartilage easily enough after being cooked.

Place the pieces of skate in a stew-pan and add 700 ml (1¼ pints) water, also the mace, nutmeg, bouquet garni and salt. Bring all this to the boil, cover and leave to simmer for 15 minutes. Then discard the bouquet garni, remove the skate and keep it hot. (Any further removal of cartilage can be done at this stage.) You will find that you have about ¾ cup of cooking liquid left in the pan.

Melt the butter, stir in the flour, add the ¾ cup of cooking liquid and a very little salt. Then add the cream and wine. Bring to a boil, then let the mixture simmer gently and thicken for 3 or 4 minutes.

Put the pieces of skate in the sauce and serve hot.

1987

Seafood Through a Fish-eye Lens

Fish need to see all around them and have eyes constructed accordingly. This is why one device which can be fitted to a camera is called a 'fish-eye lens'.

It is odd that, although seafood is a category of food with unique and interesting characteristics, few authors have given any general account of these. This essay provides an occasion for a broad look at the subject through a fish-eye lens.

Variety. No one has tasted every kind of seafood; and I dare say that no one ever will. Edible kinds of seafish, crustaceans and molluscs number thousands, and the number of 'sea vegetables' (formerly 'seaweeds') which we consume in one way or another is steadily increasing. The sum total of species is so vast that even Norwegians and Singaporeans, who head the league table in per capita consumption, can only expect to sample the range; and there are people, such as Tibetans, who don't even achieve a sampling.

Confusion. The number of species is quite enough by itself to cause confusion. But the confusion has been compounded by muddles over common, vernacular names. These muddles are far, far worse than those which afflict, say, fruits and vegetables.

Of the two main sorts of fishy confusion, one may be regarded as natural and viewed with tolerance. This is the confusion caused by the fact that even within one language, indeed sometimes within one dialect, the same fish will have a range of different names. These reflect local practice in small coastal communities, which were often isolated from each other in the past by poor overland communications. In Italy, for example, the common grey mullet, *Mugil cephalus*, has more than forty different names. Thus someone who has grasped that this species is officially called *cefalo* may go shopping in Palermo, be offered *mulettu tistuni*, and think that this is a different species; whereas it is the same.

The other sort of confusion applies to European languages, especially English, and is a by-product of colonisation. Its effect is quite the contrary – to make it seem that there are fewer families or species of fish in the world than there really are. What happened was that early English colonists, to take the main culprits as our example, applied familiar but inappropriate names to the species which they encountered in the New World, Australasia and elsewhere. Consider, for example, what fish have been dubbed 'salmon' in Australia and New Zealand. None is a salmon. And some of them are not even related to each other. The 'Murray cod' of Australia is not even a sea fish, let alone a close relation of the true cod. No doubt it would be unfair to reproach the early colonists, especially the convicts who were sent to Australia, for not being ichthyologists. Even so, the heart sinks on contemplation of some of the errors they made.

Fortunately, international and national authorities are doing something to rationalise commercial names for the species; and more and more authors are adopting the practice of identifying the species they mean by its scientific name as well as by popular ones.

Even without these linguistic muddles we would have a problem over hidden relationships, because the same fish will anyway have different names in different languages. This alone is enough to obscure the fact that most families of fish (and *fruits de mer*) are global in distribution and that the difference between species within a family is often without significance for the cook or consumer. Indeed, there are many species which are the same right round the world: *Mugil cephalus*, referred to above; *Xiphias gladius*, the swordfish; *Katsuwonus pelamis*, the skipjack; and the famous bluefish of North America, *Pomatomus saltator*, which is the equally famous lüfer of Turkey and tailor of parts of Australia, and has dozens of other names elsewhere.

Quite apart from this, fish fall into broad groups from the point of view of the cook, according to their size, shape and fat content, and substitutions rarely present a problem.

The term 'wild' applies to all seafoods except for the tiny proportion which are the subject of fish farming; but the term is rarely so used. I have wondered whether this is because 'wild' may mean ferocious as well as non-domesticated, and most of the creatures are perceived as gentle of habit. The oyster, for example, is conspicuously innocuous; and the Roman poet Ovid praised the grey mullet for its blameless life, browsing on vegetation and never partaking of flesh. But this won't do. Most forms of seafood gobble up other forms relentlessly; and we do, after all, refer unhesitatingly to wild flowers. The explanation must rather be that since virtually all seafoods are wild, there is no point in so describing them unless one wishes to distinguish between, say, wild and cultured mussels. Seafoods indeed constitute by far the largest resource of wild food in the world; the only resource which still gives scope for 'hunting' on a large scale.

Seafood is also the outstanding example of a natural resource which has not yet been fully exploited. Fishing by the Russians and the Japanese (and the French — I recently met a fishing vessel from Brittany in Tahiti) is now on a global scale, but even so there are many species and some regions which offer great scope for the future.

Humanitarian considerations are only applied selectively to sea creatures, in contrast to the land animals (especially mammals) and birds. It has recently become unseemly for anyone except the Inuit (Eskimos) to eat marine mammals, and concern is often shown over how to kill lobsters and crabs painlessly; but compassion rarely extends to fish. (Why the crustaceans should attract more sympathy than a fish is a mystery, but they do. An unusual case in Edinburgh a few years ago involved the prosecution of a restaurant for grilling a live prawn on a hot-plate. This did seem, to the court as well as to the public, a clear example of what not to do. But positive advice is more dubious. An ironic feature of the situation is that the advice often given on killing them, although well meant, is such as to prolong their suffering.)

There is one interesting point which applies to fish generally and has not attracted much attention. Considered as a source of protein, and compared with land animals or birds, they have one great advantage. Because the water supports their weight, they need a less elaborate skeleton and therefore provide more flesh in relation to weight.

For those who flinch from eating 'bony fish', this last point may seem odd. The shad, to take a notorious example, is often considered to be impossibly bony. An American Micmac Indian legend relates that when the Great Spirit Manitou created the animals, one discontented porcupine asked to be changed into something else. In response, the spirit 'seized the animal, turned it inside out, and tossed it into the river to begin a new existence as a shad.' The tale is apposite, but even if the shad has as many bones as a porcupine has quills, it has less bone, weight for weight, than a porcupine or any other land animal.

Mention of the shad, whose roe at least is a bonefree delicacy, brings to mind another feature of fish (and of other edible sea creatures). They provide the smallest eggs which we normally eat. Those of relatively small fish are so tiny as to constitute no more than a granular mass. Those of the larger fish, especially sturgeon and salmon, are easier to see and count, and, in the case of sturgeon caviar, so valuable as almost to deserve counting.

Consumption and appreciation of seafood date back to what are rightly, albeit vaguely, called 'the earliest times'. One of my favourite books is indeed called *Fishing from the Earliest Times*;* and another is *Ancient and Modern Fish Tattle* by the Reverend C. David Badham (1854), which has more ancient than modern material in it.

The earliest evidence is mute: the middens of empty sea shells which have been uncovered on many prehistoric sites and which reveal, for what it may be worth, that primitive people in Scotland feasted on limpets and periwinkles, and Australian aborigines on certain clams. Harvesting such foods, which conveniently sit waiting to be gathered in the intertidal zones, needs no technology. Catching any fish, on the other hand, needs some. But it can be very simple, as the techniques still used in Africa and Oceania demonstrate. When there weren't many people, there was no need for ocean-going trawlers and all their scientific apparatus.

Even so, in early historic times the art of fishing and the scale of consumption developed rapidly. The works of early Chinese writers and of classical Greek authors, although some survive in mere fragments, exhibit a sophisticated range of specific fishing techniques and considerable discrimination between the species. Commenting on the history of fishing, Radcliffe observes that techniques have changed less over the centuries than have corresponding techniques in, say, hunting (changed by the introduction of the gun); and that the spear, the line and hook and the net have remained pre-eminent.

Classical Roman authors yield the first evidence of phenomena which are still with us, namely gastronomic gush and undue emphasis on the merits of this or that particular species. It is odd that the Roman admiral Optatus should have taken pains to introduce the parrotfish (Latin *scarus*) from the Carpathian Sea to the west coast of Italy. No one in the Mediterranean pays much attention to this fish nowadays, although it is known in the Aegean and (as marzpan) in Malta. Perhaps its vivid colouring, often bright green, attracted the admiral's eye, much as the kiwi fruit has recently excited practitioners of nouvelle cuisine.

Roman enthusiasm for another fish, the red mullet, is easier to understand, but was attended by financial greed and morbid practices. Many Roman authors testify to the red mullet fever which gripped their contemporaries in the first centuries A.D. One symptom was an undue preoccupation with size, which caused the price of large specimens to rise to absurd heights, equivalent to many hundreds of pounds in the 1980s, for a really big one. Another was the habit of keeping red mullet in captivity and arranging for guests to enjoy the highly specialised

* William Radcliffe, 2nd ed., London, 1926.

aesthetic experience of watching the colour of dying fish change. The moralist Seneca attacked the practice with savage irony, claiming that a Roman would no longer attend the bedside of his dying father, however much he desired the father to die(!), if the rival attraction of a dying red mullet was on offer.

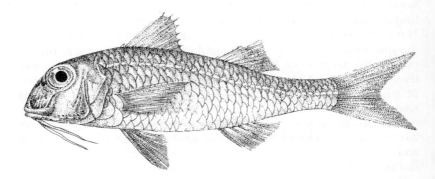

In medieval times, when the pomp and luxury of the Roman Empire had vanished, attitudes were more practical. This was the age when the demand for fish, stimulated by the Christian Church's insistence on meatless days, began to have a perceptible influence on the political and economic history of the western world. This development was linked with the realisation that stocks of such fish as cod, in northerly waters, were truly enormous; and it prompts some reflections on the contrast between cold-water and warm-water species.

It is commonly believed that fish from cold waters are somehow better than those from sub-tropical or tropical seas. I have never been able to detect a general difference of this sort myself, and suspect that the notion is based on the fact that fish keep better in cold climates, and perhaps on a vague puritanical idea that fish which swim in chilly waters acquire merits which are unattainable by those which laze among warm coral reefs. Be that as it may, there is one clear difference. It is a characteristic of warm waters that there are very numerous species present, but each in relatively small numbers; whereas in cold waters one typically finds fewer species but in huge quantity.

So, at least in Europe, the whole business of fishing and trade in fish took a new turn as the Dark Ages came to an end and northerly peoples such as the Scandinavians emerged from relative obscurity. The powerful Hanseatic League, centred on the Baltic Sea, was based to a considerable extent on its near monopoly of the trade in salted and dried fish; and these fish came from the huge stocks of the North Atlantic. Indeed, the subsequent colonisation of North America was certainly stimulated – some would say largely caused – by the search for ever more effective ways of exploiting these stocks and by the competition between the maritime powers for them.

The effects of all this activity are still with us. The salted and dried cod of medieval times survives today as an important article of commerce, under Scandinavian names such as *klippfisk*. (The same thing, dried but not salted, is stockfish.) In many parts of the world people who now have better means of preserving fish continue to eat these products because they have acquired a taste for them. The same applies to the famous *lütefisk* which Swedes, for example, devotedly eat at Christmas despite all the bother involved in preparing it. Indeed it applies to many kinds of cured fish, including the hundred and one forms of cured herring such as kippers and bloaters, red herring and rollmops. Not only have these preparations survived, but the practice of smoking herring, originally intended only to preserve the fish, has been extended for gastronomic reasons to other species such as mackerel, marlin, swordfish and tuna.

The process of fermentation was applied to fish in classical times, so as to yield the fish sauce which the Romans knew as garum and which figures in almost all their savoury recipes. Traces of this survive in the Mediterranean, for example in the Provençal *peïsalat*, but it is in South-East Asia that the tradition really thrives. There, alongside the preservation of fish by drying and smoking, large quantities are still used to make the garum-like fish sauce which the Thai know as *nam pa* and the Vietnamese as *nuoc mam* (see page 223).

In recent times, developments such as canning and freezing, in conjunction with the emergence of steam- and then diesel-driven fishing vessels, have wrought and are still wreaking great changes. Episodes such as the Anglo-Icelandic 'cod war' and the tangle of problems associated with fishing limits and quotas echo the manœuvres of the Hanseatic League and the era of colonisation and remind us that food is the very stuff of which politics are made. But it would be true to say that in much of the world techniques were already available in the Middle Ages for utilising almost indefinite quantities of the ocean catch, and that northern Europe and the Orient seem to have been the two regions where most inventiveness was shown in this respect.

In another respect, however, there was a clear difference between East and West. The Chinese have a consistent record, stretching back for more than four thousand years, of recognising the nutritional (and

often the medical) value of most seafoods, and of honouring fish. As
Bernard Read remarked:*

> Owing to its reproductive powers, in China the fish is a symbol of
> regeneration. As fish are reputed to swim in pairs, so a pair of fish
> is emblematic of connubial bliss. As in water fish move swiftly in
> any direction, they signify freedom from all restraints. . . . Their
> scaly armour makes them a symbol of martial attributes, bringing
> strength and courage; and swimming against the current provides
> an emblem of perseverance. The fish is a symbol of abundance or
> wealth and prosperity.

In the West, the fish was a symbol of Christianity and prescribed as
Lenten fare; but opinions were divided on its merits, even on its
suitability, as food. In Britain, for example, the evidence of eighteenth-
century cookbooks indicates increased consumption of fresh fish from
the sea, but the literature of dietetics shows a strong counter-current
flowing from some medical authorities. As recently as 1835 Graham, in
the sixth edition of his treatise on *Modern Domestic Medicine*,
declared that fish 'affords, upon the whole, but little nourishment, and
is, for the most part, of difficult digestion, and this appears to be the
general sentiment of intelligent medical men.' If this would raise
eyebrows now, what of the book *On Leprosy and Fish-Eating* by
Jonathan Hutchinson† whose avowed intent was to demonstrate, in
400 pages, that the fundamental cause of leprosy was 'the eating of fish
in a state of commencing decomposition'? These examples remind us
that it is only in the present century that seafood has been fully accepted
in the West as an admirable source of nourishment.

But these glimpses of history have not included anything about
cooking fish. Who were the pioneers in this field? If one holds, as I do,
that nothing can beat a good fish which is freshly caught and broiled
over charcoal with the simplest of added ingredients – the olive oil,
lemons, thyme and other aromatics which the Mediterranean region
supplies – then one is looking back a long way. But the art of fish
cookery is more than that, and due honour must be paid to the more
complex dishes and those who devised them.

Here I think that pride of place should probably go to the Italians. No
disrespect to the French, who must be high on any list and who share
with Spain alone among European countries the great advantage of a
double coastline, one Atlantic and one Mediterranean. But the Italians,

---

* *Chinese Materia Medica: Fish Drugs*, Peking, 1939.   †London, 1906.

for their part, have an enormously long coastline, so that no Italian town is really far from the sea and a high proportion of the population has been able to enjoy fresh seafood from early times.

And the Italians score in another respect. Their cookery is relatively homogeneous, with less of a contrast than is found in France between 'haute cuisine' at one end of the spectrum and peasant food at the other. The competitive feats of the great French chefs of the eighteenth and nineteenth centuries had a magnetic and distorting effect in France, pulling everything upwards in the direction of sophisticated and expensive dishes. Thus it has come about that *bouillabaisse*, the archetype of simple fish soups made by fishermen with the day's catch, has developed into a costly and elaborate preparation into which, in complete reversal of its original purpose, rare delicacies such as spiny lobster are introduced for the spurious gratification of so-called 'gourmets' and uninformed tourists. (For more on this subject, see page 185.) There is no parallel phenomenon in Italy. The three score or more of traditional fish soups have not undergone a process of gentrification; and many of the best Italian seafood combinations, especially those involving pasta, and many forms of pizza, are classless and ubiquitous.

So, in Europe, I would choose Italy for the enjoyment of seafood. In Asia, the choice is more difficult; but I would turn to Japan rather than China; and to Indonesia (possessed of even more coastline than Italy) before India.

However, such competitive surveys are less interesting than an open-minded study of the different techniques of fish cookery which are practised in various places, and of the different supporting casts of ingredients. For anyone brought up in a single culinary tradition – as most of us have been – this can yield a host of new ideas. I have a weakness for fish fried in batter, in beef dripping in the style of Yorkshire, where I spent much of my youth. But, having later been able to eat fish fried in a wok in peanut oil in China, I would not say that one was better than the other; each is a treat. And who is to compare, say, fish simmered in coconut cream (south India, Sri Lanka, Thailand, Indonesia, etc.) with a similar fish cooked in an aromatic Mediterranean mixture? Both, to my mind, are equally good.

When it comes to steamed fish, on the other hand, the Chinese and the Thai, to take two examples, have much to teach Europeans and Americans. Plain steamed fish, traditional fare for Anglo-Saxon invalids and convalescents, is dull indeed when compared with Haw Mok (Thai curried fish steamed in artichoke containers).

Fortunately, the trend which has been developing in our time – and developing at a startling rate – is towards the intercontinentalisation of seafood and seafood cookery. A generation ago, in Britain, anything written about fish simmered in coconut cream would have been strictly for reading. Now it's for cooking, and in London at least the wherewithal is easily found. People are beginning to realise that although fish are much the same the world around (despite the tangle of common names which obscures the relationship between, say, red mullet and goatfish), the methods of preparing them vary widely. Ditto the way of serving them, and the choice of beverage. The marriage of seafood with wine may have been consummated most satisfactorily in France; but there are simpler nuptials which seem appropriate in other places, involving beer and tea, and these can be transplanted along with the dishes to which they pertain. This topic would, however, need another essay, and here I wish to say more about fish cookery, notably one fundamental question: how to calculate cooking time. Practice removes the need to calculate; but those who do it usually do it wrong.

A fish is cooked when its innermost parts have reached a temperature of about 63°C. In conventional cookery (I am not talking about microwave cookery) heat travels from the outside to the inside. So the determining factor is the distance to be covered. Since the shape of fish varies greatly it is obvious for a start that the weight of a fish is not a good guide. It couldn't possibly work for both a long, thin eel and a chunky grouper. Realisation of this prompted the promulgation of the so-called 'Canadian method', which calls for basing the cooking time on the maximum thickness of a fish. That is right. But if it is going to work, it has to be applied in accordance with the relevant law of physics, which is this: *The time taken for heat to penetrate is not in simple proportion to the thickness of the object, but to the square of the thickness.* One might think that a piece of fish two inches thick would take twice as long to cook as a piece one inch thick. Not so: if the heat has to go *twice* as far it will take *four* times as long. That many people are unaware of this explains why a thin piece of fish is often overcooked and a large fish risks being partly undercooked. It also explains the importance of scoring the sides of fish, a practice which is found worldwide but is done with particular care in China. If the scoring is done at the correct intervals, and deeply enough, the result may be to halve the maximum distance which the heat must traverse to reach the innermost part, and therefore to reduce cooking time to a quarter of what it would have been.

Incidentally, the same principle applies to all foodstuffs. I just happen to have taken special note of it in connection with fish cookery, and to have observed how many people misunderstand the situation in this context. (When I was in the United States recently someone gave me a gadget which was supposed to enable cooks to apply the Canadian method by measuring the thickness of the fish. The gadget was calibrated in inches and minutes. Alas, the manufacturer did not know his physics and had got the relationship wrong: one inch – ten minutes, two inches – twenty minutes, and so on. I hope that this device is not being seriously used!)

But does seafood need to be cooked? The Japanese, with their sashimi, have demonstrated that really fresh seafood is very good when eaten raw (especially so if it is presented with Japanese artistry). And the famous seviche of Latin America provides a method of 'cooking' without cooking, applicable in particular to seafood. What happens here is that the marinating of seafood in lemon or lime juice causes the denaturation of the protein in much the same way as the application of heat in conventional cooking would do.

Both sashimi and seviche are in the process of spreading round the world, and the former in particular seems sure to modify habits of seafood consumption; both directly and indirectly too, for the Japanese conception of what is a fresh fish in the market is gaining ground, and slowly tightening up lax standards elsewhere. (Not always so lax. In the nineteenth century, fish merchants kept cod alive in floating wooden chests for the London market. And even now it is possible, indeed customary, to buy live cod in Bergen in Norway, and live plaice in Denmark.)

It is true, of course, that the currents of culinary change eddying round the world affect all kinds of food, not just seafood; and that some of the currents reflect nothing better than passing fashions, crazes and fads. But seafood is, in my belief, a category especially susceptible to and ripe for genuine and lasting changes of attitude and practice. It is also one which offers the twin prospect of greater gastronomic pleasure and improvement in world food supplies. All that we need to give culinary history a push in this respect is an enquiring spirit.

Indeed the seafood enthusiast should never be content with knowledge and experience already acquired. When in the early 1970s I wrote about the merits of angler-fish (American goose-fish) and explained why the tail-end alone was marketed, I thought that I was doing a service to British and American readers and telling them all they really needed to know about this fish. Now, a mere fifteen years later, I find that people are asking me whether I realise how good it is, and that its availability and price in London shops have increased dramatically. But I also find that I had only told part of the story.

Even while I was writing this essay a letter from a Mr Thomas Flögel (whom I have never met) in Taiwan arrived. From this I quote:

> Another point regards the fabulous angler-fish, which provides one of the greatest delicacies the sea has to offer: ankimo, the liver of the angler-fish (angler being anko in Japanese, liver is kimo, which is telescoped into ankimo), which, when I first saw it in the fish market of Tsukiju/Tokyo impressed me by its incredible dimensions even before I had tasted it. It is rolled in bamboo-mats and then steamed, the greyish slices with some orange in it (I don't know where this comes from) melting away in the mouth like the best foie gras. In Japan I have mostly eaten it with grated radish sharpened by a little bit of chilli, chives and ponzu sauce. I especially like the idea that no force-feeding is necessary to obtain this delicacy, the angler obviously being such a glutton that he does this out of his own free will.

So, this fish will yield new, unexpected pleasures, and my self-education can be carried a stage further if I proceed to Japan. Like the Roman cookery writer Apicius, who one day heard someone vaunt the size of prawns taken off the Libyan coast and hired a vessel on the spot to take him to Libya (with results which I shall not record, for they are unpropitious), I must act quickly on this new information. I have told Mr Flögel that I shall revisit Japan, and Taiwan too (for he has more information to impart, on the delights of eating the stomach-sac of the scallop), before the year is out.

Seafood, after all, is still the greatest domain open to gastronomic explorers; and seafoods are so various and ways of preparing them so many that one lifetime, expanded though it may effectively be by jet travel, can never be enough.

1984

Fish in the Bosphorus

If one's subject is Mediterranean seafood, there is no shortage of delightful places in which to pursue one's researches. None is more delightful or more interesting than the Bosphorus, whither I have gone several times and where I was greatly aided in my studies by residents with a really deep knowledge of the subject; in particular, the late Mr Hugh Whittall, who patiently and enthusiastically corresponded with me about it. He also kindly furnished me with a comprehensive essay of his own composition, which was an invaluable mixture of public statistics and personal observation.

It has been fashionable for some time to speak of the Mediterranean as a dying sea, or even – with pardonable exaggeration – as one which is virtually dead. The perils of twentieth-century pollution are indeed serious; but in the very dim and distant past the Mediterranean came far closer to death. That was in the Pliocene Age, when the Straits of Gibraltar were closed and the Mediterranean was an inland sea. Because of the warm climate, it loses a lot of water by evaporation; and the inflow of water from the rivers which discharge into it has never been sufficient to make up for this. So it was shrinking, and had indeed shrunk into a series of large lakes (corresponding to what are now the deeper areas) which seemed doomed to end up as mere brackish lagoons incapable of supporting more than a few survivors of the hundreds of species of fish which had been there.

Fortunately, the situation was saved. An enormous convulsion opened up the Straits of Gibraltar, permitting water from the Atlantic to flow in, which it has been doing ever since. Water flows both ways past Gibraltar, but more flows into the Mediterranean than out, and it is the net gain of water from the Atlantic which has kept the Mediterranean alive.

However, although the Atlantic waters are a condition for the survival of the Mediterranean, they are not the only helpful factor. The Mediterranean is also the gainer in its exchange of waters with the Black Sea, through the Bosphorus. The Black Sea is generously fed by rivers, and contributes its surplus to the Mediterranean. Since the waters of the Black Sea have a lower salt level, it is easy enough to follow their course as they fan out into the Aegean. This movement is more pronounced, naturally enough, at those times of year when the rivers discharging into the Black Sea are in full spate. The best time is the winter.

The Mediterranean is rich in marine fauna, in the sense that there are very many different species there, albeit in relatively small quantities. (The situation in the North Atlantic is the reverse. The general pattern there is that there are fewer species, but large populations. This sort of contrast prevails generally when one compares tropical or near-tropical waters with colder oceans.)

The Black Sea, on the other hand, contains fewer species: say, 120 or so as against about 400 in the Mediterranean. The low salt level of the Black Sea is the main reason for this. Many species which would otherwise migrate through the Bosphorus into the Black Sea cannot tolerate such a low level and therefore stay in the Mediterranean. The species which find the Black Sea water acceptable include, not surprisingly, many of those which like brackish waters, such as grey mullet; and species which live in the sea but habitually ascend rivers, for example sturgeon and eels, and also the relatively rare Black Sea salmon trout, *denizala* in Turkish.

The Black Sea species also include mackerel, bonito and tuna among the so-called pelagic fish – those which swim on or near the surface over deeper waters – and a number of flatfish. Some of them are unique to the Black Sea, for example *Alosa pontica pontica*, a kind of shad. (By the way, the Soviet cookery book favoured by Stalin, *The Book of Tasty and Healthful Foods*, speaks of this fish in a proprietorial way as the 'Kerch herring' and extols its virtues along with other products of the Soviet Union. Maybe Stalin really thought that it could be caught only in Soviet waters.) But most are found in the Mediterranean too, and also of course in the Bosphorus, to which I now come.

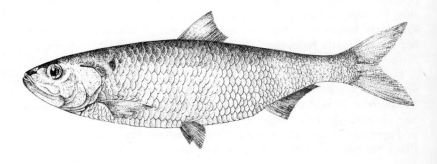

The Bosphorus, linking the Black Sea to the Sea of Marmora, normally has a surface current, southwards, of 3 or 4 knots. This is because, as we have seen, there is a movement of water from the one sea to the other. This main current is so strong that the Bosphorus has been compared to a great river. But the main current is not the only one. It sets up counter-currents, running north, close to the banks. And below the surface there is a northerly current. The water in this northerly current does not pass into the Black Sea, or anyway not much of it, but is swept upwards by a threshold at the northern end of the Bosphorus and becomes part of the southward surface current. So it has little significance. However, it produces some curious effects. A fishing boat with nets lowered may find that the pull of the deep-down northerly current on the nets is so strong that the boat itself is propelled northwards although the surface water in which the boat is riding is travelling south!

It also seems that certain currents have posed serious problems for the Bosphorus crabs in some places, since these find it almost impossible to make their sideways progress against the force of the current where it is strongest, for example round a promontory. One such, by Arnavutköy (the 'Albanian village'), is called the Cape of the Current, and since classical times the tale has been told that crabs would come out of the water and cross the promontory on the rocks, across which they gradually wore down a path, which the Greek writer Aelian declared that he had seen with his own eyes.

What with all these currents, and stormy weather, the Bosphorus can be a dangerous stretch of water. Writing of the northern entrance, Byron penned these lines:

> *There's not a sea the passenger e'er pukes in*
> *Turns up more dangerous breakers than the Euxine.*

And in the villages along the shores of the Bosphorus many tales are told of how people were asleep in their villa on the edge of a cliff and were suddenly awakened by a crash, to find that the prow of a cargo ship had penetrated their wall; or had just set the table for lunch on the verandah when the yard-arm of a passing schooner, swept too close by the treacherous currents, neatly brushed everything off it.

The visible traffic through the Bosphorus consists of ships and ferries. The traffic of fish is largely unseen, although it is reflected in the fish market. Forty or fifty years ago the main migrations of fish southwards from the Black Sea would start around late October or November, when the weather and water temperature grew cooler. According to Mr

Whittall, who made careful observations over half a century, there was a noticeable change in the period from 1940 to 1970. The cold came later and later, until it was starting in January rather than November. The migrations of the fish changed correspondingly. It seemed clear that the signal for the migration was a drop in the temperature, and that the fish were travelling south – not necessarily very far – to find warmer waters in which to spawn, so that changes in the climate affected their timetables.

What fish are these migrants? Here are some of the more important.

Sardelya, the sardine, migrates south – and onwards through the Marmora and the Dardanelles – towards the end of the year, and comes back to the Black Sea, after spawning, in the spring.

Hamsi, the anchovy, follows a similar pattern, although a few weeks behind the sardine. Small though it is, it ranks high among fish so far as the Turkish people are concerned, arousing remarkably intense feelings. These have found expression in folk poems, one of which reads in part:

> *A flourish of trumpets should sign its coming,*
> *To the men of Trabzon it's a hero.*
> *A basketful is enough to give blood to the feeble,*
> *All the people in the world hear its call.*

Lüfer, the bluefish, is another species about which Turkish people are keenly discriminating. The extent of their interest is shown by the fact that there are five different names for this fish, according to its size. (Indeed I have heard people talk about the lüfer as though it was special to Turkish waters. It may be special *in* Turkish waters, or anyway in Turkish kitchens, but it is by no means special *to* them. On the contrary, it is an intercontinental fish, pervading not only the Mediterranean but also both sides of the Atlantic. A parallel phenomenon is observable in North America, where fishermen who go out after the 'blues' find it hard to credit that the fish is known anywhere else.) The southward migration of the lüfer takes place towards the end of the year. Mr Whittall observed that in some years great banks of them would form off the Princes Islands near Istanbul, in early January, and there would be a glut in the market. But if they had not been caught they would press on through the Marmora and into the Mediterranean, and only return in May. Fishing for the lüfer is carried out in the Bosphorus itself with the aid of large lamps, at night, and the early winter, during the southward migration, is the best period.

Iskumru and *kolyoz*, the regular Atlantic mackerel and the chub mackerel, behave in much the same way, and *istavrid*, or horse mackerel, a less well favoured migrant, follows a similar pattern. (Istavrid is a fish for which the Greeks nourish a passion, echoed rather faintly in Turkey and not at all in some other countries.)

Palamut, the bonito, is related to the mackerel family, but larger. Its seasonal migrations are comparable. But when we move one size further up the scale, to the tuna family, we find different behaviour. The tuna migrates north into the Black Sea for summer spawning, and comes south again in the autumn and winter. These fish pass the Golden Horn in great numbers on their way north; indeed Pliny believed that the name Golden Horn had been given because of their abundance. It is certainly true that they appear on many Byzantine coins.

There is another large fish, *kılıç*, the swordfish, which behaves likewise. It is likely to be on its way north through the Bosphorus in the spring, and comes back down in August. A seventeenth-century historian of Istanbul, Evliya Celebi, has given a description of how swordfish were caught at the village of Beykoz (the name means 'Prince's walnut') and at certain other places along the shores of the Bosphorus.

There is a *dalyan* or structure for the capture of swordfish; it is composed of five or six masts, on the highest of which sits a man who keeps a lookout for the fish that come in from the Black Sea. When he sees them approaching, he throws a stone into the sea in order to frighten them, wherein he succeeds so well that they all head for the harbour, where they expect to find security, but instead swim into the nets laid in wait for them. The nets being closed, at a signal from the lookout, the fishermen flock round to kill them without their being able to make any resistance with their swords. The fish if boiled with garlic and vineyard herbs is excellent.

Finally, so far as this short list is concerned, the famous Black Sea turbot, *kalkan*, the kind with large nail-like protuberances on its back, ventures into the Bosphorus, and more rarely as far down as the Marmora, in April and May.

Thus the pattern of fishy migrations varies considerably and at most seasons of the year at least one species is apt to be making its passage in one direction or another.

It remains to add that there are many species which exist in both the Black Sea and the Mediterranean, and no doubt in the Bosphorus too, but which do *not* perform migrations of the sort we have been considering, for the simple reason that they have no need to do so. Broadly speaking, these species fall into two groups. *Anadromous fish* go up rivers to spawn. By definition they do not need particularly salty water, so the ones which live in the Black Sea just go up local rivers. *Demersal,* or *bottom fish* are less affected by changes in water temperature (which occur at the surface more than deeper down) and do not therefore have to make a major move in order to spawn. These species include flatfish and a whole lot of more, or less, familiar fish which are brought up in trawls. Among them are the red mullet, of which there are two principal species in the Mediterranean, known in Turkish as *barbunya* and *tekir* (*Mullus barbatus* and *M surmuletus*). The former is established in the Black Sea, but in the form of a sub-species, *M b ponticus*; while the latter, in Hugh Whittall's words, 'just pokes its nose out of the northern end of the Bosphorus'. The two kinds are closely similar, although cooks usually prefer tekir, and it is remarkable that one should have adapted to life in the Black Sea and the other not.

Sciaena umbra (Turkish *eşkina*) has two white balls in its head; its other names are *halili* and *degirmenci*, the latter meaning miller, the idea being that these otoliths, as they are called, resemble millers' grinding stones.

There are many famous, yet unpretentious, fish restaurants to be visited on the shores of the Bosphorus. At Kum Kapı there used to be one which was called 'The Dead Fish', until some spoilsport revealed to the owner that this name was not alluring to visitors, and it was changed. I do not believe that this caused an increase in trade. The old name, precisely because it was so inappropriate, had exercised a considerable attraction!

1984

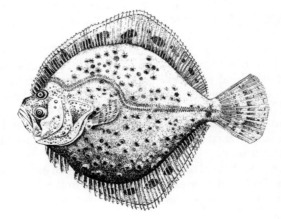

The Harlot of Marseilles

I know but one and I don't like her at all. I refer, of course, to the meretricious '*bouillabaisse*' which is served in tourist-trapping restaurants around the Old Port of Marseilles, and of which obnoxious echoes are to be found all round the world.

Why be steamed up over this steaming dish? Well, perhaps one shouldn't be; we all have to earn a living, don't we, and maybe exacting high prices from tourists for a tarted up version of what was once a simple fisherman's dish is a venial way of setting about the task. Why be purist, why harp on history, why swim against the tide? Meanings change and *bouillabaisse* is whatever people mean when they use the term, not what a bunch of other people long installed in their graves meant when they used it.

Musing one day along these tolerant and enlightened lines, I came upon an item which sharply restored my rebellious feelings on the subject. There is a book, appropriately called *An Odd Volume of Cookery*, by Louise Lane Morrisey and Marion Lane Sweeney. It was published by the otherwise reputable firm of Houghton Mifflin in Boston in 1949. In it there is a recipe for bouillabaisse. This begins: 'Put one can tomato soup and one can pea soup in top of double boiler and heat.' The recipe contains no fish, no herbs and no olive oil.

This is going too far.

So I decided to recall the history of the dish and seek to set some suitable boundaries to the use of its name; an enterprise which brought some disconcerting surprises.

All round the Mediterranean, but particularly on its south European coast, fishermen have been at work since antiquity, and there is plenty of evidence for the natural supposition that they had their various ways of supping off the day's catch, especially that part of it which had least value in the market.

It was from this background that various Mediterranean fish soup/stew dishes such as the Greek *kakavía*, the Catalan *suquet* and the Provençal bouillabaisse evolved.

However, to trace the evolution of bouillabaisse requires at least a

working definition of what it is. Here are its distinguishing characteristics, as perceived by me, and more or less as I described them in
Mediterranean Seafood.

- the dish requires a wide variety of fish, including *rascasse*, some fish
  with firm flesh (to be eaten) and some little ones (to disintegrate into
  the broth), and maybe some inexpensive crustaceans (small crabs,
  cigales de mer, etc.);
- onions, garlic, tomatoes, parsley are always used – and saffron too
  (though this item is costly);
- the liquid used consists of water (some white wine is optional) and
  olive oil, a mixture which must be boiled rapidly;
- the fish (i.e. the ones to be eaten, not the ones which disintegrate) are
  served separately from the broth, which is poured over pieces of
  toasted bread (of which there is a special sort at Marseilles for the
  purpose).

The early French cookery books were more concerned with dishes
suitable for the well-to-do than with the homely fare of fishermen; and
writing about the regional dishes of the south of France did not really
start until the nineteenth century. So I was not surprised to find that
descriptions of the dish in cookery books do not date further back.
Indeed, it is probably safe to say that the first relevant published recipe is
that given by Jourdain Le Cointe in his *La Cuisine de Santé*.* This
recipe, along with much other pertinent information, was kindly
brought to my attention by Philip and Mary Hyman. It is not for
'bouillabaisse', but represents a sort of proto-bouillabaisse. Le Cointe
called it '*Matellotte du Poisson*', and it reads as follows, in translation:

> Most of the fishermen of the coast of Languedoc and Provence,
> when they have removed from their nets all the large fish destined
> for sale, are wont to use the fry, gobies, and other little fish to
> make excellent and renowned 'matelottes'.
>
> On the very bank of the river where the fishermen disembark,
> their wives light a clear fire and place on it a small cauldron half
> full of good wine and an equal quantity of fresh water. They
> throw in small white onions, chopped parsley, bay leaves, a large
> clove of garlic, salt, pepper, nutmeg, and sometimes a couple of
> spoonfuls of olive oil. They boil all this together and, when their
> husbands arrive, they empty all the little fish from the nets into the
> boiling liquid; then continue cooking for half an hour, checking

* Paris, 1790, Vol. 3.

that the fish are only just covered by the wine and that the amount of broth is not too great. When the fish are cooked, they take them out, reduce the sauce and pour it over their 'matelotte', which is really good, delicate in flavour and wholesome.

This is recognisable, but there was no tomato (then a rarity, certainly not something which fishermen's wives would have had to hand); no saffron (expensive); the olive oil (also expensive at that time) is optional; and the cooking of the very small fish seems unduly long. We are not quite there yet; and we haven't yet met the name bouillabaisse.

Indeed, according to *Le Petit Robert*, the best French dictionary for this purpose, the first recorded use of the term bouillabaisse in print was nearly fifty years later, in 1837. In fact, they appear to have overlooked *Le Cuisinier Durand* (1830), which gave two recipes under that name. Here is one of them in translation.

BOUIL-ABAISSE A LA MARSEILLAISE

Put a little chopped onion in a casserole with a little olive oil and leave it on the fire for a moment. Next, cut into slices sea-fish such as the moray eel, rascasse, sea bass, whiting, langouste, etc. Add these to the casserole together with a little parsley and a little garlic, both well chopped; a slice of lemon; a tomato cut into pieces, from which you have squeezed the water and seeds. Season with salt and pepper, and a little saffron. Sprinkle good olive oil over it, then moisten it with a glass of dry white wine mixed with some fish broth (made with the heads of your fish, if you don't have some to hand already). The liquid should completely cover the fish.

Set this to cook on a high heat and, when the liquid is reduced by three-quarters, pour it out on to a concave platter, wherein you have already set out fairly thick slices of day-old bread.

The fish should be served separately.

Revelation One. The first known recipe advises using sea bass and langouste, high-class and expensive items characteristic of what I deemed to be the harlot version.

Durand's recipe was followed quite quickly by another, in *Le Cuisinier Méridionale* (1839, anonymous). This goes as follows – often echoing Durand, but with important differences:

BOUILLABAISSE A LA MARSEILLAISE

Cut your fish into slices half an inch (1.3 cm) thick.

Cook separately the debris, such as heads, tails, bones, in a pot with a clove of garlic, an onion with a clove stuck in it, a bouquet of herbs and a little *petit salé*; then strain the resulting broth, which will serve as the liquid you need.

Put olive oil and chopped onion in a casserole, [heat and] allow the onion to take colour for a moment, then put in the slices of fish with parsley and garlic, both chopped; a slice of lemon, pips removed; and a de-seeded tomato. Season, but with little salt if you think that the broth you have made will be salty enough. Add a pinch of saffron and olive oil. Add white wine mixed with the prepared broth so as to cover the fish entirely. Cook over a high heat and, when the liquid is reduced, pour it over slices of fresh bread and serve the fish separately.

All kinds of fish can be used to make bouillabaisse. Using sea-fish improves it. Nonetheless, the bouillabaisse acquires a more delicate flavour if a mixture of sea-fish and freshwater-fish is used. If only the latter are used, the dish will have a stronger taste.

The sea-fish which are appropriate are sea bass, whiting, langouste, turbot, mackerel, rascasse, moray eel, sole, etc. The freshwater-fish are: grey mullet, barbel, pike, carp, crayfish, eel, perch, trout, etc.

Revelation Two. One of the earliest recipes advises using at least some freshwater-fish.

It is commonly said that when a recipe appears in print it has already been in existence for some time. This is a logical notion, and can often be shown to be correct. But in this instance it may be true in one sense (people were already making a dish like those described in the above two recipes) but not in another (such a dish already existed under the name bouillabaisse). The fact is that there seems to be no earlier mention of bouillabaisse. And it is surely significant that when the first Provençal restaurant in Paris, Les Frères Provençaux, opened in the early years of the nineteenth century, there was no listing of bouillabaisse on its menu. Where did the name come from?

At this point, I decided to see whether the derivation of the name offered any clues about the origin of the dish. So we now descend into the etymological arena, where swords have been glinting in endless strife since the question was first considered.

The warring etymologists agree that the word comes from or at least corresponds to the Provençal *bouiabaisso*. What, then, did that mean? There are three main views:

1 *Le Petit Robert*. The word is a corruption of *bouillepeis*, or *bouillir* and *peis*, thus meaning 'boil the fish'. This makes perfectly good sense; everyone (except Morrisey and Sweeney!) agrees that the dish involves the boiling of fish.

2 Littré, *Dictionnaire de la Langue Française* (1883, Vol. 1). The expression should be interpreted as *bouillon abaissé*, literally 'broth lowered', i.e. the level of the broth is lowered by evaporation during cooking – or, as we would say, it is 'reduced'.

3 *Le Grand Dictionnaire Universel du XIX Siècle* (Larousse, 1878, Vol. 2). This work also separates the term into *bouillon* and *abaisser* ('boiling: lower'), but explains that the meaning is that the heat is lowered (by removing the pot from the fire) once the liquid comes to the boil, since (it adds) just a moment's boiling is enough to cook the fish. An unorthodox idea.

But we should not consult dictionaries alone. We must also look in an erudite work, by '70 French doctors', called *Le Trésor de la Cuisine du Bassin Méditerranéen.** In this work we find yet another explanation:

4 The word splits into *bout*, meaning 'boils' and *abaissée*, meaning 'lowered down'; and the explanation is that the pot was lowered right down into the fire (to promote rapid boiling).

Take your choice. I would have opted for (1); but it seems highly unlikely that the Provençaux, who continue to the present time to write 'Boui-Abaisso', could have confused 'peis' with 'abaisso'. Of the others, (2) makes good sense; (3) doesn't; and (4) seems rather contrived and implausible.

So my conclusion was that the notion of boiling and reducing is what underlies the term.

However, the fine print examined during this little investigation uncovered a subsidiary battle: that between those who insist that the dish requires protracted rapid boiling and those who think that just a brief one suffices, or that it need not be rapid.

The reason for this point being disputed is, I think, confusion about what rapid boiling is meant to achieve. I have seen it said that it is necessary if you include crustaceans in the dish, since they take longer to

---

* The revised edition of this (*c.* 1930) had a preface by Prosper Montagné, who, after Alphonse Daudet, was a spearhead in the militant campaign to establish a Provençal cultural identity, including of course a culinary identity, which would be visible to the outside world, as it now is but used not to be.

cook through. But this would point to longer boiling, not to more rapid boiling. The usual reason given for the rapid boiling is that it is necessary to achieve the amalgamation of the oil and water (or oil, water and wine).

This took me, and takes us, into a new area of discussion: what exactly are the requirements for 'amalgamating' olive oil and water? Do they form an emulsion? If not, what can be meant by 'amalgamation'? If yes, is there an emulsifying agent at work, and if so what? Can vigorous, rapid boiling have anything to do with it?

Well . . . consulting the best authorities on emulsions (and in particular the best, Harold McGee, *On Food and Cookery*)* suggested to my mind that the thing would be impossible. Sorry, no bouillabaisse! High temperatures are fatal to emulsions. Vigorous movement may hinder rather than help. Anyway, there would have to be an emulsifying agent, and the proportion of water to oil would have to be within certain boundaries.

But I detected some gleams of hope, on the following lines:

- the rapid boiling would reduce the amount of water so that the proportion between it and the oil is compatible with an emulsion forming;
- the gelatin from the fish could act as an emulsifier; and
- this particular kind of emulsion (unlike some others) may be compatible with a high temperature and rapid motion.

But, could one count on the fish producing enough gelatin? In this connection, is there significance in the insistence in many recipes that the fish chosen should include, for example, eel of one sort or another, or angler-fish, all rich in gelatin?

I pondered all this, and was thinking that an experiment was called for; but we only had extra virgin olive oil in the house and if I was found boiling some of that vigorously with a lot of water I might be in trouble.

Fortunately I had been continuing to share my thoughts with the Hymans in Paris, and Mary Hyman was meanwhile going right ahead and doing what I shrank from doing. She reported: 'I put a fair amount of water and some olive oil in a pot and brought it to a rapid boil. At first, as might be expected, the oil simply sat on top of the water, but it then began to foam up, and formed a thick, pale yellow, bubbly layer, through which the furiously boiling water could still be seen underneath. I allowed the mixture to boil until I could see almost no more

* New York, 1984; London, 1986.

unmixed water, then removed from the heat. I lightly whisked this thick foam, mainly to make the bubbles smaller, and the result was for all the world like a *beurre blanc*! If allowed to sit, it loses the greater part of the bubbles and looks more or less clear, but a flick of a whisk makes it opaque again and, in any case, it is definitely thicker than oil and definitely an emulsion.'

She went on to say that, with the added presence of bits of gelatinous fish, such a water–oil emulsion would doubtless be of a most pleasant, creamy consistency even without whisking.

Revelation Three. We really are creating an emulsion, and we know why the rapid-boiling school is correct.

At this point I returned to the 70 doctors, hoping to find support for my anti-harlot, use-inexpensive-fish view. Of the five doctors who gave recipes for bouillabaisse, Dr Magnan was the most comforting, as these extracts from his recipe show:

> The fish to be used are: *lei peis de roco*, rockfish with firm flesh, notably the rascasse (a sine qua non), wrasse, gurnard, angler-fish, John Dory, moray eel, and five of the little crabs called *favouilles* [*Carcinus mediterraneus*] at Marseilles and Toulon.
>
> Use also small fish such as the rainbow wrasse and small members of the sea bream family which, being of smaller size, will be crushed after the cooking and, after being passed through a *tamis*, will serve to bind the sauce. . . .
>
> There you have the Provençal dish which enjoys a universal reputation. Together with the national anthem, it has carried the fame of Marseilles to all parts. One should not allow its composition to be changed. If one were graciously to agree to the inclusion of, say, whiting or *langouste*, one would thereby shatter a secular institution and fall into culinary anarchy, which is the worst kind of anarchy.
>
> All the same, I accept a modification which consists of adding to the fish a crustacean which one finds in the summer and which the experts call *Scyllarus arctus* and the public *cigales de mer*. This creature is not much more than 15 cm long, so it has to be caught when fully adult. It has a special aroma – not at all a dominant or strong smell. It is modest and discreet and has been adopted by a number of gourmets who appreciate *fruits de mer*. Since it is only introduced for the sake of its aroma, two or three are sufficient if the bouillabaisse is being made for five people. They go into the pot at the same time as the rascasses, of which there must be at least two.

Admirable! However, surveying the by now rapidly thickening dossier of evidence from the Hymans, and refreshing my memory about the contents of what are probably the two best-known cookbooks of Provence, I found new cause for disquiet. Reboul (*La Cuisinière Provençale*, 1895) distinguishes between the true bouillabaisse (of Marseilles) and others, but allows that use of the name for the latter is not improper, and gives recipes for several, including *Bouillabaisse Borgne*, in which there are no fish, but pride of place is taken by potatoes and eggs! And Escudier (*La Cuisine Provençale et Niçoise*, 1953) devotes a whole chapter to bouillabaisses, including *Bouillabaisse aux Epinards*, which also has no fish.

Revelation Four. My incredulous disdain for the Morrisey/Sweeney recipe was exaggerated. The ladies could cite Reboul and Escudier to show that their recipe, although way out, is not quite beyond the pale.

So where did all this activity leave me? I had a better understanding of bouillabaisse. My feeling that the simple inexpensive version is the most appropriate was still intact. But the evidence of history had largely restored my earlier tolerant attitude towards deviations. When next in Marseilles I may even be tempted by harlotry and have the version with langouste . . .

Meanwhile, for the benefit of any readers who have got this far, and who may be thinking that they fancy making the dish but still haven't had a reasonably detailed and fully recommended recipe, I give my favourite. It is not from a cookbook, and is not laid out in professional cookbook style. But its credentials are excellent. It was added, in a short appendix of recipes, to a book which is essentially about fish and fishing in the Mediterranean: *Les Pêches d'Amateurs* (1961) by Professor Jean Euzière, with a preface by Professor J. M. Pérès, then director of the illustrious marine research station at Endoume near Marseilles. It has the advantage of incorporating instructions for making *rouille*, a frequent but not invariable accompaniment of bouillabaisse, which I have not so far mentioned.

BOUILLABAISSE

This can be prepared in various ways, but always with fish which are very fresh, and using the largest possible number of species, especially of rockfish. The fish traditionally used are:

RASCASSES [the large red one called *chapon* and others are suggested];

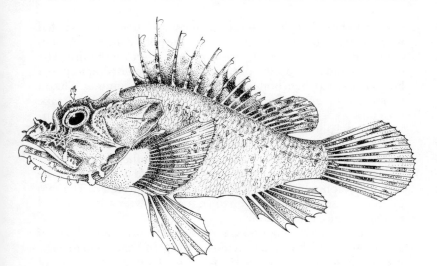

STAR-GAZER [*Uranoscopus scaber*, locally called *rat*];
CONGER EEL and MORAY EEL;
ANGLER-FISH;
WRASSES [*tourdre vert* or *tourdre blanc*, *Labrus turda* and *L. merula* respectively; also *serre*, *L. viridis* or *L. festivus*; and *séné* or *cocotte*, *L. mixtus*; and the smaller species called *girelles*];
SERRAN [*Serranus hepatus*] and its relations:
GURNARDS;
etcetera.

To these should be added some crustaceans, such as langouste, Norway lobster, *cigales de mer*, crabs. Old fishermen also add *escargots de mer* [such as top-shells or periwinkles] sea anemones, and *tomates de mer*.

The various ways of preparing bouillabaisse are all derived from the archetype of the dish, which the old fishermen used to prepare on the beaches of their creeks with a fire of dead wood. This is the most ancient and the simplest method, and I give the recipe for it first.

It is got ready by assembling in the pot, an hour or two before the time for cooking, the fish (scaled and gutted), the crustaceans, the *escargots de mer*, potatoes (peeled and cut into large pieces or into slices 1 cm thick), olive oil, finely chopped onion, several cloves of garlic (crushed), a bouquet garni and pepper. All this is stirred from time to time.

Half an hour before the meal, a lively wood fire is set going, fed with small branches. Water is added to the pot – a little more than is needed to cover everything – and the pot set on the fire. The flames should envelop the pot, to bring the contents rapidly to a boil and to keep them boiling violently for twenty minutes. The oil will then form an emulsion with the water, and the broth will take on a milky appearance. Therein lies the secret of the preparation.

When the potatoes are cooked, remove the pot from the fire and add saffron. Then pour the broth on to slices of bread arranged on a platter, and put the fish and potatoes on another.

The slices of bread may be toasted and rubbed with garlic, or be stale bread on which grated cheese has been sprinkled. The two platters are served at the same time, together with a sauce called *rouille* because of its colour.

To prepare *rouille*, pound vigorously in a mortar two cloves of garlic (from which you have removed the germ) and a red pepper, previously soaked. Add a little soaked breadcrumb, a few bits of the cooked potato from the bouillabaisse, and an egg-yolk. When all is well pounded, add olive oil slowly, stirring, to finish it, just as you would if making an aïoli.

In the preparation of a bouillabaisse in this manner, only the fish with firm flesh, such as conger, moray, rascasse, gurnard, remain whole; the fish with soft flesh such as the wrasses [etc.] disintegrate and give the broth an excellent flavour.

It is in order to make better use of the fish that some people only introduce those with soft flesh five minutes before cooking is complete. This method permits serving them whole, but the broth will have less flavour.

The above instructions do not call for browning anything. It is possible to make a bouillabaisse with browned onion, but in my view this procedure results in the loss of much of the savour of the dish.

1988

Part Six
Asia

The Traditions of Laos

'Try one of these,' said the beautiful princess. Having announced to her my interest in Lao foods and cookery, I had to suppress the suspicious expression with which I would otherwise have regarded the platter, and do as invited. 'Delicious.'

'Yes, they're deep-fried grasshoppers. And their nutritional value is quite high.'

'Oh, really? That's good.' So saying, I casually manœuvred myself in the direction of a platter of fried chicken. The piece I picked up was a gizzard, and it brought a foot with it, which I vainly tried to shake off with seemingly casual motions of the wrist. The kind Princess Marina had followed me. 'Ah,' said she, 'you know which are the best parts of the chicken.'

The scene was the royal palace; the occasion, a reception given by His (then) Majesty the King, shortly after my arrival in Laos about ten years ago. And the result was that I had a very thorough introduction to Lao dining. One part of the lesson that only sank in later was that the food served in the palace was basically very much the same as that which ordinary Lao would prepare in their homes for special occasions. One exception was the rare 'Lao caviar' from the giant (500 lb, 227 kg) catfish of the Mekong. This was reserved for royalty.

The most striking differences in Lao diets are not found between the rich and the poor but among different parts of the country; and even these are not very remarkable. What is remarkable is that a distinctive cuisine exists in this small country surrounded by its larger and numerous neighbours: China, Vietnam, Cambodia, Thailand and Burma. One might think that little Laos would be no more in the world of cookery than a confused reflection of the cuisines on the other side of her five frontiers. But communications are poor, for geographical reasons (the mountainous area on the Chinese–Laotian frontier is a mysterious no-man's-land) or political ones. The only interchange that involves import or export of food is between Laos and Thailand, and the parts of Thailand which border on Laos are anyway inhabited by ethnic Lao who represent a sort of gastronomic transition between the two countries. Laos, moreover, differs from all her neighbours in having no coastline and in being a country which is still not merely undeveloped but which has remote mountain jungles that are to a large extent unexplored.

There are a number of characteristics of Lao cookery and eating habits which, although not all uniquely Laotian, combine to make the cuisine of the Lao people truly distinctive.

The first concerns rice, the staple food. There are other Asian countries where sticky or glutinous rice is appreciated, but Laos is the place where it is most markedly preferred. The Lao do eat non-sticky rice too, but the typical Lao meal will certainly include a woven basketful of sticky rice, which is taken little by little with the fingers, kneaded slightly, and used as a 'pusher' or for sopping up juices. It replaces bread for the Lao and also to some extent tableware. Lao do not use chopsticks, indeed, often enough nothing but the fingers, sticky rice and salad leaves. They use salad leaves to wrap up mouthfuls of mixed ingredients, and they do it very neatly. So it is in Thailand and Malaysia, but the practice is most noticeable in Laos.

Though they use a sauce of small salted fermented fish, which is common to other South-East Asian countries (in Thailand it is called *nam pla*, in Vietnam, *nuoc mam*, see page 223), they also have a fish sauce more specific to Laos and northern Thailand called *padek*. This sauce contains pieces of fermented fish as well as rice husks. It has a very strong smell indeed, and the Lao keep their large earthenware jars of padek on a verandah or some such airy place outside the house. I have asked Lao friends in London whether there is any other product they would regard as an acceptable substitute. They agree that Swedish *surströmming* (fermented herring, also strong smelling, so much so that Swedes will tell you that a bird flying over a freshly opened barrel of the stuff will drop dead to the ground) does very well despite the absence of rice husks. Rather more to my surprise, they find our regular canned anchovies satisfactory.

What other flavourings do the Lao use? Herbs are not much in evidence. Coriander is popular, and you see mint, basil and occasionally dill. But the Lao are much more apt to add lemon grass (also known as citronella), which is a large grasslike plant which thrives like a weed in those countries lucky enough to have the right climate. It has a strong and convincing lemon flavour. The other principal flavours are those of ginger and the more delicate galingale. (The latter, whose name is spelled in various ways, was a popular ingredient in medieval English dishes. As with ginger, which it looks like, the rhizome is the part normally used, either fresh or dried.) The curries of India and Malaysia and Indonesia have not made any noticeable impact on Lao cuisine. But

I might add one oddity: one used to see cannabis in the markets. When I asked about this, I was told that it was for adding to soups. Ah, I thought, a likely tale! However, it was true – an old Lao custom.

Lao cooking methods and equipment are very simple. Cooks can improvise little ovens and bake small cakes, for example, but they usually confine themselves to simmering, frying and barbecuing. A Lao barbecue is an exciting affair. I remember once being present, with the then Prime Minister Prince Souvanna Phouma, at the annual occasion when he allowed the local population the rare opportunity of plunging into one of the largest fish ponds on his country estate to catch what they could. The pond, already murky, was swiftly transformed into an opaque brown mass of turbulent water, in which golden bodies and silver fish threshed about in what seemed like complete confusion. However, all was sorted out within an hour and the lucky fishermen proceeded to light fires, impale their fish on stakes, and plant these in the ground so that the fish were held at an angle of about fifty degrees over the fire. It was a condition of the Prime Ministerial concession that a proportion of the catch be reserved for consumption by his guests. So, while he sat benignly under a canopy, puffing at his usual Havana cigar, we all fell to and devoured our share of the fish, certain of one thing – that it was freshly caught.

The simplicity of the actual cooking equipment is more than compensated for by the elaborate equipment for preparing foods, and the time the Lao will devote to the process. They use pestles and mortars of various sizes, including giants which are set on strong wooden pillars outside village houses and take several kilos of, say, chilli peppers at a time; and a whole armoury of chopping knives, large and small but mostly large (one may see a Lao woman using what we would call a meat cleaver to chop up spring onions). Great virtuosity is displayed in making food into packets for steaming or broiling; the cooks wrap them in pieces of banana leaf secured with slivers of bamboo or tied with thin 'strings' of rattan. Time spent on this kind of work is not grudged. On the contrary, it is an enjoyable activity, especially if carried out in groups, a procedure to which the Lao 'extended family' is well adapted.

Finally, a Lao meal is served with gracious simplicity. It is usual to lay out all the main dishes and the soup (there is always a soup) at once, together with the greens, and let people help themselves. They do so in accordance with various rules about 'elders first' and so on, but this is all taken for granted so much that a stranger would be unaware of any structure in the process (and would be forgiven for breaking any unwritten rules, for the Lao by nature are extremely tolerant).

Wherever possible, a Lao cook will prepare more food than is needed, especially if guests are present, since it is considered a slight on the host's reputation if everything is eaten up. This, however, rarely happens, since it would be considered bad manners for a guest to consume one hundred per cent of what was served to him. (With so much attention to good manners, everyone is bound to win!) Though the idea of separate courses is absent, an exception is made for desserts, which will be served last. The Lao themselves tend to finish their meals with fresh fruit, and play down the role of desserts.

1982

More Bell-flower Root, Please

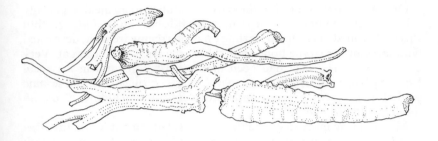

There is no lack of places to eat in Seoul, but places where a non-Korean can both eat Korean and find out what he is eating are relatively few. One such is the Korean restaurant in the Shilla Hotel. It is genuine, and most of the diners are Korean, but there is a menu in English, and the chopsticks can be discreetly supplemented with cutlery. I found that a couple of meals there tuned me in admirably.

You can forget bread in Korea; but you will find that what they do with rice (theirs is relatively glutinous, as in Japan), noodles and pancakes makes a memorable substitute. Korean foods and cooking techniques show, naturally, considerable resemblance to those of north China to the west and Japan to the east, but they are still distinctive and this shows in the inventive fillings of pancakes as much as in anything else. They like to cook with vegetable oil, by the way, and sesame oil is their favourite.

They put a lot of emphasis on soups, great brimming bowls with surprising mixtures of ingredients, such as chrysanthemum leaves with thin diamonds of cooked egg and sliced matsutake mushroom. (In their choice of mushrooms the Koreans resemble the Japanese more than the Chinese. When I was there, the Shilla had a special mushroom menu, featuring Japanese favourites.)

Koreans like to have just about all the dishes on the table together, so you can eat the dishes in much the same order as you would western food. I recommend starting with pine-nut porridge. It is smooth, white, delicious; and I can't think why I haven't met it in Europe and America (perhaps it is a question of cost). And finish with either a Korean apple (better than the pears), or my mystery bowlful of pale pink water (?) with two slices of (?) pickled walnut in it; this had the Shilla waitress shilly-shallying over the name – 'Korean dessert' was all she could manage in the end – and it was only later that I identified the dish as made with dried persimmons. The taste was great and the aroma most refreshing.

One needs something refreshing to end a full Korean meal, especially if it has included one of their famous beef dishes. I took *bulgogi*: thin slices of broiled beef served sizzling on an earthenware dish, decorated with large pieces of the bone from which the meat had been cut. Very good indeed. The beef had been marinated beforehand in a typical Korean preparation of soy sauce, garlic, sugar, spring onion and sesame seed. But beef comes in countless other ways, including *p'yonyuk* (boiled) and *yuk p'o* (dried).

Myself, I lean more to vegetables, fruits, salads, and it was in this area that I found the real high spot of the meal: pickled bell-flower root with red pepper threads. Months later, I established what the root was (*Campanula rapunculus*) and that it grows elsewhere too. But only the Koreans seem to have 'discovered' it. It is like a super-salsify, firm but delicate, its pale cream colour and subtle flavour highlighted by the amazingly fine threads of red pepper. This was what I asked for more of, and it came with a smile – Koreans are pleased if you like it.

Koreans are also, of course, pleased if you like *kim'chi*, the pickled cabbage (or oriental radish or cucumber – it isn't always cabbage) which is the one Korean dish which has got into the international vocabulary. It is spicy and hot, and the liberal use of chilli pepper in it reminds you that this is Korea, not Japan or north China. You don't ask for it, it just comes, and it is fine in its way, but not a revelation like bell-flower root.

I am told that Korean beer is good, but the standard beverage with a meal is *bori cha*, barley 'tea' made with water and toasted barley. Koreans have never acquired the habit of drinking real tea. They will tell you that others, like the Chinese and Japanese, had to take to tea because they had no pure water, whereas in Korea the water is as pure as water can be.

Korean cuisine has gradually been making its presence felt around the world. I had the first of my real Korean meals in Vientiane, Laos, in 1973, and have since enjoyed them in London, New York, Paris, Seoul,

Taipeh and – of course – Los Angeles. I say 'of course' because Los Angeles has such a large and organised Korean community that their part of it is known as Little Korea. There are numerous Korean stores, displaying the full range of Korean foods, and about forty Korean restaurants in the area around Western and Wilshire. They are probably all good; it is rare, perhaps unknown, for a Korean restaurant to offer anything but good food and good value.

1985

Plum Meal

A revolution in Taiwan, encouraged by the government? Yes. I recently saw, in the bookshops of Taipei, ample evidence of this phenomenon, which is occurring in the culinary rather than the political domain.

The Recipe of Plum Meal. Every shop had this title. The five English words on the dust jacket, everything else in Chinese. An enigma to me. Could they be milling dried plums into some sort of additive to bread flour? Had someone mistranslated Plum Pudding? Or was it a piece of obsolete American slang (this recipe or meal is 'a real plum')? I sought help from tiny Taiwanese Mimi who, with her giant German husband Thomas, was guiding me around.

The explanation was simple. The government thought that too much time and effort were going into the preparation of elaborate traditional meals with many dishes. They had decided that five was enough. The new style was symbolised by the five-petalled plum flower, which is also the national emblem of Taiwan. A Plum Meal is one composed of five dishes only, and the book offers numerous quintets of recipes suitable for this purpose.

Meanwhile, so far as I could see, most eating in Taiwan is still done in the streets, from the stalls which cluster everywhere. The government campaign is directed at an audience largely invisible to the visitor. The one person whom I observed buying the Plum Meal book had the air of someone who was planning to upgrade rather than downgrade the fare in her home.

Food at the stalls is usually a one-dish affair, since the stalls are specialised (like the snake stall I visited, with dozens of strong cages containing live snakes, hooks on which the chef impales them prior to slaughtering and flaying, and big pots in which a variety of snake soups are made for curing ailments as well as for gastronomic pleasure). If one wants a second dish, as one might after having snake soup, one goes to a second stall. But the helpings are large, and one dish is usually enough; or more than enough, as I found at the stall called 'Sanshi Lau Li Dou Sha Mien', number 206 in the South Gate Market in Taipei.

This is quite a famous stall, where the food is typical of *Sanshi* province on the mainland: a region where wheat, not rice, is the staple.

Lau Li is 'old Li', the owner. *Dou Sha Mien* means knife-shaving-noodles. The person who shaves the noodles, with an unusual horse-shoe-shaped cutter made by Mr Li himself, is Ms Shu, and she has been doing it for eighteen years, of which four were spent as an apprentice. Her dough is made with only wheat flour and warm water. Folded over and pressed into a long roll, which is held up in the left hand, it is then sliced at dazzling speed with the right hand into long thin strips. These are cooked in a huge wok, big enough to cope with eighteen large helpings a time. The water in which the noodles are cooked is served as 'plain noodle soup', and is faintly milky and sweetish.

I had a bowl of the soup before tackling my mound of noodles, which were accompanied by four side dishes: 'delicious pork jelly', soya bean sauce, sesame oil and vinegar. The noodles were very good, but I began to falter when I was still some way short of finishing. Mimi kept right on, and Ms Shu was watching, so I had to make it to the end, but that was definitely that. No scope for a visit to one of the dessert stalls.

As I left, I passed a bookshop displaying 'Plum Meal'. My goodness, thought I, if this is how One-Dish Davidson feels after his light lunch, what sort of people are those for whom five dishes represent a kind of abstinence? They can't all be as big as Thomas, since he towers above the crowds in the street and indeed constantly attracts public comment on his size.

Such musings simply reflected my inadequate knowledge of eating patterns. That very evening I had a near-Plum Meal in the home of a Taiwanese artist: four dishes, and no trouble at all, because it was self-help and you took just what you felt like eating.

I began to see light; not all eating is done in the street, the Plum Meal publicists have their sights on meals in the home, and these are very different from stall fare. But one question gives way to another. The artist's wife had asked me into her kitchen to watch the cooking, and I saw that she had but two Calor gas burners with which to operate. Mimi told me later that that was standard, and that anything more elaborate, like a third burner or an oven, would be highly unusual. Now why in the world would one have to preach to people with only two gas burners the desirability of not preparing more than five dishes?

1985

Taking Coffee Seriously

Andreas, my host, and his wife knew about my morning needs. 'Where shall we go for coffee?' he asked. 'How about Trois Bagues? They are very meticulous, always keep their coffee water at precisely 92°C.' 'Or George V?' said she. 'Such patient people. They take six and a half minutes to drip the water through the coffee, using a special cloth filter.' She added that their water is either boiling (100°C) or at 88°C, depending on the blend you choose.

I realised that at either of these places my attitude to water temperatures might strike the management as too casual, so I settled for Tom, where there is a choice of 21 coffees.

Puzzle, where was I? Nowadays, there can only be one answer: in Tokyo.

Making my way there via California, I had met a coffee broker in Los Angeles. He lamented that the Japanese were now bidding keenly for all the best coffees and driving prices up beyond his reach. A new trend, inconvenient for him. Why couldn't they stay with their teas?

In the 1950s and 1960s one could find coffee shops in Tokyo, called *miluku hawlu*, milk hall. But no one wrote home about the coffee served in them. The real vogue for coffee started about fifteen years ago, and in this short space of time the Japanese, with the sensitivity and thoroughness which they have for long applied to their tea ceremonies, have graduated to be the world's leading connoisseurs of coffee.

Having coffee in a *kissaten* or *kohi shoppu* in Tokyo is quite expensive, say £1 a cup, but worth it if you are really interested in coffee and not in a hurry. The establishment is likely to be small, if it is really serious, and intimate in atmosphere. Initial greetings and the arrival of iced water and a little rolled-up moist towel (hot in winter, cold in summer) are followed by a pause while you read the list of coffees available and decide which you want and what roast.

'Blue Mountain, Arabian Mocca, Colombia Supremo, Guatemala, Brazil Santos, Kilimanjaro . . .' So starts the list at Tom's, whose young proprietor, Mr Minoru Nagai, has been in business for eleven years. He likes to discuss the coffees with you, and insists that the mere list is not sufficiently informative. Guatemala, for example, is not just Guatemala; the water content of the beans will depend on age, conditions of transport and other factors, and your choice should be influenced by precise information on all this. You could spend an hour absorbing all the information you ought to have before deciding. Fortunately, you can keep your reputation as a connoisseur without losing an hour; ask for his 'Straight Coffee of the Day', thus complimenting his personal choice and also saving yourself a few cents.

The choice made, you wait while the coffee is prepared. Allow ten minutes for this; not wasted time because it is a joy to see the *mastah* (master of the house) or one of his chief lieutenants at work. Techniques vary from one place to another, or even within one place according to the nature of the coffee, but there is no difference in the finesse with which every stage and gesture is accomplished, right down to the delicate stirring of the froth. Your coffee costs a lot not only because it is the best but also on account of the time which is ungrudgingly devoted to making it.

Naturally, the cups themselves will also be superior. At Kohi-Ya your coffee may be served in any one of 500 cups, no two alike; an unusual feature which ups the price per cup to around £1.50 or more. But anyone who enjoys unique experiences is bound to try this one, especially as they roast their coffee beans over charcoal.

Or how about Tai-Bo in downtown Ayoama? There you are expected to state the exact temperature of the water, as well as how much water and what weight of coffee beans, thus, 'Mexico, medium roast, 93°C, 100 cc, 25 grams.' Tai-Bo, by the way, means 'great monk', but any monkish atmosphere is dissipated in the evening when they serve alcohol and there is good jazz.

The places mentioned so far are small and just right for serious coffee drinkers. But there are other kinds of coffee shop where the attention of the management is less sharply focused on coffee because other things are on offer, like something called 'pizza toast'; or *Kola-fuloto* (Cola float – just the familiar Coca Cola with a ball of ice cream floating on top, but a popular novelty with the Japanese young); or French and German pâtisseries which appeal to ladies who are on a shopping spree in town and want special refreshments in a special ambience. These places are often quite large and elegant, for example the Juchheim in the Ginza area.

Foreign names are common. The Japanese are in the grip of a real passion for American and European names, which are often bestowed and admired without any comprehension of what they mean. (The owners of bags inscribed 'Only Very Good' or 'Feed a Child' probably

think, if they give any thought to the matter, that these are the names of
New York couturiers.)

The way-out eateries have crazy titles, but the image of coffee
drinking is sedate and the coffee shops generally have unremarkable
names like Mozart, Renoir (a big chain), Cozy Corner or St Germain.
Even so, some are mildly startling, such as 'The Gland' (which must
have been the result of the oriental inability to pronounce an 'r').

Wherever you choose to go, your coffee will be brought to you with
the formula '*Omatase itashimashita*', which means 'I have kept you
waiting', which is certainly true in the $6\frac{1}{2}$-minute drip place. And your
cup will be set down so that the handle is on your left, leaving the right
hand free for stirring with the coffee spoon, as is correct.(Or is it? One
coffee house, Yoshidaya-Kohiten, is frequented by people who don't
use spoons at all and who constitute the 'No-Spoons-Club' – title in
English, of course.)

You never pay at the table, since food and drink are not to be
contaminated by money. (In the old days, members of the samurai class
never even touched money. Relics of this attitude are very much in
evidence, such as the practice of paying rent or other sums in an
envelope.) There are other points of etiquette too; but knowing how to
behave in a coffee shop is much easier than mastering the etiquette of
the special tea-houses, where the possibilities of making comical – and,
to the Japanese, disturbing – gaffes are numbingly numerous.

Cold coffee beverages are on hand as well as hot. The most remarkable is the 'Dutch coffee' served at Tom's. This is made by letting cold
water drip very, very slowly through a glass bulb filled with ground
coffee. The process takes six hours, and is done overnight. The result,
usually drunk cold, is astonishingly powerful, too much so for some. If
you flinch at the prospect, persuade your companion to order it, then
have a sip, but be content yourself with an 'Iced Junior' (iced café-au-
lait with cinnamon).

Is all this a temporary craze? If you go to Japan next year, or next
century, will you find that all these amazing coffee shops have vanished?
I think not. Traditions are strong in Japan, but that applies to new as
well as old ones. When the Japanese take a proper hold of something,
they keep hold. And they now have a very tight grip on the best coffees
in the world and on the art of serving them nearer to perfection than
anyone else.

1985

The Size of Things to Come

Pausing in Los Angeles en route from Miami to Seoul, I was struck again by the current fad for miniaturised foods. Tiny ears of corn, the spindly enokitake mushrooms, the smallest carrots you ever did see. (Sleight of hand here. In the kitchen of a famous restaurant I asked to see the wee things in their fresh state. The chef produced a carrot about 1 foot (30 cm) long and 2 inches (5 cm) thick, and showed me how with a sharp knife he could produce several dozen 'babies' a minute from it.) Anyway, I wondered whether additions would ever be made to the clutch of clichés typified by these table tots.

A month later, after Korea and having flown from Taipei to the Pescadores Islands (forty minutes, heading south-west over the China Sea towards the mainland), I had the answer: yes, and soon. In these windswept isles, where winds of 90 mph are commonplace and jets need a runway of but 100 metres to take off against it, a devoted Japanese expert, Mr Ochimizu, has finally succeeded in culturing commercial specimens of *Chlamys nobilis*, an engaging little scallop which comes in colours like primrose yellow, mauve and cherry red (and some new colours, for Mr Ochimizu has been busy crossbreeding). The scallops are marketed when they reach a size of nearly $1\frac{1}{2}$ inches (3.5 cm), and make delicious semi-mouthfuls. At this small size, they are eaten whole. And the shells can be sold separately, for costume jewellery, at $1 a pair.

Mr Ochimizu's work is his life. He came from Japan fifteen years ago, but his little house still looks as though he was shipwrecked yesterday. The bedroom furniture is typical: one bed; one attaché case containing, presumably, one change of clothes; one pair of binoculars hanging on the wall by the window which looks out to sea – that's it. He is amiable, and joins one in a cup of coffee, but his thoughts are patently elsewhere, on the freshly deposited spat.

Commercial know-how is provided by Mrs Che Te Jung, a very small and very lively Taiwanese businesswoman. Her private beach at Makung, with aquaculture tanks and offices alongside, hums with activity. It is she who raises two species of grouper, notably *Epinephelus akaara*, for the Hong Kong market, where they fetch sky-high prices

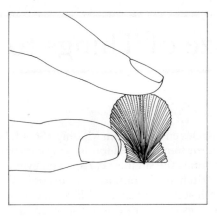

when alive and in good condition. And she has a production line for black pearls, a line which ends in a massive safe, for these are really valuable. But the bright little scallops are closest to her heart. In the States, she confided in me, in California, for example, there are restaurants where they serve everything small. I concurred. 'Wait till they see my scallops,' she laughed. 'They will be a sensation, something really new . . .'

I hope that these enthusiasts in Makung catch the tide before it ebbs. Food fashions, especially in America, grow as swiftly and luxuriantly as tropical plants, but they die away rapidly. Symptoms of impending death include a tendency to make fun of them. The quiche suffered in this way just before it was ushered out of the back door; and now the first signs are appearing of humour being brought to bear on miniaturised foods. A New Yorker who was recently in the Napa Valley, north of San Francisco, found material for satire on the supermarket shelves there. They were like the baby area of a hospital maternity ward, she reported, with criblike baskets alongside each other, each clearly identified by a label: 'Baby Carrot', 'Baby Dill', 'Baby Corn', and so on.

A small portent, perhaps, but not to be lightly disregarded. Could it be that when Mrs Jung crosses the Pacific with her samples of tiny scallops they will be greeted in California with hoots instead of hypes? If so, she may have to look for markets nearer home. Chinese emperors of the Ching dynasty arranged for *Chlamys nobilis* to be caught from the wild (no easy task) and served to them at dinner. On the assumption that this tradition has endured, although not practised for many centuries, it is easy to imagine exciting possibilities. And the dynamics of the situation are such that, if an accommodation between Taiwan and mainland China proves to be essential for the health of Makung's new industry, I even wonder whether . . .

1985

Hallo, Halo-Halo

Warmth of climate really does seem to generate warmth of behaviour. I moved south from Japan and Korea, through Taiwan, to the Philippines. Expecting to find brows heavily knotted over economic and political problems, I was taken aback by everyone's apparent good humour, and my first meal in a Manila restaurant was a revelation: people were laughing and singing, expressing their enjoyment and relishing the food and drink with an exuberance which struck me as unseemly until the mood infected me too. Thinking back to Japanese restaurants, I realised that such enjoyment had been suppressed in their colder climate.

Filipino food is good, but its perceived merit is increased by a large factor because of this tropical-rejoicing syndrome. How is it, then, that the most revered cuisines of the world all belong to temperate climes, where they are handicapped by the muted appreciation which is all that people there can muster? The question waits to be addressed by a Brillat-Savarin whose horizons extend beyond Lyons and right down through the Mediterranean to the Equator. And there is a companion question waiting to be answered, about cookery books.

We may think that every possible category of cookery book is represented on our bookshop shelves, but one is missing, and it is one which abounds in the Philippines: the emotional cookery book, or recipes as a vehicle for expressing love, fostering comradeship, and honouring the dead.

The phenomenon is mainly manifest in introductions. An English author is apt to state his or her aims, modestly, in a page and a half, concluding with some mild expressions of gratitude, scrupulously emasculated (or effeminated), to sources of inspiration and to the family for putting up with all the recipe-testing.

How wanly such prose reads when compared with the preambular matter in, say, the book of the collected recipes of Maria Y Orosa, where testimonies to her wartime heroism (she died in 1945, hit by Japanese shrapnel) are mingled with touching anecdotes about the devotion with which she pursued nutritional studies, colour pictures of replicas of cakes of her time (kitsch, we would say here, but not if we were in Manila, where the simple charm of their decoration is immune to sophisticated criticism), jokes that she made about herself ('She loved to picture how funny she looked, wearing coats which were too small or too big for her . . . all hand-me-downs and give-aways. She could not afford to buy any.'), and the text of the plaque in the Maria Y Orosa Memorial Hall.

Having absorbed all this, and knowing that Orosa had been a covert captain in the guerrilla army, and had fed prisoners of war on a soybean food of her own devising, we respond as we should to the pages of recipes for using *saba* banana flour in baking, creating cassava cookies and *tikitiki* (rice bran) muffins, utilising the obscure but nourishing roselle fruit, and making a *palayok* oven. Out of context, shorn of the personal background, their power to fascinate would evaporate as fast as vitamin C from roselles cooked the wrong way.

A symbol of the Filipino joy in eating is the dessert-cum-drink called *halo-halo*. The name is Tagalog (the official language of the Philippines) for 'mix-mix'. Luning Bonifacio Ira, contributing an essay to *The Culinary Culture of the Philippines,** explains the flexible rules for

* Ed. Gilda Cordero-Fernando, Manila, 1976.

making it in both simple and 'special' form. Either way, she declares, it is a 'supercooler', a 'defrazzling continuum', a 'glacial spectacular'. 'Here, epitomized in a glass, is the hallmark facility to blend, to create distinctive variations and to emerge an identity greater than its parts. That extra dimension is Filipino exuberance.' She's right.

Halo-halo was born when ice came to the Philippines, in the 1920s. Its badge is a mound of shaved ice at the top of a tall sundae glass. Below the ice sits a scoop of ice cream. Below that are the cooked fruits: cubes of sweet potato and of *saba* banana, slivers of jackfruit, red beans, spoonfuls of purple yam jam, cubes of *gulaman* (agar-agar gelatin) bathed in coconut milk, sugar-palm seeds and chickpeas. These are in layers; the mix-mix is for you to do when you are consuming it. You can have as many different layers as you please, but you still have an ordinary halo-halo unless you add the three requirements for a 'special': *leche flan* (egg-yolk custard, top Filipino dessert), *makapuno* (the rare kind of coconut which is full of soft meat because of a recessive gene), and a sprinkling of sugar and toasted *pinipig* (whole-rice flakes).

This is, evidently, composed with art and skill. But Filipinos don't go on about that. Nor do they pronounce with awe the name of the chef who composed what you are mix-mixing. They just urge you to enjoy it and laugh with pure and innocent pleasure when you do. Quite a relief.

1985

Sticky Fingers

In Santa Barbara, I had *sushi* at the longest sushi bar in North America, with six Japanese sushi chefs behind it and thirty eager Californian customers to my left and right. The repeat performance in Japan was at one of the shortest sushi bars anywhere, only nine feet long: room for two other customers, me, and the two friends with whom I was staying in Kamakura, an hour's train ride from Tokyo.

These friends had pondered how to give me a supreme sushi experience and had decided that their neighbourhood *sushi-yan* (sushi-maker) was second to none in skill and more interested than most in talking about this to ignorant foreigners.

When the word 'sushi' was first recorded, in the eighth century AD, it simply meant a way of preserving fish by salting and pressing them. Later, this evolved into a technique of curing fish by laying them on a bed of vinegared rice; but only the fish was eaten. Later still, someone must have tasted the rice with the fish, and had a pleasant surprise, for now the most familiar form of sushi (the most familiar of dozens) is the hand-shaped mound of vinegared rice with a piece of raw seafood on top of it. This is the Tokyo style, and this was what I was to taste.

We went late, and soon had the undivided attention of the sushi-yan. Seemingly without effort, he confected for us sushi after sushi: marinated mackerel with ginger on top; the expensive 'red clams'; thin, thin fillets from the back of a flounder; tuna of the highest quality; the rare Japanese geoduck (a bivalve shellfish usually thought of as a delicacy belonging to the north-west of the USA, and pronounced gooeyduck).

In between, our palates were refreshed by oriental radish (*daikon*) which had been cooked in soy sauce, rice wine and rice vinegar, etc. and was served in long, thin, brown strips. I worked hard, making notes of what the sushi-yan said about how he had chosen the seafood at the giant Tokyo fish market early in the morning, how the flesh of the red clams was still alive, how carefully one had to fan the rice after cooking it, and so on.

But this was not all. The sushi-yan made a pronouncement which, from the changed tone of voice, I could tell was of a different kind. It was explained to me that he was inviting me behind his bar, to try my hand, literally, at making sushi. It was also explained that this was an honour and a privilege.

So there I stood, happily without an audience except for my friends, with the tub of vinegared rice on my right, also the bowl of (? vinegared) water, and the sushi knife on the spotless working surface between me and the chilled compartments of raw seafood.

It soon emerged that I had more than the normal human quota of thumbs, and that they and my fingers had a glutinous quality like sticky rice. The rice being used was not the really sticky kind, but of an intermediate stickiness (the choice in the Orient is not between non-sticky and sticky but from a whole spectrum). But it was too sticky for me. My mounds of rice fell apart, clinging in ragged lumps to my fingers. I was remembering to dip the fingers regularly in the vinegared water. I had got that bit straight. But I lacked the necessary speed and lightness of touch in shaping. A split second's delay is too long.

The next lesson, after my mounds had been reconstituted, was laying on the smear of *wasabi*. This is a green paste, made from a perennial herb, *Eutrema wasabi*, which is not related to horseradish but resembles it in flavour.

The wasabi-smearing was child's play, and my performance of it applauded. But my use of the knife put me back at the bottom of the class. I had watched the sushi-yan dip the blade in water, then tap it lightly so that the drops jumped off, and I could do this too. But how to make cuts eluded me. The blade was amazingly sharp – no problem there – but somehow things stuck to it, and what I cut through with it changed shape disconcertingly, and altogether I began to see myself as a prize dunce. The sushi-yan was kind enough to tell my friends that I had made a promising start, and that he thought he could make something of me in five years; but I didn't really believe him.

1985

Three Meals in Phuket

Phuket, the island which lies just west of the southern tip of Thailand, is rich in tin, seafood, and unusual eating experiences. Driving in from the airport with Vagn, a Danish fisheries expert, I observed some fairly lavish new houses. 'The homes of the tin millionaires?' I asked. 'No, the homes of their number two wives. The big shots and the number one wives live in nondescript-looking houses downtown. Real wealth does not advertise itself here. But number two wives like to make a splash.'

That night we dined at a Chinese restaurant. Others (the millionaires, and if so which wives were with them?) selected very expensive dishes. A soup which involved whole chickens stuffed with entire birds' nests was one. Indeed soups seemed to be the most costly items, with the extra special shark's fin kind costing a sum which made me doubt my pocket calculator.

We too had a shark's fin dish, but an economical one: little lettuce leaf cups filled with tiny fried strips of the fin, bean sprouts, crabmeat, crab eggs and hen's egg. We also had turtle egg. I asked the obvious, anxious question. 'Oh no, not from an endangered species – and the number taken is strictly controlled.' The effect was slightly spoiled by a subsequent sly smile, but by this time I was holding the egg, white and like a puffball, over my soupbowl and pinching it open, as instructed. 'You could boil it for hours and it would *never* set,' I was told.

I preferred the crab dishes. There were huge claws of the mangrove crab (*Scylla* spp) cooked with soy sauce, ginger, lemon grass, garlic, coriander. But the best were the small 'crabs' (beetle-like sea cicadas, *Hippa asiaticus*) of which as many as 20,000 at a time may be ordered for state banquets in Bangkok (yes, I wondered too, but that's what they said). These were fried whole and then dipped in jungle honey. Jungle honey is gathered from the wild and has a strong, fine flavour which overwhelms the faint marine character of the tiny crustaceans. Indeed their role is mainly to provide crunch.

That place was three stars, Phuket style. The next evening we settled for no stars except those in the sky, choosing to eat grilled squid and fish at Rawai beach, where the sea gypsies are to be seen at monsoon time (they live at sea for the rest of the year).

The 'restaurant' there consisted of some long tables between the narrow beach and the first line of nodding palms; a corrugated iron roof; and the grill. This was an interesting arrangement, rather like a bread oven with the top sliced off. The fuel, coconut husks, was introduced down a funnel at ground level. Above it, and across the open, circular top, the fish (*Caranx sexfasciatus*, one of the better species of scad) was suspended on a wide-meshed metal grid. Above that were placed sheets of corrugated iron, to reflect the heat back down. It worked very well, but we could see that the long experience of Nai Tan Mookdi, the 'Number One Proprietor', was needed to judge just how soon the fish, invisible under its cover, would be ready. He did this to a nicety, and provided three sauces to go with it: the best was soy sauce with small red onions chopped into it and a dash of lime juice.

I forgot to say that the restaurant equipment included an old-fashioned mangle, no doubt inscribed 'Birmingham 1908' like the one I had met in the north of Laos. This was for the dried squid. A squid 6 inches (15 cm) long was passed through it and came out at 18 inches (46 cm), slightly corrugated. It was then cut into three and the pieces grilled for two minutes. A delicacy, but it tasted like breakfast cereal to me.

The third dinner was home cooking. Vagn made a curry-type dish of chicken, attributing it to Nang. Nang just means 'Miss', and the young woman thus vaguely identified had come to cook for him from one of the small islands. She was a marvellous cook, he said. 'What a waste, after two years she was summoned back by her family, returned to the little island with her savings, and that was that!' I tried to think of the episode from Nang's point of view, and wondered how it looked to her. I also copied out Vagn's notes of exactly what she did.

NANG'S CHICKEN DISH

1 chicken (1½ kg, 3 lb)
2 coconuts
2 pieces galingale
9 stalks lemon grass (fresh if
    possible)
15 tiny onions

1 large head garlic
10 small chilli peppers
5 Kaffir lime leaves (bay leaves
    aren't the same but a couple
    of them would do)

Dismember the chicken. Use the two coconuts to make 1 cup of thick and 5 of thin coconut cream. Put the 5 cups of thin cream into a large pot, put the pot on the fire, and add the chicken pieces after a couple of minutes.

Cut the galingale into small pieces. Cut the lemon grass (soaked if you have to use dried leaves) into pieces of 2–3 cm and beat them to make them soft. Add both to the pot. Peel and crush the small onions and the cloves of garlic. Add them and the chillis too.

Simmer until the chicken is tender, then add the cup of thick coconut cream, bring almost back to the boil, add the Kaffir lime leaves (torn into pieces), remove from the heat and serve.

(If you have access to a good oriental food store, you should be able to get the ingredients, including products which serve as short-cuts for making coconut cream.)

1985

Vietnamese Food

I have not enjoyed Vietnamese home cooking. No, that is ambiguous, what I mean is that I haven't had any. My visits to that country date back to the time when the war was still going on, and it was only because of my official status that I was able to go both to Saigon and Hanoi, with some side excursions from each capital; but the programme never included private hospitality.

What I had plenty of were meals in restaurants and meals in British Embassies. The latter had a certain interest, due to the confrontation between the supposed requirements of diplomatic entertaining, including efforts to feature the cuisine of the home country, and the natural instincts of that most stubborn breed, Vietnamese cooks. The result can by acronymically summed up as WYGIWYME (what you get is what you might expect). But the restaurants – yes, in Hanoi too, except for the main hotel which had fallen under the influence of the Cubans who built it – did offer real Vietnamese food. This is good, sometimes very good, often subtle in flavouring but always the sort of thing you can enjoy in a relaxed kind of way.

There is one thing to grasp before you start. The basic condiment is *nuoc mam*, 'fish sauce'. This is a fermented fish product, often referred to misleadingly by foreigners as made from rotten fish, or in some other off-putting way. In fact, except for some inferior grades which you won't meet in any respectable restaurant, it is not at all off-putting and indeed not particularly fishy. In chemical composition and taste it resembles closely the soy sauce which is the stock condiment further north, in China. It has a salty taste and, like salt, is to be used in moderation. Remember that, like salt in western countries, it will already be in many of the dishes you eat, and the bottle on the table, like our salt cellar, is for adding more if you wish. (For more about *nuoc mam* see page 223).

The strong points of Vietnamese cooking are their spring rolls (smaller and crisper than the Chinese kind), noodle dishes, all available seafoods, and soups. They have one soup, crab and asparagus, which was our favourite when we lived in South-East Asia. Ask for Súp Măng Tây Cua. It was the French who introduced asparagus to Vietnam (where it was promptly dubbed 'western bamboo'), and this is an example of how the Vietnamese cuisine, a classic one in its own right, has absorbed French influences as happily as those from China.

Lemon grass is one ingredient typical of South-East Asia which the Vietnamese use to good advantage in their fish dishes. They employ ginger much less, but are free in their use of a whole range of locally available mints.

The Vietnamese use sticky, short-grain rice much more than the Chinese. Rice also appears in the form of *banh pho* (rice sticks), which fall into the category of noodles. The 'cellophane noodles', made from mung beans and also common in China, are the most popular. My feeling about these is that a little is fine, but a dish in which they are the main ingredient is unlikely to score top marks with me.

Pork is the most popular meat. A lot of chicken is eaten. It is often a pleasant surprise to find, in a soup, or stew-type dish, or a stir-fry, chunks or slices of fresh pineapple treated like a vegetable.

But I would advise you to opt for seafood, and ask particularly whether you can have an unusual prawn dish called *Cháo Tôm*. This is what we would call a 'starter', but it is worlds away from the banal prawn cocktails etc. to which we are accustomed. Raw prawn (shrimp to Americans) is pounded together with garlic, egg-white, rice powder and other ingredients, then moulded into a sort of egg shape on the end of a four-inch section of sugar cane. The whole thing is baked in the oven or barbecued. Let the waiter guide you on how to eat it.

There is one really exotic ingredient which you will be lucky to encounter. If you see a waiter going round with what looks like a medicine dropper and releasing a couple of drops of colourless fluid on to a dish, signal your desire to have some too, costly though it is. A secretion of a kind of water bug, its collection is a laborious business: one large, live water bug yields only a tiny amount. (See also page 228.)

Finally, a caution. The Vietnamese have adopted from the Chinese (who took it over from the Japanese, all quite recently, in this century) the use of monosodium glutamate (MSG) as a flavour enhancer. This occurs naturally in many foodstuffs, and it does have the ability to intensify flavours, while having none of its own. But, at least in its commercially produced form, it doesn't agree with everyone and too much of it can produce the undesirable symptoms – such as short-lived headaches and palpitations – which are generally referred to as the 'MSG syndrome'.

I once discussed MSG with a Japanese scientist and gastronome who works for Aji-no-moto, the biggest producer of the substance. He said that the trouble was that other, less discriminating people (he meant

Chinese and Vietnamese) had let the whole business of using MSG, which the Japanese do with the utmost care and moderation, get completely out of hand. This certainly applies to some Vietnamese cooks, so it is often wise when entering a Vietnamese restaurant to announce that MSG doesn't suit you and ask that the chef be informed.

1987

Nuoc Mam: the Fish Sauces of Vietnam and South-East Asia

'*Nuoc mam*? Isn't that some sort of smelly fish sauce from Vietnam?' That's the sort of reaction which many people give if nuoc mam is mentioned. And it isn't entirely wrong. Nuoc mam *is* a fish sauce, being made from fermented fish; and it *can* be smelly. But there's much more to it than that.

First of all, nuoc mam of good quality is a real delicacy. Secondly, it is a vital source of protein for scores of millions of people in South-East Asia, and their principal condiment, used as often as we use salt. Thirdly – a piece of information which may surprise people who haven't tasted both – it is remarkably similar to soy sauce, in composition as well as in function. The role played by soy sauce in Chinese, Korean and Japanese cookery (and in most of Indonesia) is the same as that played by nuoc mam and the other fish sauces of South-East Asia* in that region. The salty taste, rich flavour and chemical constitution of both products are alike, although one comes from a plant and the other from fish.

Although good nuoc mam is a treat, it must be admitted that low-grade nuoc mam is not. Like the little girl in the verse, when it's good it's very very good, but when it's bad it's horrid! The difference depends on lots of factors, including the care and skill with which the sauce is made. To emphasise the point that it really is a skilled business, let me invoke the words of a French author: 'By the complicated work which it requires, the delicate decanting needed and the time taken to achieve the best results, [the manufacture of nuoc mam] recalls quite closely the preparation of fine French brandies.'

The high official who wrote these words, under the pseudonym 'le

---

* These fish sauces are: *nuoc mam* in Vietnam, *tuk trey* in Cambodia, *nam pa* in Laos, *nam pla* in Thailand, *ngan-pya-ye* in Burma, and *patis* in the Philippines. They are not to be confused with the fish or shrimp pastes which are also popular in the region and which have names like *terasi* and *blachan* (in both Malaysia and Indonesia) and *bagoong* (in the Philippines). These are another story.

Nestour', did not set out to be a best-seller. The only copy of his book *La Pêche en Cochinchine* which I have ever seen (in the national library at Hanoi) bears an inscription which suggests that he had only 100 copies printed. However, he was as expert on everything to do with fish in Indochina as he was on the foods and wines of his own native country. That he should have drawn an analogy between fish sauce and brandy, at least in the finesse required for making either product, is enough to make the most sceptical sit up and pay attention. A visit to a fish sauce factory and a tasting (which one might almost call a *dégustation*) of the products are definitely indicated.

In the mid-1970s I was living in Vientiane, the capital of Laos. As Laos is the only country of South-East Asia to have no coastline, I was pleasantly surprised to discover a fish sauce factory on the outskirts of Vientiane, whose owner was not only ready but anxious to show us round. No one could have seemed less likely to be a fish sauce manufacturer than this chic young woman, wearing a summer dress of a delicate yellow material which shimmered brightly against the background of large earth-coloured sheds in which she supervised her operations.

There *was* a smell inside, but it was mild, even in the vicinity of the concrete vats in which the fermentation takes place. These measured nine or ten feet square and two or three deep. One was empty, being cleaned out. The other five were full of fish sauce in various stages of maturing.

'We have a mixture of sea fish and freshwater fish, about 20 per cent to 80 per cent,' Mrs Pheuy told us, 'and that gives a very good flavour. The Lao prefer it to a *nam pa* [fish sauce, the Lao term] made from sea fish alone, which is what you can get from Thailand. And it costs much less, since Lao fishermen catch thousands of small fish which aren't much use for anything else.'

She lifted back the corner of the bamboo matting which covered the otherwise open top of one of the vats. In the murky liquid within we could make out what were evidently masses of these tiny fish, partly decomposed. 'This lot has been in the vat for two months, and will stay for another three or four weeks. To start with, we add about one part of salt to three of fish. Those are the only ingredients. If we were making *padek* [a kind of soupy fish sauce with whole bits of fish in it, which the Lao particularly relish] we'd be adding rice husks, but this nam pa is very simple and very pure. Now see what comes out of a vat which is ready.'

The adjacent vat was about to be tapped by drawing off the first batch of liquid through a bamboo spigot. A small bottle was filled for our inspection. The liquid was peaty in colour, like Scotch whisky, and smelled good.

'The first to be drawn off is the best quality. But we haven't finished with it yet. Before we bottle it we let it mature in the sun for a few weeks.'

Led outside, we saw hundreds of enormous pottery jars standing in the courtyard, each full of fish sauce and all in the strong sunshine. Mrs Pheuy slipped on her elegant Japanese sun glasses and posed for a photograph beside one of the jars. It struck me that she could just about have fitted into the jar if it was empty. Meanwhile, she was explaining that the pottery would absorb certain traces of unwanted odour, and that the heat of the sun would bring out the full flavour of the sauce. We found this very easy to believe!

Later, in Saigon, I met another fish sauce manufacturer, again a beautiful young woman. She smiled with amiable tolerance when I told her of the Lao factory (Laos being regarded as a small and backward country by the Vietnamese) and said that she would let me have a bottle of her own 'extra special 4-star' sauce which was reserved for her family's use and as gifts to important customers. This came in a square bottle, containing only half a pint, and it was quite superb. The difference between it and a cheap ordinary brand was as great as that between a fine vintage Bordeaux and a bottle of *vin ordinaire*.

Such a degree of difference in quality is the result of many causes, including the choice of fish (anchovies are preferred in Vietnam); whether the whole fish or parts only are used (Cambodians make a traditional fish sauce from the livers of a kind of catfish and a fish called 'snakehead'); the proportion of salt used (generally around 25 per cent); whether there are additives such as pineapple juice, which speeds the breaking-up of the fish protein; the duration of fermentation and of subsequent maturing; and so on. It is a complex business, which has in recent decades been thoroughly investigated by scientists. Their conclusions, broadly speaking, are that the South-East Asians had worked out for themselves over the centuries the combinations which would yield the most nutritious and flavourful sauces.

No one knows how far back the history of nuoc mam stretches. But we do know that a strikingly similar product, which the Romans called *garum*, was made by the classical Greeks and Romans and that they regarded it as an indispensable ingredient for every kind of savoury dish. Roman gourmets distinguished between various kinds of garum, according to where it was made and how; and they were willing to pay a lot for what they found best, which was a kind made from the fermented viscera and blood of mackerel. Other 'oily' fish, from the huge tuna to the tiny anchovy, were also used. To this day, some people in the south of France prepare from anchovies a product called *pissala*, which is a direct descendant of garum. It is a purée of salted and fermented fish, very popular in the region of Nice as a flavourful condiment or spread; and it gives its name to *pissaladières*, which are onion tarts whose surface has been smeared with it before they are baked.

It seems clear that the Romans enthused over garum because they liked the flavour, not because they saw it as a way of preserving fish. But in South-East Asia the aspect of preservation is equally important. It is less easy there, in the moist climate, to use the age-old technique of drying fish to keep them. Fermentation offers a convenient alternative. And, although it requires skill and care, it does not call for advanced technology, nor any apparatus for chilling and freezing, nor any complex arrangements for storing and distribution. I guess that these are the reasons why the use of fermentation has continued so vigorously in South-East Asia but has dwindled since Roman times in the Mediterranean and Europe to a mere vestige of what was once a flourishing tradition.

There are also dietary considerations. The diet of South-East Asians is based on rice, vegetables and fruit. These foods go a long way towards giving them adequate nourishment, but need to be supplemented by more protein. Fish sauce is a highly concentrated form of this, since much of the protein in the fish has been broken down by fermentation into free amino-acids (including the so-called 'essential' ones, i.e. those which the body needs but cannot make for itself). So the custom of adding fish sauce to rice (which I used to do for breakfast in Laos, and quite enjoyed) is nutritionally sound. It is also cheap, since the abundance of fish, especially freshwater fish, in South-East Asia means that fish sauce, of the ordinary kind, is not at all expensive. A young Vietnamese scientist, who earned his doctorate by a study of the chemical analysis of various fish sauces, told me in Saigon that nuoc mam is really vital to the health and well-being of the peoples of Indochina, and urged me to increase my own consumption of it (which explains the rice and fish sauce breakfasts).

Fish sauces can be used as a condiment, straight from the bottle, or they can be used in cooking. Most South-East Asian dishes of a savoury kind (except in Indonesia, where soy sauce is generally preferred) call for some. But one of the simplest and best ways of enjoying them is to use them as the basis of a made-up sauce such as the Nam Prik of Thailand or the Nuoc Cham of Vietnam. The former is just a saucer containing a mixture of fish sauce and lime juice with some tiny bird chillis. The latter is made as follows:

NUOC CHAM

1 *fairly small red chilli pepper,*	6 *tsp sugar*
seeded	¼ *lime, juice and pulp*
2 *cloves garlic, peeled*	4 *tbs nuoc mam (fish sauce)*

Chop the chilli pepper and pound it in a mortar with the garlic cloves and sugar until you have a smooth paste. Mash this up with the lime juice and pulp, add the fish sauce and about 6 tbs water (more if you don't like a strong sauce), and give everything a final mix together. Serve as a sauce with almost any savoury dish. Use with discretion.

However rare and costly the very finest nuoc mam may be, it will never rival another extraordinary flavouring of aquatic origin which is used in Indochina, especially Vietnam.

The first official dinner which I attended in Laos was given by the (South) Vietnamese Ambassador for the Prime Minister, Prince Souvanna Phouma. When the main dish was served, I noticed that a Vietnamese girl of aristocratic appearance (no serving maid, evidently) knelt by the side of the Prime Minister and held up a medicine dropper for his approval. He nodded and she squeezed two drops of fluid from it on to his food. Goodness me, I thought, this must be some sort of oriental medicine intended to help his heart condition. But the girl then did the same for the Defence Minister. Could he suffer from the same trouble? And for the other notables, and eventually myself. By this time it had dawned on me that her mission was a culinary, not a medical one, so I too nodded and thus made my first acquaintance with this rarest South-East Asian 'sauce'.

I learned later what it is: a glandular secretion of which a few drops may be expressed from live specimens of the water bug *Lethocerus indicus*. I had it again, when I was feeling less bewildered and more analytical, in Hanoi in 1975. There is (or was) a restaurant there called simply 'The Fish Place', with one speciality, Cha Ca Lao Vong (literally, 'grilled, cut up fish meat of the old fisherman'). The Fish Place had managed to survive in Hanoi from the 1930s through the Second World War and the Vietnam war. The young women whose charms had attracted French officers there some forty years back were now quite elderly, but still beautiful and as expert as ever in their kitchen. They produced their speciality and proudly offered, as an 'extra', the medicine dropper whose significance I now knew. I had two drops, and afterwards sought words to convey the effect which they had. No word is quite right, since the flavour is unique. But 'musky' is quite a close approach. I wrote in my notebook that it was so potent, and such an exciting gastronomic experience, that it must be counted very good value at $10 a drop!

Buying Fish Sauce

Buy from an oriental provision merchant. Check the prices. If you are in a store where South-East Asians shop, the more expensive fish sauces will almost certainly be the better ones. And this is definitely an area in which it is worth paying more for higher quality. Personally, I recommend Thai fish sauce, of those which are most easily available, but I know that many would recommend *patis* from the Philippines.

1982

European Eels in Japan

When I began eating and learning about eels in Japan I supposed that I was dealing with the native Japanese eel, *Anguilla japonica*. But the matter turned out to be much more complicated.

En route from New York, where eel consumption is minimal ('Ugh' is the normal American reaction to the idea), to China, I was turned loose in the village of Narita, near Tokyo's airport, with Paul Levy, the notorious 'foodie' (one of the very few who willingly answer to this somewhat obnoxious term, the explanation being that he and Ann Barr invented it). We strolled down the main street, Paul exclaiming as usual with feverish excitement over every item of food on display. 'Look, potatoes! Amazing!' And so on.

But then we came to something which really did seem unusual, a small restaurant which clearly served nothing but grilled eel. The eels were being grilled right up front, almost on the pavement. I too became excited. Had we, by chance, stumbled upon a uniquely specialised establishment? We must sample the eel, though breakfast was but an hour behind us. It was great! Soon we were in the air again, boasting to our companions about the treat which we had had and they had missed.

Next time, I stayed much longer in Japan and the restaurant in Narita fell into context as only one of hundreds, perhaps thousands, of such places. Eels are big business for the Japanese, and have been since antiquity. In the eighth century the famous poet Otomo-no-Yakamochi addressed a friend, who was clearly a thin man, thus: 'Let me tell you, Imawaro, that you should eat an eel, which they say is good for you after you have lost weight through the heat of the summer.' This notion is still prevalent; indeed the eel is thought of as a very valuable source of nutrients and vitamins. It is recorded that a celebrated thief called Nihonzaemon, who was executed in 1747, could see in the dark, an achievement which he attributed to eating a lot of eel and which he would have ascribed specifically to the large amount of vitamin A in eels had vitamins been discovered then.

However, it is not just for nutritional reasons that the Japanese eat over 60,000 tons of eel annually. They count it as an exceptionally tasty food, especially in the form of *kabayaki*, a term which has become almost synonymous with eel. This dish, which seems to have become fully established in the mid nineteenth century, is always prepared by specialists, never in the home. There are two principal techniques, Tokyo-style and Osaka-style. In the former, a live eel is fixed to the cutting-board through its head by a sharp tool, then opened up along the back, gutted and boned. Next, head and tail are cut off and what is left is cut into two, the head end and the tail end. These are pierced with several skewers and grilled; then steamed; then grilled again. For the second grilling, the fish is basted repeatedly with a thick sauce composed mainly of soy sauce and *mirin* (sweet rice wine used only for cooking). The Osaka style differs in that the fish is opened along the belly, not the back; the steaming is omitted; and the fish is cooked with head and tail on (but served without). In Tokyo, *kabayaki* is usually served on a bed of hot rice; in Osaka between two layers of hot rice.

Sometimes eel is served after the first grilling. This is called *shiroyaki*. And the prized liver of the eel is often served in a clear soup (*kimosui*) as an accompaniment to *kabayaki*; or grilled and served as an hors d'œuvre while the diner waits for the *kabayaki*.

The specialist cooks of Japan are not troubled by false modesty about the time it takes to master their skills. In the case of eel, the saying is: 'Three years for filleting, eight years for steaming, and a lifetime for grilling.'

Kabayaki restaurants always have a tank in which live eels are kept, and the cooking is often done in the front part of the house so that the aroma of eels being grilled will attract the passer-by, as it did Paul and myself in Narita. A Japanese friend wrote to me: 'I have a strong childhood memory of standing in front of a neighbourhood eel restaurant for as long as half an hour, looking curiously into the tank full of long, smooth, twisting fish and admiring the chef's handling of the slippery things – which sometimes go on wriggling after being beheaded, gutted and boned.'

A popular method of fishing for 'wild' eels is to lower sections of bamboo (about two feet (60 cm) long and up to four inches (10 cm) in diameter) into the water and then pull them up after eels have taken refuge in them. But this fishery has declined greatly and now accounts for only about 2000 tons a year. In contrast, eel-farming, which began in 1879, has grown into a large industry. About 40,000 tons of eel are produced by farming each year, and a further 20,000 tons of farmed eel imported from Taiwan. The eels used to be raised out of doors, in fishponds, but nowadays they are reared in indoor tanks.

This industry depends, naturally, on a regular supply of infant eels, the 'elvers' which arrive annually from their distant oceanic breeding grounds and swim up rivers to establish themselves in fresh water. But this supply fluctuates, and in 1969 there was a serious shortage, prompting the import from France of elvers of the Atlantic eel, *Anguilla anguilla*.

Such imports have continued. So when I ate my Japanese eel in Narita I may have been eating a fish with a curious history. It could have begun life in the Sargasso Sea, whither its mother would have swum from Europe (and where this same mother would have perished after completing her biological function by spawning). Then, as a mere larval speck, it set out on the journey of thousands of miles to the European coast. Two years later, now several centimetres long but still transparent, it arrived at the mouth of a French river. At this point, it was scooped up in a Frenchman's elver-catching basket, then flown in a jumbo jet to Japan and transferred to a tank in a fish farm. There it was kept at the right temperature and fed a nutritious diet until it reached marketable size and landed up on our plates.

It is curious to reflect that if this same eel had been selected for *kabayaki* treatment in a factory and thence for sale, ready prepared, in a supermarket, and if it had happened to be in a batch imported as an exotic Japanese delicacy by a gourmet shop in New York, it would have achieved a complete round-the-world journey, finishing up to the north of its birthplace but in much the same longitude.

1985

Part Seven
Cheese

British Cheeses: a Historical Introduction

'Hard cheese, old chap,' says one character in a novel by P. G. Wodehouse to another, meaning that the latter has suffered some misfortune and deserves sympathy. The phrase is an odd one to find thus used in England; for one of the outstanding features of British cheeses is that they are mostly hard, in contrast to the numerous and well-known soft cheeses of France.

Perhaps this is because we in Britain (like our neighbours, the Dutch) often make a meal of bread and cheese, whereas for the French a cheese course is but one element in a meal. If you eat a lot of cheese at one time, it is more practical to choose a hard cheese – less messy and less rich.

Whatever the explanation, we certainly favour hard cheeses; and it would be natural to think that hardness in a cheese would be counted a virtue by us. So it is, up to a point. But cheese can be too hard, even for us. It used to be said of Suffolk cheeses that they could, if necessary, be used by millers whose grinding stones had broken. It was this sort of possibility that gave rise to the phrase 'hard cheese'; and it is no doubt because our cheeses are no longer prone to exhibit such extreme defects that the phrase has dropped out of use.

The use of the same names for our most famous cheeses, such as Cheddar and Cheshire, over many centuries would suggest that they had remained much the same since we first hear of them (usually in the sixteenth or seventeenth centuries, sometimes earlier) until the present time. The truth is otherwise. In this first essay I shall say something about the history of our cheeses, to make clear that what we now enjoy are rather different from what our forebears enjoyed, or failed to enjoy.

Failed to enjoy? Have not cheeses been one of the sources of British national gastronomic pride from time immemorial? The answer must be an Irish 'yes and no'.

Whether and in what way cheeses were made in Britain before the Romans arrived is, so far as I know, a matter for conjecture. What is certain is that the Romans were highly sophisticated and enthusiastic cheese-makers – witness the long and detailed passage about the manufacture of cheeses in Columella's manual of husbandry (first century AD); and what seems almost equally certain is that they must have made cheeses in Britain and bequeathed the art to us when they left. It is interesting that the Romans used their word for cheese as a term of endearment, almost equivalent to 'sweetheart', and that until recently the word 'cheese' had a secondary meaning in English, namely something which is 'just right'. (Etymologists tell us that the English usage stems from the Urdu word 'chiz', meaning 'the thing', and this may be so; but the coincidence is still suggestive.)

From early times the various English cheeses were mostly known by the name of the counties in which they were made; thus Cheshire, Leicester, Gloucester and many others which have ceased to be made. Cheddar was an exception. Logically, it should have been called Somerset cheese; but the most famous area for its manufacture was along the base of the Mendip Hills in that county, and the village of Cheddar, because of its famous Gorge and numerous visitors, was the most popular point of sale and hence gave its name to the cheese. Stilton, to which we shall revert in another essay (page 248), was another exception. So were the soft cheeses, such as Slipcote, which loom large in eighteenth-century books, less large in the nineteenth century and have almost vanished in the twentieth.

The cheese trade was well organised even two or three hundred years ago. Thus we read that in the eighteenth century sixteen ships were kept busy bringing cheeses from Liverpool to London. And the names to which I have referred had real significance, for cheeses from different areas had their own recognisable characteristics. But the quality was uneven. The scientific production of cheeses still lay in the future; and despite the skill and experience of the farmers' wives and daughters who made the cheeses (like all dairy work, the task of women), faults were common. Thomas Tusser, writing in 1557, warns his imaginary dairy-maid Cicely against ten possible disasters. Some were obviously avoidable (hairs in the cheese), but others were not, because at that time no one possessed scientific knowledge of exactly what happened when a cheese was made. Thus the presence of unwanted 'eyes' (holes) in the cheese, or its puffing up, had often to be shrugged off as inexplicable phenomena, to be avoided only by the empirical lore of the experts. The Cheddar which Londoners ate in those days was often a very different product from that of today.

An excellent and early survey of the regional cheeses was provided by Thomas Fuller in *The Worthies of England* (1601). He said that the biggest and best in England were those from Cheddar; but he seems to have thought Welsh cheeses even better, basing his opinion on that of mice, whom he considered to be the most discriminating judges and who, when they had a choice, 'have given their verdict for the Welsh'. This titbit of information presumably came from a warehouse where cheeses from the different regions were stored together in conditions which were not mouse-proof.

The great change in English cheese-making came in the nineteenth century, when the factory system of production was introduced. This arrived in Britain a little later than in the United States; but by the middle of the 1870s there were half a dozen factories operating in Derbyshire, and during the next two decades the system became established throughout the cheese-making counties. As this process took place the number of different cheeses being made was gradually reduced. The economics of mass-production and distribution awarded a strong preference to cheeses which are relatively easy to manufacture; whose quality can readily be controlled and standardised; which have good keeping qualities; and which are simple to transport. To these factors must, of course, be added the requirement that they should be pleasant to eat! But this, alas, was not the overriding factor. Some delicious cheeses which are only suitable for 'farmhouse production' have disappeared or are in danger of doing so.

The British public in general adopts an acquiescent attitude towards cheese. Shoppers do not exercise much discrimination. Fortunately, however, one small and special market for cheeses has always exercised a beneficial attitude on the quality and variety of cheeses available. This is the institution known as the British club, which exists mainly in London and which is supported by members who have a strong interest in cheese and who very definitely know a good one from a less good one.

Even so, the clubs themselves are now able to offer only a limited selection of British cheeses. He or she who would like to sample the full range must go outside London for the purpose, catching a train from Paddington to Goring-on-Thames. A pleasant walk of ten minutes then brings the pilgrim to Major Patrick Rance's store in the village of Streatley.* It is here, surprisingly, that the full range of British cheeses will be found arrayed on shelves which attract cheese enthusiasts from all over the country. Major Rance is himself the greatest enthusiast of all, and it is thanks to his dynamism and persistence that certain rare cheeses are still made in a few farms which would otherwise have abandoned the business for lack of an outlet. With what a gleam in the eye do people who visit Major Rance perceive for sale pieces of Windsor Red (a moist Cheddar with elderberry wine veining from Tythby Farm);

---

* The shop is now run by Major Rance's son Hugh. (A.D., 1988)

of properly matured Lancashire from Goosnargh and Inglewhite; or of the only Double Gloucester still being made in Gloucestershire by the traditional methods, using milk from the only Old Gloucester herd still on permanent pasture! The Major has some soft cheeses, but a survey of his stock bears out the British preference for hard or semi-hard cheeses, and allows us to obtain the best glimpse we can of the range which used to be available.

To conclude this brief historical essay it is fitting to choose an old recipe. Most of the cookery books of the seventeenth and eighteenth centuries, if they deal with cheese at all, tell us how to make the cheeses themselves, or give recipes for cheesecake, and no more. One of the first to have a cheese cookery chapter is also one of the early English cookery books which was reprinted in the United States: *The English Art of Cookery* by Richard Briggs, who proclaims himself to have been cook at many taverns in London and at the Temple Coffee House. The first edition was around 1788, and the first American edition came out in Philadelphia in 1792. Briggs gives recipes, among others, for Welsh rabbit (a dish which figures on page 254), Scotch rabbit and English rabbit. This last is distinctive and delicious. Here is how you make it:

ENGLISH RABBIT

Toast a slice of bread on both sides, put it into a cheese plate, pour a glass of red wine over it, and put it to the fire till it soaks up the wine; then cut some cheese in very thin slices, and put it thick on the bread; put it in a tin oven before the fire, toast it till it is brown, and serve it up hot.

These instructions need only a little clarification. For a piece of toast 4–5 inches (10–12 cm) square and nearly an inch (13 mm) thick, you will need 4 to 5 tablespoons of wine. (It will soak up a little more than that, but the wine flavour is too dominant if you saturate it.) And you will need 2 oz (60 g) cheese, finely sliced. Once the toast, kept warm in a pre-heated fireproof dish, has had the wine poured over it, little by little, and has been topped with the thin slices of cheese, place it under the grill for about 3 minutes, so that the cheese has mostly but not quite all melted and has started to bubble and brown on top. Then serve it piping hot.

1980

The Hard Cheeses of England

Cheddar is the archetypal English hard cheese; and since the name now refers rather to a technique in making the cheese (whence the ungainly verb 'to cheddar') than to its place of origin, it has gained currency in many parts of the world. American, Canadian, Australian, New Zealand and even French 'Cheddars' sit on the shelves beside English Cheddar. What they have in common is that they have all been subjected to a similar process in their manufacture: a method of draining, cutting and drying the curd which brings it to just the right point for being salted and packed into moulds. At this stage the curd is in pieces rather like potato chips. When it is taken out of the mould twenty-four hours later these pieces have been pressed together into a recognisable cheese shape. The newly born cheese is then bathed with very hot water to melt and seal its exterior surface, bandaged in cheesecloth, returned to the press for another twenty-four hours, taken out again and kept at a temperature of about 50°F (10°C) while it matures. Nor does it rest in peace while maturing. It has to be turned over daily, and excess mould brushed off the cheesecloth.

The last part of this description applies to cheeses made by the traditional method, such as those produced at the Cheese Dairy at Chewton Mendip, which is the place to go if you wish to find a cheese which is a true Cheddar by provenance as well as having been 'cheddared' in manufacture. There are few establishments of this kind. Most Cheddar cheese, after undergoing the initial process of 'cheddaring' as described above, is packed in plastic in the form of blocks. This method has the advantage – for the merchant – that the cheese loses no weight thereafter and is rindless. But it has the disadvantage that it does not produce a full-flavoured cheese. The product is wholesome, and can be eaten without distaste, but it does not bear comparison with a 'real' Cheddar of the Chewton Mendip pattern.

A good Cheddar should be a year to eighteen months old if it is to be savoured at its best. To produce such cheeses obviously requires a considerable investment of time and effort, all the more so since the Cheddar normally is and always has been a big cheese. Cheddars used to be called Corporation cheeses in Somerset, because they were made by all the dairies of a parish putting their milk together. The results were impressive. One of the most weighty contributions to Queen Victoria's wedding celebrations was a Cheddar cheese over nine feet (2.7 m) in diameter and registering 1250 pounds (567 kg) on the scales. (Two villages had combined to make this monster.)

However, small quantities of milk left over from making the big Cheddars were used to make small ones, in the form of a little round loaf called a 'truckle'; and it is still possible in the west of England to buy farmhouse truckles which have an excellent flavour, full and 'nutty' as a cheddar should be, and with the right firm but creamy texture and the pale glow which are the marks of real quality. These truckles are worth seeking out, although the true connoisseur is likely to prefer a piece cut from a 50 or 60 lb (23–27 kg) Cheddar, provided that it has been properly matured. This is one area in which it is reasonable to say: 'the bigger the better'.

After Cheddar comes Cheshire, the only other English hard cheese which is sold on a large scale. Cheshire is red in colour, although it need not be. The red colour is produced by the addition of annatto, a natural colouring agent which is also used to make butter yellow. (It is obtained from the fruit of the annatto tree, *Bixa orellana*, found in the West Indies, Brazil and India. The pigment involved is known as bixin.) Annatto is added to Cheshire cheese, because northerners like their cheese red, whereas southerners prefer the natural pale gold of Cheddar. The reason for this difference has not yet been satisfactorily explained. Nor is it clear just where the dividing line runs. Leicester cheese, from the heart of England, is also coloured red; and Double Gloucester, even further south, is sometimes so treated. (Double Gloucester, by the way, is the only Gloucester cheese normally available now. It used to be distinguished from Single Gloucester by some technical features of production and by being twice the size of Single. But Single Gloucester, as it used to be, is made no more, or only rarely, and Double Gloucester is now usually of the size which Single Gloucester used to be.)

How different from each other are these various hard cheeses, if we leave aside the question of colour? The answer is that the differences are there, but that they are relatively small. Cheshire is a little less rich in flavour than Cheddar, but a good Cheshire may be superior to a mediocre Cheddar. Cheshire is also a little more crumbly in texture; Leicester still more so, but rich in flavour; and Gloucester more mellow, with a close and crumbly texture.

These distinctions are clear enough to the expert, when dealing with prime cheeses which have been matured for the right length of time; but they are not always easy to make for the amateur who buys pre-cut and pre-packaged wedges. Always try to buy your cheese from a specialist cheese shop. And, if you are lucky enough to have one in your neighbourhood, ask about some of the less common English hard cheeses. These include white Stilton and Lancashire. The latter, being a northern cheese, is another reddish one and it has two merits. One is the flavour, which is very rich and devoid of any acid taste, once the cheese has been properly matured. The other is its texture, which is spreadable, making it an excellent cheese for toasting, a process which actually improves its flavour.

The toasted cheese sandwich, or variations on the Welsh rabbit theme, are the most usual ways of cooking cheese in England. Next, perhaps, comes the use of cheese to make cheese sauce, often served with fish and also with certain vegetables such as cauliflower. There are those who make cheese soufflés. But I have chosen for my recipe in this essay the following:

CHEESE STRAWS

Straws is the wrong word, and I don't know how it came to be used. What you produce are oblong bars.

Preheat your oven to 450°F (230°C, mark 8). Meanwhile mix together in a mixing bowl 4 oz (125 g) flour with 8 tablespoons of butter, 4 of milk, 10 of grated cheese and a quarter teaspoon of salt. Form the mixture into a dough, using your hands, then roll it out on to a floured board until it is about ¼ inch (6 mm) thick. Cut this into oblong pieces about 2 inches (5 cm) long and ½ inch (12 mm) wide, arrange these on a baking tray so that they are not touching each other, and bake them in the oven for 15 minutes, by which time they will be golden-brown.

1980

Soft Cheeses Revived

As a result of acquiring a lot of books to do with food history, we have some surprising visitors at our house. Trish Murphy, for example, came through our front door with her bicycle. 'Hand-made,' she explained briefly, 'a man who works right by Waterloo Bridge. Fantastic crafts-manship. Daren't leave it in the street.' With that she emerged from the protective cocoon of luminous and waterproof garments which cyclists in central London are well advised to wear, produced her notebook and descended to my library to check on what some eighteenth-century English writers had to say about making soft cheeses.

They had plenty to say, especially those such as Richard Bradley (first Professor of Botany at Cambridge University) and William Ellis (an Essex farmer) whose works on cookery and food were based on a sound knowledge of agriculture and dairy-farming. Bradley, in *The Country Gentleman and Farmer's Monthly Director* (1726) and *The Country Housewife and Lady's Director*,* wrote in detail of more than a dozen cheeses – hard, blue and many soft varieties – and Ellis in *The Country Housewife's Family Companion* (1750) described yet others. The making of soft cheeses was a major activity on farms in their days; and the variety was great. People used to read eagerly about the best way of making a rennet bag; about Queen's Cheese and Sage Cheese in Chequerwork; and about the other niceties of this traditional domestic industry.

Trish Murphy's interest in all this was both academic and practical. She wanted to know the history of these old-time cheeses; but she also wanted to know which could be made and sold again today, without contravening twentieth-century regulations. Her assignment was to set up a specialist dairy, located in a hidden courtyard near Covent Garden, which had been London's fruit and vegetable market for centuries. The area, which had once been known for its 'rope houses' – a kind of doss house in which the poor could pass a night on ropes slung across the room, off which they were lifted in the morning – was then hovering between decay and revival. Trish was a revivalist.

Neal's Yard – that is the name to remember – is one of those enchanting surprises which most great cities of the world still hold for the persistent searcher. It can be reached from two streets, Monmouth Street and Neal Street, but is visible from neither. All you see from the street is a kind of tunnel which looks as though it leads to nothing in particular, maybe even to nothing at all. But walk through the tunnel and you will turn into something not unlike the courtyard of a medieval inn, bustling with activity, decorated with flowers and offering a range of excitingly different food shops, of which the main one is devoted to the sale, in large unadorned packs, of grains, dried fruits, nuts, herbs, fruit juices and honey.

This was the complex to which a dairy was to be added and, despite formidable difficulties, has been added. Here, since the summer of 1979, you can buy numerous soft cheeses (Coulommiers, Colwick, Crowdie, Cottager's, etc.) made from cow's milk, three others made from goat's milk, a trio of different yogurts, cultured buttermilk, crème fraîche, whey cream butter from Whitchurch, frozen unpasteurised goat's milk, and superb ice creams made on the premises.

Trish Murphy, the designer and technologist of this new establishment, which I believe to be unique, has returned to her academic work

* Part I, 1727; Part II, 1732; both parts reprinted by Prospect Books, London, 1980.

and to research in developing countries. But she keeps in close touch with her creation, speeding to and fro on that hand-made bicycle of hers. She gave me a vivid record of the problems which she overcame (no. 1 of many: no milk tanker could get through the tunnel to the dairy!) and of the experiments which led her eventually to discover which soft cheeses could still be made according to the almost defunct traditions. In all this she was greatly helped by a course in cheese-making at the Cheshire College of Agriculture, and also by studying US Department of Agriculture publications. Here is her account of the principal cheeses which she finally brought into production, followed by the recipe for her own 'favourite oddity', which is as delicious to eat as it is striking in appearance.

Trish told me that, working in her tiny premises, she decided to start with only three categories of soft cheese. First, Coulommiers, unripened and ready to eat in three days. Secondly, Colwick; and thirdly the 'bag cheeses', descendants of the simplest hung cheeses, which probably go back to Roman times.

She suspects that *Coulommiers* was an import from France in the nineteenth century, and is not really part of the old English tradition. She knew, however, that it was the best known of the few surviving soft cheeses; that recipes for making it were still to be found in recent official publications and in *Farmer's Weekly*, as well as in the current cheese-making-at-home books; and that someone at Wells in Somerset was still making the tall, round, two-piece Coulommiers moulds. Also, she thought that the cheese deserved its popularity. It looks like a Camembert in shape and size, has a pleasantly mellow flavour and is of a soft, creamy texture. Made from full cream cow's milk or goat's milk, the curd may be layered with parsley and garlic, or coarsely crushed black peppercorns. The cheese can be eaten fresh or left to ripen naturally for a week. (Note, however, that uncontrolled ripening may be disastrous. The high moisture content of these soft cheeses makes them an attractive home for just about any micro-organisms – moulds, yeasts and bacteria. Some may enhance the flavour, but others spoil the cheese with off-flavours or taints.)

Colwick, which takes its name from a village near Nottingham, is a larger cheese of $1\frac{1}{2}$ pounds or so. It is made in a perforated mould like a cake tin, lined with cheese cloth. As the curd drains in the cloth-lined mould, the edges of the cheese cloth are pulled upward and inward, causing the top of the curd to sag into a concave shape. It is this characteristic 'dished' centre – excellent when filled with cream and fresh strawberries for dessert – which makes Colwick so charming.

The term 'bag cheese' refers to cheeses which are hung in bags to drain. For those who would like to try this technique, here is the procedure.

MAKING BAG CHEESES

Pasteurised milk or cream is first coagulated either by the addition of starter bacteria (a 50–50 mix of *Streptococcus cremoris* and *S. lactis*) and rennet, or with the starter alone. (The latter procedure produces the flavourful, tangy Cottager's cheese, which bears no resemblance to bland, factory-produced 'cottage cheese'.) The curds are then gently ladled into sterile cheese cloths, the corners tied and the bags hung to drain. Draining is best continued for two days. After the first day, the cloths are changed and the firm curd on the outside of the nascent cheese is scraped down into the centre to ensure uniform drainage. When ready, the cheese is salted or flavoured to taste. Garlic, chives, fresh herbs or spices may be stirred in, or fresh cream added.

Trish's 'favourite oddity' is variously called York, or Cambridge or Bath – no doubt because in past times it was made in each of these three places. A special rectangular mould used to be available for making it, but is unfortunately no longer made. However, one can improvise a substitute, by using square or rectangular cake tins with the bottom cut out. Here is the recipe, with acknowledgements to the Cheshire College of Agriculture.

YORK, CAMBRIDGE OR BATH CHEESE

If you use 15 pints (8 litres) of milk you will finish up with two cheeses weighing about 12 oz (350 g) each (and, of course, a lot of whey!). Each cheese will have a coloured stripe running right through its centre, an effect which is achieved by colouring one third of the curd with annatto (see page 240). This is not difficult to obtain. Nor is the starter, which can be obtained from specialist firms. And the equipment is simple.

EQUIPMENT
2 bowls or buckets, 1 holding 10 pints (5.6 litres), the other 5 (2.8 litres)
a thermometer
a ladle or large spoon for slicing the curd
2 moulds – use, e.g. a pair of square, 6 × 6 inch (15.2 cm) cake tins, but
    beware of sharp edges and replace whenever rust sets in

wooden cheese boards or wire cake racks for draining the cheeses
either straw mats (traditional) or a double thickness of cheese cloth to
 go between the draining boards and the cheeses
a large container, e.g. a big roasting pan, to set under the draining
 boards to collect the whey
(all utensils to be sterilised beforehand)

INGREDIENTS
15 pints pasteurised milk or cream
1 teaspoon cheese 'starter' (see above), or substitute buttermilk
1 teaspoon cheese rennet diluted in 5 teaspoons water
$\frac{1}{4}$ teaspoon annatto

METHOD
Heat the milk or cream to 90°F (32°C); for goat's milk to 85° F (29° C).
Add the starter to the milk, then divide the milk into the two containers,
one of 10 pints (5.6 litres) and one of 5 (2.8 litres). Stir the annatto into
the latter until the colour is uniform. (It is important to add the annatto
before the rennet, since the curd must not be stirred too much once the
latter has been added.) Then distribute the teaspoon of rennet (diluted,
so that you have 6 teaspoons of liquid altogether) in the proportion of 2
to 1 between the containers. Stir for a minute or two, very gently.
Rennet starts to act quickly, and you must not break the curd as it is
being formed. Cover both containers and leave for 1 to 1½ hours until
the milk is set and the curd comes cleanly away from the side of the
containers.

 Now set the moulds on their padded draining boards and ladle the
thinnest possible slices of curd into them. First ladle about two thirds of
the plain curd, then the coloured curd, and finally the remaining plain
curd. Cover the moulds with paper and leave them to drain in a room
which has a temperature of 65–70° F (18–20° C).

 Let the cheeses drain in their moulds for 2 to 3 days, emptying the
whey container daily. The cheeses set by themselves and need no
turning or other such treatment. When they are firm enough, remove
the moulds, revealing the blocks of cheese, each with its coloured layer
roughly in the centre.

 This cheese was traditionally cut into three equal pieces and not
salted.

FINAL ADVICE
Respect the curd. If there is a ritual of soft-cheese making, then the curd
is the sacred element. A fragile structure, comprising the coagulated

milk, protein and casein, it is a delicate sponge which traps water and fat. It is easily ruined by over-stirring or rough treatment, which will result in thin, rubbery cheeses. Be patient; don't rush the cheese!

Lost and Gone for Ever?*

There are many soft cheeses which have disappeared from the English rural scene. Here are three which may be met by readers of eighteenth-century books.

Queen's Cheese. This was a three-week mature variety, made from milk and cream enriched with sugar and egg yolks, between Michaelmas (29 September) and Allhallowtide (1 November).

Sage Cheese in Chequerwork. Sage cheeses still exist, e.g. Sage Derby, but they are hard cheeses. This chequerwork one was a soft cheese, assembled from curds of which part were coloured green with sage and spinach juice. Shapes were cut with metal cutters and then interlocked or inlaid, green into white and white into green, to produce a mosaic or chequerboard effect.

Slipcote (or *Slipcoat*). A name with various meanings. It was sometimes used for a Colwick ripened between two plates; or for any cheese which separated from its outer coat, which would then slip off. It was also used for a Stilton which went wrong and 'blew its coat', whereupon it was hastily renamed slipcoat to suit its condition!

 Why did the range of soft cheeses diminish after the eighteenth and early nineteenth centuries, and why was production reduced? The explanation is complex, but the main factors were the transformation of cheese-making in Britain into a commercial industry, and the tendency to encourage farmers to sell all their available milk to provide daily milk deliveries (the British daily 'pinta') for the ever-increasing city populations.

1981

* This seemed to be true when I wrote it, but I was too pessimistic. Slipcote at least has reappeared, and I was able to buy it at Neal's Yard, although it isn't on their 1988 list. Trish Murphy's work, by the way, has been carried on by Randolph Hodgson, who decided after a while to transfer production of soft cheeses to more spacious premises in Kent. All cheeses are still 'finished' at the Neal's Yard Dairy, where expert advice is readily given to customers.

The Noble Blues

There are five blues, but I doubt whether five thousand people could be found who had tasted them all. Stilton is famous and readily obtainable. The other four are elusive, and one is downright evasive – a blue cheese made in Inverness-shire in Scotland but marketed as 'Shropshire blue'. So far as I know there is only one way to join the select band of under five thousand, and that is to appeal to Major Rance (see page 237). He has all five cheeses, although not necessarily all at the same time, and he mails them all over the world, taking due account of travelling time, climate of destination and other relevant factors.

These factors are important when valuable and delicate cheeses are being exported. I once had occasion to give a dinner in Laos for Prince Souvanna Phouma, who was then Prime Minister. Knowing his appreciation of good cheese, and knowing how often the French Ambassador furnished him with the finest cheeses of France, I determined to go one better and produce a Stilton in perfect condition. A young woman from the Foreign Office in London was due to fly out to Vientiane at just the right time. I briefed her to go to Paxton's in Jermyn Street, London's finest cheese shop, and explain the situation. 'Ah,' said the head cheesemonger there, 'Laos . . .' He reflected briefly. 'Can you tell me the exact date of the dinner, and whether the cheese will travel as hand baggage or in the hold?' He was told. Thereupon he ran his eye over the range of Stiltons behind him on the shelf, inserted his thin cylindrical testing scoop into one, withdrew a long sample, examined it, rammed it gently back into place and tapped the tiny piece of rind on the end to reseal the cheese. That Stilton was not suitable. But the next one was. It travelled to Vientiane, the dinner took place on the appointed day, and the cheese was at its peak of perfection. But if expert judgement had not been brought to bear on the matter we might easily have found ourselves serving a Stilton which the Prince (and, perhaps worse still, the French Ambassador, who was of the company) would have known to be under-ripe or over-ripe.

Stilton is made in the summer from the richest milk, or milk to which cream has been added. It is inoculated with *Penicillium glaucum*, which is responsible for the blue veining; and it counts as a semi-hard cheese because it is not pressed like, for example, Cheddar. It has proved possible to make a satisfactory Stilton in New Zealand, but attempts to do this in other countries have been unsuccessful. This is interesting, because although the process of manufacture is complicated and prolonged it does not, so far as one can see, require any unique setting, like the caves in which and in which alone Roquefort can be produced.

A Stilton is fully ripe after six months or so, and is best eaten within three months of ripening. Do not, by the way, be misled by the advice sometimes given to add port to it. This is quite wrong, although it might do something towards salvaging a Stilton which has been allowed to become dry. The risk of drying out can be averted in two ways. One is to buy a small Stilton, such as often comes in a fancy pot, and eat it up fairly quickly, which is usually no problem. But the best Stiltons are the full-size ones (5 lb, 2.3 kg at least, but 16 lb, 7.3 kg is an even better weight), which are traditionally consumed by removing the top and scooping out the cheese with a special silver scoop. This is fine if the company is large and the whole cheese is destined to be eaten within a few days, as would happen in a London club, for example. If, however, an ordinary family buys a large whole Stilton it is better to cut it across, removing a whole round for immediate consumption and then fitting the upper part back on to the lower part to ensure that what is left will keep well and not dry out.

Stilton can be traced back to the early eighteenth century, and interesting debates (not entered into here, for they would require several pages) can be held on its exact origin. But it may not be the oldest of English blues. The Blue Vinny of Dorset is certainly of great antiquity. Vinny, by the way, is simply a corruption of 'veiny', referring to the big blue vein which can be induced to spread through a Dorset cheese made from hand-skimmed milk. The process is somewhat uncertain, and the rate of failure used to be very high, especially when quaint traditional methods, such as dipping old leather harnesses, or even boots, into the milk churn, were practised. (No bad idea, since the blue mould flourishes on damp leather; but in our enlightened days there must, I feel sure, be regulations forbidding these methods. A certain recondite and subdued pleasure may be obtained by imagining the debates in the relevant committee of the European Economic Communities and the summoning of lawyers to stop up loopholes such as Dorset farmers might find, for example the use of dismantled or even shredded boots: 'the European Court of Justice determined that a fragment of the upper leather of a single boot did not constitute a "boot" within the meaning of the Regulation.') Anyway, this is solely a Dorset cheese. Just as

Bulgarian yogurt is distinguished not, as many people suppose, by the use of special bacteria (on the contrary, the Bulgarians use the same bacteria as do yogurt-makers in many other countries) but by the incidental effects of 'rogue' micro-organisms which flourish in the atmosphere of Bulgarian farms but nowhere else, so Dorset Blue Vinny seems to depend on fortuitous combinations of factors which are peculiar to Dorset. Thus the supply of this cheese will always be very small.

Blue Cheshire, like Stilton, is made in the summer and takes a long time to mature. Since Cheshire is normally coloured red, and the veins are greenish rather than blue, the coloration of the cheese is striking. It has a fine, full flavour and a creamy texture. These are characteristics which it shares with Blue Wensleydale, from Yorkshire. This prized cheese can trace its lineage back to the great Yorkshire abbeys of medieval times, when the monks made cheese from ewe's milk. Later on the makers of Wensleydale changed to cow's milk. White Wensleydale is available, and not to be despised, but the blue is what enthusiasts demand. It comes in 9 lb (4 kg) weights, often from another Yorkshire dale, Dovedale.

All these blue cheeses are best eaten as they come. The thought of cooking them would strike most people as a heresy; but I did once make a sauce for fish with blue cheese, following a recipe given to me by a Paris restaurateur, and it was good.

BLUE CHEESE SAUCE

Take about ¼ lb (125 g) blue cheese and work it into a paste at the side of the stove. Separately, take 2 pints (1 litre) of white sauce made with fish stock and work 3 egg yolks into it. Then work in the blue cheese paste. The sauce will be quite thick, and will be sufficient to cover 6 fish steaks in a suitable recipient. (The fish steaks may have been previously fried, or poached – they should have been cooked in one way or the other.) See that the sauce is spread evenly over the fish, then glaze the dish in a hot oven for 4 or 5 minutes.

A simple variation for use with cold fish is the following. Combine a cup of cream with a few ounces of blue cheese, previously worked into a paste, and pass the resulting mixture through a fine sieve. Add a pinch of cayenne and serve cold but not chilled.

1980

Welsh and Scottish Cheeses

In my first essay on British cheeses (page 235) I quoted an opinion voiced in the year 1601 that Welsh cheeses were the best of all. I doubt whether anyone would say that today, or make a corresponding statement about the produce of Scotland. But in both these parts of Britain good cheeses are made, and it is worth knowing about them and taking care, when speaking to people of Welsh or Scottish origin, to avoid the error of counting them as 'English' cheeses.

There are those who would say that, so far as Wales is concerned, this would be no error, since the one cheese for which Wales is known, Caerphilly, is mostly made in south-western England; and that the cheeses most suitable for making Welsh rarebit (or rabbit) are all English. This may be true. Certainly, as I found out for myself by going there, the town of Caerphilly, dominated by its picturesque ruined castle, is not the best place in which to try to buy Caerphilly cheese. However, a Welshman to whom I put this point had his answer ready. Caerphilly was indubitably of Welsh origin; and if foreigners such as the English had adopted it and taken over much of the work of producing it, that was to be taken as a tribute to its excellence.

It may also be a tribute to the ease with which it is made. Although it counts as a hard, or semi-hard, pressed cheese, it has a relatively high moisture content and does not need, indeed must not have, a lengthy period of maturing. Since it is quickly sold, it does not lock up capital, but produces a rapid return. And its attractive features ensure a steady demand for it.

The attractions of Caerphilly have been described by some experts as blandness and an agreeably moist texture. I think, however, that it is a mistake to dismiss it as 'bland'. It is not a cheese with a strong flavour, such as would make it unacceptable to some people, but the flavour is definitely there – mild, pleasant and faintly salty. It is said that Caerphilly came into being, probably in the early part of the nineteenth century, to fill a particular need, that of the Welsh miners who sweated as they toiled and who required for their midday snack a cheese which had a high moisture and salt content.

Most Caerphilly cheese now comes from Somerset. It is made all the year round, but is at its best in the early summer. It should be bought and eaten about three or four weeks after being made. If it is kept longer it will begin to go dry and crumbly and, although still satisfactory to eat, it will not be 'right' any more. Incidentally, if you have a whole Caerphilly, which will be in the form of a round about 2 inches (5 cm) thick and 9 inches (23 cm) in diameter, and if you have to keep it for a while after starting it, wrap it in a cloth which is barely damp (*not* wet).

To enjoy Caerphilly at its best, eat it with plain unsalted crackers and without any additions like mustard or pickles which would overpower its mild flavour.

Turning now to my native country of Scotland, I wish that a skirl of bagpipes could announce that there, north of the border, are to be found the finest of all British cheeses. But I must be content with saying that they are good. The principal Scottish cheese is Dunlop. It has its merits, but no one has ever become ecstatic about it. It is a good plain cheese, mild in flavour and resembling a slightly soft version of Cheddar. The name Dunlop is doubly appropriate. It is the name of a parish in Ayrshire, in the south-west of Scotland, where the Dunlop cow (which later became famous as the Ayrshire cow) was bred. This cow produced so much milk that it became obvious towards the end of the seventeenth century that the natural fate of much of it was to be made into cheese. At about this time a young woman called Barbara Gilmour, who had fled to Ireland to escape the Covenanting persecutions and had learned something of cheese-making there, returned to Ayrshire, married a farmer called Dunlop and began to produce Dunlop cheese – and no doubt Dunlop children too.

Dunlop has a very thin rind and an even texture. In its original form, it was moist like Caerphilly, and for a similar reason; the miners of Lanarkshire and parts nearby required a moist cheese to eat in the pits. Subsequently, however, following complaints about uneven quality, the Ayrshire Agricultural Association imported a Somerset cheese-maker to instruct the local farmers and their wives; and since then Dunlop has resembled Cheddar more closely and has had a lower moisture content. It does not, however, keep as well as Cheddar. It should be eaten between six weeks and four months after manufacture.

Earlier Scottish cheeses have vanished. Marian McNeill, in *The Scots Kitchen*,* recalls that milk products, often taken in the form of drinks such as whey or buttermilk, were very popular among the Scots and that curds, i.e. unprocessed cheese, were a natural by-product. Thus 'Curds

---

* 2nd ed., London and Glasgow, 1963.

and green whey' was a street cry in Edinburgh. Dorothy Wordsworth enthused over the whey when she visited Scotland. Some, like Miss Muffet, enjoyed both. Others went for the curds. And some had a special taste for the 'beestings', which is the name for the milk given by a cow during the three days following calving. This is technically known as 'colostrum' and is different from ordinary milk, very high in protein content and containing globulin, which has a solidifying effect. The milk taken on the second day after calving was thought to be the best for making 'beestie cheese' (surely one of the names least likely to have been thought up by an advertising agent), and the procedure was simplicity itself – and can still be followed if you know a cooperative farmer. Take the milk, add a little sugar, a pinch of salt and one or two teaspoonfuls of caraway seed, then leave it in a covered pot at the side of the peat fire (or in an equivalent position, e.g. on a hot plate at low heat) for several hours. The result can be eaten or sold at once. But I do not know where, even in the islands, you could find this today.

Mention of the islands brings to mind the other cheese for which Scotland is known nowadays, that of Orkney. This is a simple cheese to make and has been a staple item of the diet in Orkney for many centuries. The Orcadians used to keep it buried in oatmeal until they needed to eat it; and if they ate it fresh they liked to fry it in butter. There was a danger that it would become one of the 'lost' cheeses, such as the one which used to be made on the island of Coll; but it survived and is at present exported in appreciable quantities. In its most convenient form it is a one pound, rindless cheese, but it may also be found coloured and smoked. It has a firm texture and a tangy flavour.

Welsh rabbit (the term 'rarebit' seems to have come into vogue in the middle of the nineteenth century, e.g. in the first edition of Mrs Beeton's famous book, but in the earlier versions – from around 1780 to 1840 – 'rabbit' is the word used) may not have had a truly, or exclusively, Welsh origin. But there is one very good authority for saying that it has, and it is her recipe which I offer. I refer to the eccentric Lady Llanover, whose *Good Cookery* of 1867 is without doubt the zaniest book of its kind in the nineteenth century, but had a serious purpose: to help the Welsh people among whom she lived to rebuild their national identity and cultural traditions. Her Welsh recipes were supposedly communicated to 'a traveller' by a hermit who lived in a cave and was attended by two Welsh widows, Gwenllian and Marged. Here is the recipe used by this strange trio for what is described by Lady Llanover as 'this celebrated national dish of Wales' and entitled '*Welsh toasted cheese*'.

WELSH RABBIT

Cut a slice of the real Welsh cheese made of sheep and cow's milk [but Caerphilly, as made today, or Dunlop, or even English cheeses will do very well] , toast it at the fire on both sides, but not so much as to drop; toast a piece of bread, less than a quarter of an inch thick, to be quite crisp, and spread it very thinly with fresh cold butter on *one* side (it must *not* be saturated with butter), then lay the toasted cheese upon the bread and serve immediately on a very hot plate; the butter on the toast can, of course, be omitted if not liked, and it is more frequently eaten without butter.

One of my happiest childhood memories is of eating the Scots pancakes which my grandmother made in her house near Glasgow. These were usually sweet, designed to be spread with unsalted butter and home-made raspberry jam. But sometimes she made savoury cheese pancakes.

CHEESE PANCAKES FROM SCOTLAND

Put 4 oz (125 g) flour with a small pinch of salt in a basin, drop 2 eggs into the middle and gradually stir in 5 fl oz (150 ml) milk. Beat the batter until bubbles form, then add as much milk again to it and let it rest for half an hour.

Take 2 tablespoonfuls of grated mature Dunlop cheese and 2 of Orkney (*or* 2 each of two other cheeses, e.g. Cheddar and Gruyère), mix them together and stir half the mixture into the batter.

Next, put 1½ tablespoonfuls of pre-warmed cream into a pan, followed by the remaining half of the cheese mixture, with a pinch each of salt and cayenne pepper. Leave the pan on the side of the stove, so that the contents become thoroughly hot without approaching boiling point.

Now use the batter to make pancakes, frying them in a little butter in the usual way, but making them quite small (say, 3 inches, 7.5 cm in diameter). As they are done, lay them on a piece of cooking paper on which you have sprinkled some additional cheese, spread some of the hot cream-and-cheese mixture on them and roll them up. Serve hot.

1981

Part Eight
Tailpiece

A Kipper With My Tea

Why not for breakfast? Well, I have to have coffee for breakfast, and I don't think that kippers and coffee go so well together. Perhaps it is a matter of oil – kippers are of course oily and there is some oil in coffee, at least I think there is. Coffee needs to be balanced by the fresh, acid taste of citrus fruit, in fact by marmalade. Tea, on the other hand, good strong tea, complements the kipper with a touch of astringency.

Also, since a good kipper is just about the greatest treat I can think of for myself, it seems right to schedule it for my favourite meal, 'high tea'. I don't get to have this very often, having had to adapt myself over more than forty years to a life in London, or other capital cities, which prescribes 'dinner' instead. But my most formative years were spent in the north – Scotland, Northumberland, Yorkshire – and the patterns of eating learned there are still only just below the surface, ready and eager to protrude at the least opportunity.

My boyhood holidays were almost all spent with my grandparents in Bearsden, a fearsome-sounding but placid suburb of Glasgow. I will not attempt to explain why he was called Twinko and she Merdy, but there were reasons which seemed valid to the family.

Merdy rose at six, and I not much later, for the treats of the day began early. First, I was allowed to ride with the milkman in his great big, battered, open-top Humber, as he delivered the milk to the other houses in South Erskine Park. Then, having run triumphantly back down the road, I could repeat the experience with the butcher's van, a less splendid vehicle and a slower progression, for the butcher's business required more discussion. And then it would be time for breakfast.

It was many years later, long after my grandparents were dead, that I was told about Merdy's secret relationship with this butcher. When he brought her meat from the van he would whisper the name of a horse he fancied in a race that afternoon, and Merdy would give him sixpence, or even a shilling, to wager on it. Sometimes he would bring many shillings back and slip them to her. The entire operation was financed by a minuscule margin in Merdy's modest housekeeping allowance, and Twinko knew nothing of it.

This apart, Merdy was transparent, a true innocent whose pleasure it was to count her blessings (Twinko being number one), feed her hens, pick her roses, spoil – but only to a measured extent – her grandson, and exercise her skill in the kitchen.

Culinary literature abounds with references to people who declare that this or that – an apple pie, perhaps – was only really right when made by 'grandmother'; and there is frequently an implication that memory is playing tricks. I haven't myself often come across people saying such things, but I have no hesitation in saying that there were certain things which Merdy made uniquely well, and am fortified in this belief by the fact that everyone agreed at the time – it is not a case of my memory being faulty or correct but of a phenomenon which was apparent to all there and then.

We still have her baking tins, and my wife is convinced that they work better than anything of modern making – but not the way they worked for Merdy. My own mother, a good cook herself, would work beside Merdy in the kitchen, trying to duplicate precisely everything she did, and would of course produce excellent scones or whatever as a result, but scones which still lacked that Merdy-cachet. A puzzle.

Anyway, the evening routine at South Erskine Park was that Twinko, a timber merchant, would return from the city soon after five, and very soon after that we would all sit down on high-backed mohair chairs round the dining table and have a really lavish high tea. The savoury dish might be fish custard, or mince, or any of many other things – but every now and then it would be kippers. After this, and the accompanying bread and butter, would come the procession of scones, pancakes, biscuits, cakes (small) and cakes (large). For each item there was an appropriate plate, and I still have three of them, one oblong, one oval and one round. The round one was for a cake (large) which might be a Black Bun, a really rich confection which would always be eaten last.

Merdy saw to it that I ate things in something like the right order, but she was not one to restrain a healthy appetite, which I had. However, although I ate more than anyone else, I finished first. The grown-ups would be lingering over their third or fourth cup of tea, and I would be fidgeting on the mohair. At this point I was always told that I could 'get down' if I wished and go and have a sweetie.

The sweeties were kept in a decorated brown tin in the top drawer of a chest of drawers (still in my possession) in the drawing room. It was understood that, although I went in there by myself, I would have only one sweetie. Thus ended high tea. Much later, around 9.15 pm, the day would end with more tea, and tea biscuits, and I would be packed off to bed. Merdy would go to bed early too, leaving Twinko to smoke his pipe.

So there are the roots of 'A Kipper with My Tea'. The kippers which Merdy bought were, of course, excellent – the fishmonger, though not a betting man, was just as good a tradesman as the butcher – but this was taken for granted, just like the excellence of the bread, the freshness of the butter and the home-laid eggs, and so on. No one went on about how the kippers had come from this or that special kipperer.

I have since learned that there are kippers and kippers, and that without becoming a kipper-bore (potentially as dread a figure as the vinegar-bore and the olive-oil-bore whose existence was revealed by Paul Levy and Ann Barr) one can exercise a certain discrimination. Local kippers which I had in the Mull of Kintyre and in Shetland did strike me as particularly good; I have a vague resolve to go to the Isle of Man and try them there; and I and my wife have made the pilgrimage to Craster in Northumberland, where the Robson family have for long been producing extra-good ones. We certainly enjoyed the Craster kippers, but what really held our attention there was an extraordinarily cheap piece of real estate. Perched high on the cliff, looking over the tiny harbour and the North Sea – a really amazing view – was a small cottage, going for a song. When we heard about the song we started having fantasies about a second home in Craster, writing inspired by the view, kippers every day, and so on. But then a neighbour enlightened us. The cottage had been part of the kippering complex and its stone walls were so deeply impregnated with herring oil that no known technique could remove the overpowering smell.

Anyway, although having a preference for the undyed kind, I admit to liking most kippers. The one thing I feel strongly about is having them with bread and butter; and with tea, please!

1988

Index

Page numbers in *italic* refer to the illustrations